FIRST EDITION
~~15.00~~
6.50

Books By Robert Coles

CHILDREN OF CRISIS I: A STUDY OF COURAGE AND FEAR

STILL HUNGRY IN AMERICA

THE IMAGE IS YOU

UPROOTED CHILDREN

WAGES OF NEGLECT (WITH MARIA PIERS)

DRUGS AND YOUTH (WITH JOSEPH BRENNER AND DERMOT MEAGHER)

ERIK H. ERIKSON: THE GROWTH OF HIS WORK

THE MIDDLE AMERICANS (WITH JON ERIKSON)

THE GEOGRAPHY OF FAITH (WITH DANIEL BERRIGAN)

MIGRANTS, SHARECROPPERS, MOUNTAINEERS (VOLUME II OF CHILDREN OF CRISIS)

THE SOUTH GOES NORTH (VOLUME III OF CHILDREN OF CRISIS)

FAREWELL TO THE SOUTH

A SPECTACLE UNTO THE WORLD: THE CATHOLIC WORKER MOVEMENT (WITH JON
  ERIKSON)

THE OLD ONES OF NEW MEXICO (WITH ALEX HARRIS)

THE BUSES ROLL (WITH CAROL BALDWIN)

THE DARKNESS AND THE LIGHT (WITH DORIS ULMANN)

IRONY IN THE MIND'S LIFE: ESSAYS ON NOVELS BY JAMES AGEE, ELIZABETH BOWEN
  AND GEORGE ELIOT

WILLIAM CARLOS WILLIAMS: THE KNACK OF SURVIVAL IN AMERICA

THE MIND'S FATE: WAYS OF SEEING PSYCHIATRY AND PSYCHOANALYSIS

ESKIMOS, CHICANOS, INDIANS (VOLUME IV OF CHILDREN OF CRISIS)

PRIVILEGED ONES: THE WELL-OFF AND THE RICH IN AMERICA (VOLUME V OF
  CHILDREN OF CRISIS)

A FESTERING SWEETNESS (POEMS)

THE LAST AND FIRST ESKIMOS (WITH ALEX HARRIS)

WOMEN OF CRISIS: LIVES OF STRUGGLE AND HOPE (WITH JANE COLES)

WALKER PERCY: AN AMERICAN SEARCH

For Children
DEAD END SCHOOL

THE GRASS PIPE

SAVING FACE

RIDING FREE

HEADSPARKS

Walker Percy

Walker Percy

An American Search

by Robert Coles

An Atlantic Monthly Press Book

LITTLE, BROWN AND COMPANY   BOSTON   TORONTO

FIRST EDITION

T 01/79

Library of Congress Cataloging in Publications Data

Coles, Robert.
Walker Percy, an American search.

"An Atlantic-Monthly Press book."
Includes index.
1. Percy, Walker, 1916–   2. Christianity and
existentialism in literature.   3. Authors, American—
20th century—Biography.   I. Title.
PS3566.E6912Z6   813'.5'4 [B]   78-13629
ISBN 0-316-15160-2

A portion of this book appeared in *The New Yorker.*
Selections from:
— *The Moviegoer* by Walker Percy, copyright © 1960, 1961 by Walker Percy, are
reprinted by permission of Alfred A. Knopf, Inc., McIntosh and Otis, Inc., and
Martin Secker & Warburg Limited.
— "The Man on the Train" (*Partisan Review*, Vol. XXIII, No. 4, Fall, 1956, pp.
478–494) are reprinted by permission of *Partisan Review.*
— "In Memory of Sigmund Freud" from *Collected Poems* by W. H. Auden, edited
by Edward Mendelson, © 1976, are reprinted by permission of Random House,
Inc., and Faber and Faber Ltd.
— "East Coker" from *Four Quartets* by T. S. Eliot are reprinted by permission of
Faber and Faber Ltd. and Harcourt Brace Jovanovich, Inc.
— *Lancelot* by Walker Percy, copyright © 1977 by Walker Percy; *The Last Gentle-
man* by Walker Percy, copyright © 1966 by Walker Percy; *Love in the Ruins* by
Walker Percy, copyright © 1971 by Walker Percy, are reprinted with permission
of Farrar, Straus & Giroux, Inc., and Martin Secker & Warburg Ltd.

ATLANTIC–LITTLE, BROWN BOOKS
ARE PUBLISHED BY
LITTLE, BROWN AND COMPANY
IN ASSOCIATION WITH
THE ATLANTIC MONTHLY PRESS

Designed by D. Christine Benders

*Published simultaneously in Canada
by Little, Brown & Company (Canada) Limited*

PRINTED IN THE UNITED STATES OF AMERICA

To Tom Davey
To Kirk Felsman
To Alex Harris

We lay on our backs about two feet apart in silence, our eyes open, listening. The land that was under us lay down all around us and its continuance was enormous as if we were chips or matches floated, holding their own by their very minuteness, at a great distance out upon the surface of a tenderly laboring sea. The sky was even larger.

James Agee in *Let Us Now Praise Famous Men*

But as the Edsel took off, spavined and sprung, sunk at one corner and flatulent in its muffler, spuriously elegant and unsound, like a Negro's car, a fake Ford, a final question did occur to him and he took off after it.

"Wait," he shouted in a dead run.

The Edsel paused, sighed, and stopped.

Strength flowed like oil into his muscles and he ran with great joyous ten-foot antelope bounds.

The Edsel waited for him.

Walker Percy in *The Last Gentleman*

Introduction

Walker Percy is now best known as a novelist, and deservedly so. *The Moviegoer, The Last Gentleman, Love in the Ruins,* and *Lancelot* have earned him substantial but limited recognition; substantial because he has been given critical praise and obtained a loyal following, but limited because by no means has he become a well-known American writer, and some of his most avid readers still think of him as the property of a relative handful — no underground writer, and no member of a small coterie, yet someone not known in the way Saul Bellow or John Updike or Robert Penn Warren is known. Some who are familiar with his writing regard him as more than a novelist and essayist: as, rather, a philosopher, a man of special understanding and humor, a person who helps the reader think altogether differently about life, a person, too, through whom one can recognize spiritual comrades — namely those who also have found their lives strongly affected by Walker Percy's articles and books.

I may well be describing myself. I have no distance, certainly, on Dr. Percy's writing; I have liked it intensely and consistently for many years. I remember reading his articles during the 1950s, when I was learning to be a doctor, then a psychiatrist. I especially remember coming across "The Man on the Train," which appeared in *Partisan Review.* The year was 1956, and the article was recommended to a few of us stray souls who had ventured from academic libraries, or, in my case, a hospital clinic, to a seminar on systematic theology taught by Paul Tillich at Harvard. I can still hear Tillich saying emphatically, as we were leaving the classroom one day:

"Percy is a physician, I believe." I would have read anything Tillich recommended, no mind if the suggested author were a garbage collector, a madman, a theoretical physicist. For me at that time Tillich offered surcease, to use a somewhat out-of-fashion word *he* occasionally used — a relief from dogmatic, presumptuous, and all too self-confident psychiatric generalizations. If some supervisors encouraged narrow reductionism, Tillich was there at Harvard, two afternoons a week, full of passion and ready to insist upon the mystery of things, the strange and fateful "moments," he often called them, that make such a difference in our lives. The reading of "The Man on the Train" turned out to be such a moment in my life. The article was intended to bring readers up short, to prompt in them a thought or two about why they were doing what, day in and day out. It was a philosophical essay; it took up, yet again, the old Socratic question of "life's meaning," but did so in a lively, humorous way — offering psychological and sociological observations almost casually, as if they were importanti, yes, but had to be taken with a few grains of salt. It was a little harder, after reading the essay several times, and hearing Paul Tillich talk about it, to be quite so self-important, quite so sure of oneself and one's various ideas — or, in the clinic, one's "interpretations."

The fateful "mystery of things" that Tillich kept mentioning soon had me encountering Dr. Percy's first published novel, *The Moviegoer,* under somewhat unusual circumstances. I was living in Biloxi, Mississippi — stationed there, at Keesler Air Force Base, as an air force captain, in charge of a neurological and psychiatric unit at the military hospital. I was also going to nearby New Orleans almost every late afternoon in order to attend medical and psychiatric conferences and pursue psychoanalytic training. Each weekday I drove through Gentilly, where Binx Bolling of *The Moviegoer* lived. Since I was in psychoanalysis at the time, I was perhaps given to more ruminations than usual — efforts to figure out not only how I had come to be the kind of person I was, but what I ought do with my life, and, not least, what "meaning" there is in that more generic use of the word *life.*

I was making a decision about that life of mine during 1960, when *The Moviegoer* appeared; I decided to stay South, to live in New Orleans upon discharge from the air force, so that I could work with the four small black children who were then getting ready to initiate school desegregation (against persistent and violent resistance, as it turned out). I have, in the first volume of *Children of Crisis*, described how I came to that decision, after witnessing a "swim in" by blacks on a Biloxi beach, and seeing them almost killed. It was a decision that would change my life. For almost two decades I have been trying to get to know children in various parts of this country who are struggling against various social, economic, racial odds, children who manage to survive — and who sometimes show extraordinary courage rather than the various "symptoms" one like me is trained to spot and try to "treat." Walker Percy's novel gave hope to me, helped me feel stronger at a critical time, when I was somewhat lost, confused, vulnerable, and, it seemed, drifting badly. The "hope" I mention, the "stronger" sense of conviction, were personal responses to a writer whose essays I had been following, whose novel struck home with such force that I felt less bewildered and distracted than I had in a long time — and, in Heidegger's sense of the expression, more "at home" with myself.

I read *The Moviegoer* over and over again; I would be embarrassed to list the number of times. To be honest, I lost count. On each reading I discovered something new that was amusing or instructive — or provided yet another reason to return to Sören Kierkegaard, Martin Heidegger, and Gabriel Marcel, to whom (all three) I had been introduced first by Perry Miller, as an undergraduate, and then by Paul Tillich in the seminar of his I took while studying psychiatry. And then, there were the children I was getting to know in New Orleans, white and black; they, too, had good reason to stop and think about things, to question "life" in the way a severe crisis can prompt some of us to do. Here is an eight-year-old child, born and reared in that city, wondering (the year was 1962) about "things," after a long and painful stretch of months in a classroom completely boycotted by white boys and girls: "I will ask myself if it's worth it. I will ask myself why God made people like He did those white people who shout all those bad words at me. I will ask myself if it makes any sense, to keep walking by them, and trying to smile at them, and trying to be polite, when I'd like to see them all dead. I would! But the minister says we are tested — that's why we're put here in the world, to be tested. So, I guess I ought to thank those white folks. They're testing me!

"I try to talk to God when I walk past them. I ask Him please to help me do what is right — to know what I should do. It's not easy, knowing what to do. I'll bet you can find some people who have grown old, and they still aren't sure how you're supposed to live your life. They're still wondering what's it all about! My grandfather is one of those people! That's what he always asks: 'What's it all about?' He takes his whiskey when he comes home from his job, and he sits on the porch, on his rocking chair — he built it himself, and you can pull it apart and store it, and then put it back together, real easy. While he's sitting, and he's sipping, he does his asking. He asks God a lot of questions, and he asks my momma and my poppa, and he asks himself, and he'll even ask me.

"The other day, he said to me: 'Little one, why do you do like you do?' I knew what he was asking. I told him that I'd heard the Sunday School teacher tell us that we're here to do the best we can to be good, and to show God that He was right when He gave us our freedom — to be good, or to be bad. I try to be good. When those white people tell me they'll kill me, I bite my lip. I don't answer them back the way they talk to me. I try to pray for them. I don't really want to; but I do. I wonder, sometimes, if they ever stop and ask themselves why they are put here in this world. If we don't ask why we're here, we're lost in the woods. That's what I believe. My daddy says so. My granddaddy says so."

None of Walker Percy's novels features a child like her, but his main characters are haunted by the same vexing, puzzling matters she kept coming back to all the time. A dangerous social and racial struggle became for that girl not only an educational opportunity, and a decisive psychological experience, but an occasion for philosophical speculation. More than an occasion; she continued to ask herself important ethical and religious questions as she grew up. She took philosophy courses, read Dostoevski and Tolstoy, Kafka and Camus in college — and yes, the novels of Walker Percy. Somehow, in my mind, her experiences (both subjective and objective), which it was my job to try to comprehend, become linked with Walker Percy and his writing. They lived not all that far away — she on the eastern outskirts of New Orleans, near Gentilly, and he north of the city, across Lake Pontchartrain. They are both Southerners, both of their families originally from Mississippi. They have both known, perhaps, a little more anguish or despair than many others, and have both been prompted, accordingly, to look within themselves and around at others — in order to get their bearings and keep them, not only for the long haul (as in "a philosophy of life") but day after day.

And I guess I have myself shared some of their concerns. One can't spend years with children like that girl, or, indeed, the same years reading Walker Percy, without finding more and more time for some of the questions characters like Binx Bolling, Will Barrett, and Tom More ask, or Percy himself asks in various articles, or, again, a number of children ask, if given a chance to talk about themselves at any length. Much of the work I have been doing since the late 1950s, represented by the five volumes of *Children of Crisis*, has been devoted to the evocation for others of the introspective thoughts, philosophical speculations, and ethical concerns I have heard a number of different American children express during various conversations. I have relied upon Dr. Percy's ideas constantly in the course of that work — to the point that I can scarcely imagine how I would have thought about either my own life or the lives of the children, parents, teachers I have met, were he to have decided, long ago, to keep his important and instructive thoughts to himself, deny them the access to others that essays offer in one way, the novel offers in another. It is no accident that this book comes out shortly after the last of the volumes in the *Children of Crisis* series. Much is written in my profession about "methodology." Perhaps these pages furnish evidence of the kind of "research" I have attempted over the years — *search* may be the better word.

Especially the last two volumes of *Children of Crisis* connect with Percy's writing. Indians and Eskimos have no hesitation to look with open eyes and quizzically at the world — to ask rather routinely the most important of questions, the most uninhibited and far-reaching *why*'s; and as for our well-to-do children, they have often gone through some of the hurdles the author of *The Moviegoer, The Last Gentleman, Love in the Ruins,* and *Lancelot* has his various characters try to get through in such a way that they do more than shrug and grasp the next "deal." In one "country day school" north of Boston that I visited for several years a teacher told me that some of her children ("even the young ones, of nine or ten") ask questions which struck her as "existential." What did she mean?

One asks her, of course — and gets a considered reply: "They have everything, these children — except a knowledge or conviction of what to live by. No one teaches them that here. They don't go to church anymore — and even if they did, all they'd be hearing about is the value of a 'community,' or of 'mental health.' And at home it's golf and tennis, skiing or swimming, cocktails and dinner, the theatre or a trip — until you hear the parents saying that they can't figure out where all the years have gone, but now the kids are grown up. And when those kids are grown up they're ready to go on the same merry-go-round. But when they're ten or twelve, they have a question or two on their minds. I try to answer those questions. I try to talk with children who want to know — even if it's just for a few seconds — what life is all about. That's the way they often put it to me: 'What is life all about?' I tell them I don't know. I ask them to get more specific. I say pick one part of life, and maybe we can talk. Sometimes they do.

"Last week a thirteen-year-old girl asked me why so many people who live in this rich town are so unhappy. She said they never smile unless someone is in trouble — sick or falling down a ski slope or struck by a car. Then they all seem alive and full of talk. Then they talk about important subjects. Her cousin died of leukemia a year ago, and she said her parents were nicer to her during the week of the funeral than they'd ever been before or have been since. Her father actually began to wonder out loud what was the point of working, making money, going to the country club, having his drinks, and all that. But before long he slipped back to his usual ways — and I think that girl will, too. She won't be noticing as much as she does now. She won't be asking as many questions. I'm afraid that when we say that so-and-so is 'growing up,' we mean that the girl or the boy is becoming as indifferent to the important questions as most people are — as 'well adjusted,' and ready to go along with all the requirements of our comfortable suburban life."

So it goes, research, or again, the search: a teacher who herself has been a fan of Walker Percy's talks to a doctor who is interested in some of the same issues Percy keeps examining; they talk about children no less inclined to ask the same pointed, even haunting, questions Heidegger, Marcel, and Percy have posed for us in this century. Through conversations with teachers like her, and children like the one she mentions in the above quotation, I have been enabled to understand Walker Percy in the way he, perhaps, would find desirable: ideas exchanged amid a growing willingness to take risks — a step or two, while talking, in the direction of a shared trust. Certainly Walker Percy has taken risks — when he writes and, just as important, in the way he has tried to spend his time on this earth. Not that he has a taste for the dramatic, the irregular, the unconventional. He is, if anything, modest, retiring, a bit shy even, though quite approachable and affable. He is, in one sense, just another resident of Covington, Louisiana. But he has lived his very own life. A doctor, he has never practiced medicine. He has written with obvious understanding about psychiatry and psychoanalysis — to the point that he or those who publish his essays must upon occasion remind readers that he is not a psychiatrist. In fact, through both his articles and his novels he has contributed a good deal to a much needed but still incomplete social history of the feverish involvement between America's agnostic, secularist bourgeoisie and Freud's thinking. Kate in *The Moviegoer* is seeing a psychiatrist. Will

Barrett of *The Last Gentleman* has put in his time with one. *Love in the Ruins,* with its main character a doctor, has page after page of sharp observations on alienists (as they used to be called in the nineteenth century — and how ironic, that word, for those who have followed the twentieth-century existentialist literature of "alienation"). In *Lancelot,* the main character is seriously troubled, is in a hospital for the criminally insane, where (the length of the novel) he talks to a psychiatrist who is also a priest.

Percy himself has been "alienated" — from the alienated ones upon whom he has for so long kept his intent eyes. He is a loner. He belongs to no "school" of writers. He is the darling of no literary clique. As a child he lost his parents, went to live with an extraordinary relative, William Alexander Percy, himself a loner, a writer who happened to have a profession (the law). After medical school, Walker Percy spent many months in a sanitarium, virtually alone, recovering from tuberculosis — and, no doubt, from the death of his beloved "Uncle Will," which took place in 1942. There is, surely, a connection between Walker Percy's life and the ideas of those philosophers and novelists who have meant so much to him. They were all "a pretty strange bunch," he once said to me, and he did not, I think, thereby mean to establish any great psychological distance for himself. He has been relatively well-to-do, has not had to hold a job, day after day. He hasn't, that is, been compelled to make the adjustments and accommodations most people find to be a necessary part of everyday life: fit into a "work-team," fit into an "office situation," fit into the demands of a particular institution. He might have become increasingly aloof, removed in spirit as well as substance from the rest of his countrymen, who know and submit to dozens of social, economic, and psychological imperatives he has never had to experience. Yet he has tried hard to stay in touch with others; and maybe, ironically, has been enabled by his own situation to understand how the rest of us manage better than it is possible for us ourselves to do.

He immersed himself for years, as I try to make clear, in the European, Christian, and secular existentialist tradition of both the nineteenth and twentieth centuries — a tradition with its fair share of intent, and intense outsiders. But in his articles, and especially in his novels, he brought that tradition across the Atlantic to the United States of America. His has been an effort to show American readers how the abstract speculations of Heidegger, the more passionate or lyrical speculations of Marcel, have a bearing on daily life in any town of any of our fifty states. And similarly with Kierkegaard or Dostoevski. And Sartre and Camus. But, as an American, Percy has not only attempted translation or evocation; he has balanced a contemporary Christian existentialism with the pragmatism and empiricism of an American physician.

The "search" of this book's title still goes on — pursued by Walker Percy, who is now in his sixties, and by the rest of us, one hopes. I began to write a part of this book as a long profile for *The New Yorker*. I wrote another part for presentation at Yale, as the Trumbull Lectures of 1976. But I had been taking notes on Percy's writing for some time, and writing to myself "messages" or "communications" (to use two of his favorite words) for many years; and no doubt will continue to do so, if we are lucky enough to be graced with further essays or novels from him. I regard him as a pilgrim; the essays that have been collected (1975) into *The Message in the Bottle* are the notes of·a man in search of life's meaning — what in another age was called "God's gracious presence." I connect Dr. Percy, maybe out of my own peculiar inclinations, with another Southerner, Flannery O'Connor, and with two French writers, Simone Weil and Georges Bernanos — four Catholic travelers of serious purpose indeed. I hope one day, God willing, to spell out some of those connections; they keep coming to my mind as I keep thinking about those four, the life and writing of each of whom has meant so much to me. Meanwhile, this is a mixture: biography; literary analysis; and, I hope, a "response" in Gabriel Marcel's sense of the word — an act of "fidelity," he might say — to a writer, by an admiring reader.

I have tried to come up with one of those "contexts" so much mentioned by my ilk — the social scientists who worry Dr. Percy, and often prompt in him a wry smile, or the equivalent in words, a gentle touch of irony, of satire. Percy has acknowledged the influence of Kierkegaard. I have wanted in the first section to highlight some of the philosophical issues and tensions (the dialectic, as it were) that exerted a strong tug on Percy during the twenty years that followed his graduation from medical school and preceded the publication of *The Moviegoer.* As for Percy's articles, which are expressions of the development of his ideas, and, too, touching points for his work as a novelist, I have had him in mind as I pursue an *explication de texte.* There is in all his writing, and in him personally, a certain modesty and tentativeness — which, in turn, come across (as he talks or writes) as a capacity for wonder, awe, surprise, and almost childlike naïveté. The characters in his novels, of course, have that "innocence" as a chief characteristic — even half-cynical, besotted, despairing Dr. Tom More, of *Love in the Ruins.*

Some of Dr. Percy's struggles to find his philosophical bearings come across, I hope, in the second section of this book. I have wanted, through the tone of the writing, to be faithful to his quest — rather than to assume the authoritative, didactic, interpretive position all too inviting for one like me, and so anomalous when the "subject matter" is the existentialist tradition, many of whose members have fought hard against the real or fancied depredations of the academic mind. It is true, Percy has himself written for scholarly, even arcane, journals. But he has done so, often enough, with a touch of irony, if not outright innocence — an effort, often, to *regain* a certain sense of surprise and awe with respect to the things and people of the world. A surprise, an awe Kierkegaard felt to be so important, and so lacking in intellectual men and women. It is always tricky, doing commentary or exegesis, but I have tried to keep Percy's own methods in mind, and on occasion I have thought of his irreverent Dr. Tom More while working on this book's second section. As for the third part, the novels have surely prompted in Percy's various readers a range of introspective musing, and I can only join the company. There is a part of me that wonders whether anything needs to be said, ought to be said, in response to each of those novels, or all three of them. Still, one tries.

I have to mention the three good, close, fine friends whose names appear on this book's dedication page. Tom Davey, Kirk Felsman, and Alex Harris have worked with me over the years, and I with them. They have helped me a lot, taught me a lot. The quotes I have wanted entered on the record, so to speak, under their names, reflect better than any weaker words of mine can the quality of these friendships, valuable and important to me. And, to be a little presumptuous, I would like to think of Dr. Walker Percy as not only a wise person, whose every word, virtually, I have read, respected, learned from, and at times, to be honest, held onto tenaciously, gratefully, but also as someone I know to be *there* — a friend, and despite the distance between Louisiana and Massachusetts, a spiritual kinsman of sorts. Needless to say, on the level of "everydayness," his practical and concrete help in repeatedly discussing his life and work with me was essential.

There are other debts to be mentioned: Dr. Percy's brother LeRoy, his wife, Sarah, their son Billy of Greenville, Mississippi, their son Robert of Jackson, Mississippi, and, recently, Boston; Ellen Douglas and Hodding Carter III, of Greenville, Mississippi; Stanley Kauffmann, who helped me enormously in a memorable New York City afternoon and evening talk; Shelby Foote and his wife, who were similarly hospitable in Memphis; and, of course, Bunt — Dr. Percy's wife, and for me, a friend, a kind, gracious hostess, too. *The New Yorker* originally published part of this book as a profile; I again want to declare my respect and gratitude to its editor, William Shawn. As mentioned, a substantial part of this book was read to Yale faculty and students on the occasion the three Trumbull Lectures for 1976. In that connection I met and exchanged ideas about this book, then in manuscript, with a number of sensitive, kind men and women, young and older. I would especially like to mention Jane Isay, Professor Edwin McClellan, Professor R. W. B. Lewis, and, not for the first time, Professor C. Vann Woodward.

Closer to home there has been, in Boston, the continuing, sensitive, and intelligent advice of my long-time editor and friend, Peter Davison, the additional and important editorial advice of Richard Todd, who is especially in touch with the religious and philosophical tradition Dr. Percy has drawn from — and helped nourish; and the patient, thoughtful, and almost magical help extended this book, and other books or articles, by Bonnie Harris. And, as always, I make mention of my wife, Jane; to draw upon, with slight revision, the words of a novelist whose name figures rather prominently on the title page, and in the pages to follow: "Find a wife, take her charms in your arms, live a life." I have been rather lucky in the help I have had trying to heed that suggestion.

ONE

Philosophical Roots

WALKER PERCY'S COLLECTION *The Message in the Bottle* begins with an unusually titled essay: "How I Discovered the Delta Factor Sitting at My Desk One Summer Day in Louisiana in the 1950's Thinking About an Event in the Life of Helen Keller on Another Summer Day in Alabama in 1887." It is a fittingly personal and subjective start to this idiosyncratic book, yet the author has asked himself what is distinctively human — the quality he calls the "Delta Factor." A long series of relatively brief, piercing, and for the most part saddening questions follow his initial, "methodological" statement with its ironic mixture of the homespun, the unashamedly provincial, on the one hand, and the portentous language of "science" on the other hand — "Discovered," and "The Delta Factor." Some of the questions are the obvious ones that still go unanswered in this century: "Why is man the only creature that wages war against its own species?" for instance. But there are quite other questions, ones that direct the reader to Walker Percy, a particular individual: "Why was it that the only time I ever saw my uncle happy during his entire life was the afternoon of December 7, 1941, when the Japanese bombed Pearl Harbor?"

Percy's questions are both personal and philosophical. For many years he has indicated in his various writings a belief that the obsessions of the man who felt strangely affirmed and energetic early in December, 1941, and the ruminations of the man who contemplated Helen Keller's fate at his desk in (no doubt) the oppressive heat and humidity of southern Louisiana in the 1950s are not unlike those that confront and plague many of us. But we try to protect ourselves, keep secure our "adjustments," our various accommodations, if not outright surrenders. We resist knowledge of boredom, loneliness, despair — do so artfully, insistently, and, for the most part, successfully enough. News of a war, news of a tragedy, a disaster, an illness, a death, suddenly awakens us — though not necessarily to ourselves. The excitement, the sense of purpose, the appearance of enthusiasm and vitality, the evidence of unqualified commitment, can be misleading — can tell of a person's deep-down emptiness, hopelessness, or, at the least, continuing boredom.

The general calamity of war, or someone's private, crushing blow, brings us as close as many of us will ever get to a consideration of what matters, really and conclusively, in this life. But not close enough; Percy's uncle was too old to fight in the Second World War, and even if he had been young enough to enlist and go overseas, there is a limit to the "happiness" any news, any external event, can bestow on the mind. The first day's knowledge that a friend or relative has been taken gravely ill brings high drama; one questions things, many things, as never before, and, amid the sorrow or apprehension, feels the tinge of relief and exhilaration. Someone *else* has fallen; and as a result the dreary tedium of life, or its oppressive sameness, has yielded to an occasion of alarmed awareness. As never or rarely before, one asks those philosophical why's and when's — at the expense of another's suffering and danger. Percy has been asking them for many years, for over three decades now — the strange man whose temperament it is to do so in between our various Pearl Harbors, or the various reports of trouble that inevitably reach him through conversations at home, on the st 'eet, by telephone. And he would be the last one, preoccupied as he has been with the Christian existentialist tradition, to deny a connection between the personal factor and the "Delta factor." "In the beginning was Alpha," he tells us. "The end is Omega," he reminds us. Then, staking out other territory, he gives us this: "But somewhere in between came Delta, man himself. Man becomes man by breaking into the daylight of language — whether by good fortune or bad fortune, whether by pure chance, the spark jumping the gap

4

because the gap was narrow enough, or by the touch of God, it is not for me to say here."

Yet, it is for him to write that sentence, to have lived in such a way, long enough, with enough dedication and curiosity and maybe doubt, and maybe melancholy, for such a line of thought to be quite definitely and persistently *his* — a reflection of his way of spending his days, committing his energies. When Dr. Percy began writing essays he was trying to come to terms with the kind of life many people live today — Americans of the twentieth century. He saw the emptiness, the shallowness abroad in the land; he saw the "quiet desperation," if not the noisy despair. He saw the confusion, covered by hustle or bustle or faddish commitments, one after the other. He pronounced himself lost, said that to acknowledge so was at least a first, and thoroughly necessary, step. Those who are lost and don't know it are in even greater danger. And, like anyone lost, he was not only seeking a way back (seeking to find himself), but he was also upset, anxious, angry.

In the essays he would write he reveals his intellectual interests: who is this "creature," known as man, as woman, as human being, and what, distinctively, makes us ourselves? He also reveals his emotional side; he is hopeful, hence the effort he makes, but guarded, and, not rarely, the victim of a certain animus. There are enemies of various sorts: those whose words, ideas, slogans, and deeds make an always precarious and dangerous situation — our fate as particular individuals — even worse. The essays, taken as a whole, amount to an American search, an existentialism: a writer's struggle to try to dig himself and others out of a certain cultural and historical trap — the secular world, with its fast-changing, contradictory pieties, not to mention its unprecedented capacity for self-destruction.

Percy has his intellectual forebears, chief among them Kierkegaard, who saw "objectivity" to be (for many, today) a fantasy — a version of the gnostic heresy that had man able to rid himself of sin: scientific objectivity as a religion, a promise of redemption, a statement of man's perfectibility. Moreover, Kierkegaard realized that not only philosophers struggle with philosophical principles and alternatives. The two of them learned about "everydayness" by watching a lot of ordinary people rather closely — and as I try to suggest in this section, are helpful indeed to a lesser breed, the so-called field-worker of our time.

Copenhagen's nineteenth-century cripple — a man whose father was obsessed by and cringed before God — never tried to conceal himself with the cape he often chose to wear. He was an educated bourgeois, a man frustrated and disappointed in love, a Christian by hope and maybe resignation rather than conviction or ritual. His emotional, idiosyncratic temperament is never absent from his writing. Nor did he care to keep under wraps his rage or bitterness. Christ showed His anger in the temple — denounced the "powers and principalities" bluntly and with no real effort at qualification. On the Cross, for a brief but important moment, Christ even turned away from God Himself — announced to the world a feeling of aloneness, of abandonment, if not outright betrayal. Kierkegaard saw no reason to avoid following suit. *Attack upon "Christendom"* is an insistent, devastating, some would say merciless, assault upon the entire self-described "Christian world." The author, at one point, banishes millions of believers to a state of nonbeing — to Hell, really: "As I say, Christianity simply does not exist." And lest the reader settle for the abstract, in the hope that there are individuals, here and there, who *do* "exist" as faithful Christians, this observation follows: "The sort of men who now live cannot stand anything so strong as the Christianity of the New Testament (they would die of it or lose their minds), just in the same sense that children cannot stand strong drink, for which reason we prepare for them a little lemonade — and official Christianity is lemonade — twaddle for the sort of beings that now are called men, it is the strongest thing they can stand, and this twaddle then in their language they call 'Christianity,' just as children call their lemonade 'wine.' "

There is more, much more — satire and vitriol, shaking of the fist and of the head, and, alas, a level of satire and scorn, of overstatement, of withering ironic exposition, that skirts diatribe. Kierkegaard is convinced that a Christian must be an exile, a wanderer not only tormented from within but hounded from without. "Despised and rejected" is the Old Testament phrase. He asks, with John: "How can ye believe, which receive honor one from another?" That is what it has come to — Christen*dom*. When Christ's example became a mere emblem for a domain, then Christianity as a living faith died — or so a fussy, demanding, uncompromising Danish thinker and writer would see it.

One describes Kierkegaard warily; he disliked philosophy, denied himself the title of theologian, referred to himself as "a kind of poet," wrote impassioned spiritual narratives — long letters of high drama and piercing introspection, signed with suggestive, antic pseudonyms. His writing often told a story — gave an account of a particular person's psychological and spiritual struggles, his journey through a segment of time and space. He loved metaphors, similes. He called upon folklore, anecdotes, parables. He was an essayist — but willing to let his passions make him come across as an intellectual, finger-wagging pamphleteer.

He left his fellow men, lived alone, renounced not only marriage but the consolation, support, affection of his neighbors — not to mention his beloved Regina. He found no sustaining network of friends. His fight was a lonely one; no comrades stood by him. He would probably have laughed derisively at today's word *community*; maybe, somewhere in the universe, he does so. He could be called a misanthrope without too much exaggeration — and how he himself was tempted to exaggerate, to strain, caricature, overcolor, or overdraw. He was always strong-minded. He could be quite truculent. "The Christianity of the New Testament is to love God in opposition to men," he observed. Without personal sacrifice, without suffering, one's devotion to Christ remains untested, and, quite likely, puffed up or hypocritical. If one is "to receive honor from men" for being a Christian, he argued, then it will be, finally, "impossible to believe." *That* from the man who is today regarded a bit piously as the patron saint of "Christian existentialism." One has a right to suspect that were Sören Kierkegaard alive he would do his best to dispute such a designation, perhaps summoning in the effort a good deal of impatience, if not rancor.

At the end of an essay published in 1952, W. H. Auden stresses the critical importance of *Attack upon "Christendom"* in Kierkegaard's life — as opposed to his "thought." Auden refers to the "agnostic intellectuals" who "for the most part" are the avid readers of books like *Fear and Trembling* or *The Sickness Unto Death:* these books are essentially psychological essays of great subtlety, and immediate, direct precursors of Freud, because Kierkegaard took for granted at every moment, and almost casually, the existence and vast authority of what we, these days, call the unconscious. But psychological awareness or the ability to evoke with words the nuances of mental life, including the capacity we all have for self-deception, is no substitute for faith — which, in any case, for Kierkegaard, can never be taken for granted, only (to repeat) sought in a kind of battle, and against seemingly hopeless odds. He would not, were he among us, fail to pay strict and harsh attention to the position of respect, even devotion, given psychology and psychiatry by the American *haute bourgeoisie.* He recognized in his own time the seductive danger, however well intentioned, of ambitious, well-constructed analytic probes, be they into history or the mind — for instance, Hegel's *Phenomenology of Mind.* In Kierkegaard's scale of values there is no great distance between that book, for all its brilliance and depth, and the shallow, trite excesses, banalities, and absurdities of the "group encounter" movement or of something called "humanistic psychology," all riddled with categorical thinking, labels, unqualified pronouncements.

Hegel was a giant of a philosopher, and certainly intimidated by no one, including Jesus Christ. For Kierkegaard, Hegel's ideas became something of an obsession, even though (I shall try to argue) they paradoxically shared certain traits. In the *Phenomenology of Mind* and elsewhere we are given a bold and searing critique of Christianity — a faith that has prompted, historically, just the kind of subjective and self-centered line of thinking Hegel felt to be, really, a kind of madness. Christ originally tended to his flock, looked to the world as something not only *there*, but terribly important to regard, criticize, make over. Eventually, however, he became "inward," determined to find His own salvation, so to speak — oblivious, as Hegel saw it, to the fate of His followers and, by extension, to the outer world, whose claims upon us are given so much importance in the Hegelian dialectic. On the field of Calvary, God's Son had become, at least for one German philosopher, a hopelessly distracted and sentimental romanticist.

Kierkegaard's objection to Hegel was respectful as well as scornful. The former knew the power and persuasiveness of the latter's argument. Hegel distrusted profoundly the private, self-absorbed man. He had a historian's point of view, and did not question his capacity, never mind *right* (in the Christian context of "pride" as the cardinal sin), to know in advance what has yet to emerge. He saw the world to be out there, waiting to be understood and explained. Although very important, private comprehension was for him a mere prelude to public awareness. The observation that "the real is the rational and the rational is the real" was meant not only to insist upon the importance of objective, historical-minded, analytical thinking, but to dismiss the "reality" of what Hegel kept calling "the law of the heart," for him a kind of madness. And for Kierkegaard the beginning of sanity; he laughed at the notion that anyone could even *place* himself in the world's, in history's, scheme of things — never mind claim to have achieved "intelligibility," which for Hegel was the aim of philosophical speculation.

There is, though, a side to Kierkegaard that is not all that at variance with Hegel's prejudices, whatever the excesses of his conceptual and categorical thinking. Hegel's scorn for the frivolous, esoteric, or self-indulgent aspects of subjectivity is more than matched by Kierkegaard's unwillingness to make a cause or philosophical system out of his private obsessions or ruminations. Kierkegaard knew that the "leap of faith" he ascribed to Abraham — a willingness to sacrifice his son Isaac as proof of a faith in God's purposes — and posited as a "stage" for someone, anyone (but who can ever know for whom?), is an act, really, of lunacy by any conventional, sober, "realistic"

9

standards. Such a choice entails extreme loneliness, continuing personal anguish, but, most significantly, an encounter with "the absurd": in our present-day language, "passivity" in the face of the seemingly pointless loss of a loved one. Nor would he have approved of, one ought at least conjecture, the emphasis put upon the intensely personal and incommunicable by some who today call themselves "existentialists" and, doing so, call upon his name for sanction.

He did not rail against objective inquiry or the mind's rational inclinations. He did not want to take us each from the other, into a world inhabited by narcissistic, indeed semi-autistic, anarchists, each proclaiming his or her "truth," and all ridiculing anyone's effort to point out what is actually going on — the patterns of feeling, the themes being proclaimed, the order in the apparent (and apparently enjoyed) disorder. Least of all did he envision himself a patron saint of those who would mock science, or embrace with showy, even provocative, assertiveness the rituals of "introspection" or "meditation" or "faith" — the traditional or the faddishly "new." For him the issue was not what the mind did, what it saw and proclaimed, within its inevitable limitations, to be "true" or "universal"; but rather, the purpose (if any) a particular life has been put to. It is fine — more strongly, it is important — that we work as scientists or historians, that we write, paint, compose, that we build theories and out of them develop an easier, more comfortable life. For all his astringent, polemical satire, directed for the most part at the self-assured, cozy Scandinavian middle-class life, he knew better than to permit himself endless leeway in that literary direction.

It matters very much the *way* Kierkegaard condemns others, writes of their conceits or deceits — the objective he has in mind as he builds his persuasive, entrancing, and, often enough, tantalizingly obscure argument. What he demands a bit arrogantly, sometimes, of Denmark's burghers — that they give real, sustained attention to the question of "the meaning of life" — he also demands of himself, the man who observes them and evokes their pitiable and busy waywardness so tellingly. After all, articles and books can be the outcome of aesthetic indulgence, or can be all too satisfying as examples of moral conviction and personal dedication.

For all the risks Hegel took with presumptuousness or arrogance, he came close, at moments, to spotting or forecasting the similar temptations that would befall his critics. Highly personal introspection can turn into a caricature of what Socrates had in mind when he withdrew his considerable powers of observation from the natural world and worked hard to figure out what he and others were like "inside." For Hegel, the risk Socrates took was confusion — coming up with a mixture that doesn't really work: "neither fish nor flesh, neither poetry nor philosophy." Another risk, for those who take up where Socrates left off, is an ironic and fussy kind of self-importance: the determined "individual," the emphatically "artistic" personality.

Hegel would not grant much independence or authority to "intuition" or "subjectivity." Others of his age, or, certainly, ours, have been quite willing to take for granted a tension between the heart's reasons and the mind's — the old distinction of Pascal's. But Hegel brusquely waved aside the claim that there is some private realm of feeling within us — one of heartfelt emotion that can belong to a particular individual and no one else. He viewed the seemingly personal, whether an action or a fantasy, as utterly connected to the observable world, hence the proper subject of rational consideration and, yes, categorization. Uniqueness was for him an illusion; the mind is always (even that of the hermit or the rebel) embedded in a given time, place, nation, culture. As for spontaneity, originality, and empathy, the virtues of those who hail the subjective as an alternative to the legalistic aridity of rationalism, in their name (he knew long before Hitler arrived on German soil) all sorts of demonic forces can be unleashed and accorded approval. I suppose he would have gained a measure of satisfaction — he was capable of being cranky, argumentative, and all too pleased with himself — that both Carl Jung and Martin Heidegger fell for Hitler and the Nazi version of ideological romanticism.

Hegel, and with him countless "rational" or "logical" individuals over the generations, have worried that words like *sincerity*, or *authenticity*, that expressions like *openness of feeling* are, really, evidence of egotism — a means by which individuals indulge their desires, however greedy or exploitative, but obtain the satisfaction of public sanction and self-approval. Hegel was no polemical atheist, his followers notwithstanding. He saw Christianity as a historically advanced expression of ethical idealism — evidence that men could at least aspire to subordinate their various desires to the needs of a larger community, and thereby acknowledge what is, in any case, a universal truth: that even the most idiosyncratic of inward individuals is never psychologically "free," is always in his or her various "existentialist" affirmations an understandable part of a social and cultural community, however peripheral, small, or remote.

As one goes through Hegel's various essays and books, one is in the presence not only of a distinguished philosophical canon, but a particular man's at times poignant effort to imagine for his fellow man — somehow, and in some distant future — a real measure of personal freedom. Yet he never quite imagined how that "measure" would become substantial, secured, part of everyone's reasonable birthright. He had to settle for the state, the polity — the laws of a particular nation or society. Those laws allow various kinds of initiatives, forms of behavior, prerogatives, or "rights." They restrict, too — pointedly and, if need be, punitively. Let Kierkegaard mock Copenhagen, Denmark, all "Christendom"; he was, every day, a law-abiding member of a given world, and his ideas as well as his everyday actions gave constant testimony to a particular affiliation and citizenship. If he could find for himself, within those limits, a minute or two of privacy and originality, then all to the good. Hegel had his doubts that anyone was going to find much leeway for himself or herself in this world; the more a Kierkegaard learns, and even learns about his mind, the more that knowledge becomes a quite definite burden, because it carries a message that Hegel wanted no one to forget, least of all himself: the knowledge of *necessity*, of limited possibilities, of life's spiraling (post-Eden) series of demands and requirements.

Some have misunderstood Hegel, thinking him cold, arrogant, terribly presumptuous; whereas Kierkegaard has been dismissed as yet another wild, breast-beating apologist, however brilliant, for the crazier side of man. Hegel's *Spirit of Christianity*, not even published until 1907, comes ironically close to Kierkegaard's essential vision — that the spirit, and not the letter, is what matters. Actually, Kierkegaard not only possessed but used an incisive intellect, even as Hegel could, at times, take a stand against arid legalisms and insist upon moral experience as an important and proper determinant of man's actions. If anything, Hegel responded to the Holy Spirit — not the Father and the Son, perhaps, and not the disciples, and not the popes. Kierkegaard was similarly tough and mordant when sizing up religious faiths, as well as those who uphold them institutionally. He analyzed "Christendom" and only then made such an uproar about what he saw.

Hegel often had in mind Plato's remark that the philosopher is "the spectator of all time and all existence." Kierkegaard was an obsessed spectator, and perhaps troubled himself too much about the "nature" of existence. His attack on Hegel, in *Concluding Unscientific Postscript*, gives substantial evidence of being a personal confrontation with himself rather than the German metaphysician: Hegel's seeming capacity to reconcile contraries and comprehend anyone and anything must have been regarded as enviable indeed by the far-from-modest Dane. Kierkegaard's recommendation of "resignation," of an ultimately humbling renunciation, can (without stretching any psychological points) be understood as a proper antidote to substantial intellectual pride. Kierkegaard's polemics are, actually, *systematically* unsettling; he attacks "objectivity" with cold, analytic force. He is not, in principle, antiscientific, either. But he had a keen eye for idolatry, and realized that there is an important distinction between, on the one hand, a man trying hard to learn something in a laboratory, and describing his work in "objective" and morally responsible language, and — on the other hand — a man who has confused man's discoveries with God's will or Grace.

Perhaps it is a psychological tone that distinguishes existentialists, especially Kierkegaard, from the Hegelian dialecticians, or even the other philosophers of "reason." One requires hopefulness and a kind of self-assurance to keep offering explanations about an exceedingly frustrating and mysterious universe, one which, in the end, claims us all unto itself. Many existentialists — though not so much Gabriel Marcel, Karl Jaspers, and Walker Percy — have quite another disposition; they cannot overlook man's continuing and murderous follies, his pitiable pretensions, his absurd bombast, and, equally absurd, his doomed fate. Unquestionably Kierkegaard is gloomy as he surveys mankind, and there is implicit in his "stages" a pessimism with respect to most of us: we are victims of what, eventually, bores us; or we try hard to live decent and generous lives, but end up entirely missing the point of "existence."

Kierkegaard regarded most of us as without detachment, perspective, judgment — as the blind leading the blind. We live on an insignificant cinder, whirling through the universe, and soon enough, perhaps, not only will each of us die, but the cinder, too, will lose its glow, give out and crumble — again, dust to dust. Meanwhile we strut, boast, make all too much of ourselves, and, lest there be any gnawing doubts or second thoughts, resort to various forms of psychological anesthesia. For Kierkegaard, one of them is any political, psychological, or philosophical theory which claims to have figured out what is and what will be — thereby encouraging a fool's paradise. Pure whistling in the dark — that is what he thought of all such efforts. There is no real prospect, he believed, for lasting social cohesion; nor is man perfectible. The future is as bleak as the past was wretched. But some try at all costs to live it up, dance "the whole night through," and others kid themselves with that craven, sly instrument — the human mind and its bag of tricks.

Still, there *is* that mind, and it does indeed set us apart, distinguishes us from all other life on this planet. And Kierkegaard was not loath to use the mind — endlessly, brilliantly, inventively, and, some would say, quite exhibitionistically, even to the point of pride. He denounces others, shows in remarkable and painful detail how mischievous, insolent, and, always, "absurd" we are. He demonstrates the faith of the daily writer: that others can and will pay heed, so that even exclamations to the dire effect that just about everyone is a fool or living a foolish life are not altogether futile — else why come forth with them, and with so much conviction? The one who sees virtually all his neighbors hopelessly confused, deluded, or mistaken keeps addressing them. Or if not them, whom? And if no one, then why write a single sentence?

Gabriel Marcel, the twentieth-century French philosopher, was a much more explicitly *personal* existentialist. He wrote unashamedly about matters of the mind and heart, without recourse to the language of psychology — no mean feat in modern times. He regarded many of us as struggling with each other in less than futile ways and, unlike Kierkegaard, did not reserve for special occasions those breakthroughs of trust and "fidelity" that make human life — well, for Marcel — distinctively what it is. And some of Marcel's objections to rationalist or idealist philosophy apply as well to Kierkegaard, who (in spite of himself, maybe) did issue generalizations, reveal rather pointedly and heatedly an abstract willingness to define, categorize, specify according to a classificatory scheme. And did not turn on himself, consider the ethical implications of such intellectual behavior. Is it really true that any particular human being inhabits *only* the aesthetic "stage" — Kierkegaard's way of describing a sensually greedy, self-centered person's habits? Who is to judge someone "within the ethical" — a way of making a judgment about a higher, more responsible, less narcissistic life? Marcel saw us to be lonely, inclined to misunderstand and disappoint each other — but also, often enough, as longing for friendship, for a chance to show that we do understand and will not forsake "the other." And we have within us, by his lights, the possibility for transcendence — a more prosaic or ordinary kind than Kierkegaard allowed. Marcel shunned scientific or technological categories as well as social or political ones; and he refused to consign anyone, however apparently "driven" or outcast, to a particular fate. Biologists or social scientists eagerly try to pinion all of us or each of us, but for Marcel transcendence means defiance — man becoming something of genuine and enduring worth, despite the limitations of body, mind, and spirit which, at the same time, do manage to curb him.

Marcel joined Kierkegaard in regarding scientific rationalism and technological abundance as false gods of sorts; not in themselves "evil" or "wrong," but used by many of us to deceive ourselves. He was especially critical of the mechanistic side of contemporary psychology and sociology — individuals reduced to reflex patterns, or proclaimed the "products" of various "influences." A playwright and sometime storyteller, he disliked not only the assumptions but the imagery of such a point of view. And, really, he believed in God, in the Holy Spirit, in a Being, it can be said, that informs and touches and inspires and molds — the verb must necessarily be inexact — the "nature of being."

Marcel has been the most persuasive Christian existentialist of this century. He was more conciliatory toward his readers, by far, than Kierkegaard, though with no sacrifice of nuance, ambiguity, or complexity. There is in Kierkegaard a defiant, truculent side that offends not only the shallow and the pietistic, who deserve whatever they get along those lines, but sincere and thoughtful individuals, curious if the "leap of faith" has to be quite as dramatic, abrupt, and solitary as it was said to be by one man over a century ago. Kierkegaard was God-obsessed, and would have no traffic with other human beings, except to lecture them harshly or with strenuous humor. Marcel had quite another involvement with his comrades under the sun, if not the star of Satan. For Marcel God is not "on high," unapproachable, utterly inscrutable. Marcel would never have had the heart to ask us to consider Abraham's sacrificial act exemplary. Rather, he saw God as revealed in the everyday struggles each of us wages for a kind of personal integrity — one that is not self-encasing, however. Insofar as anyone becomes shut off, unable to give or receive somebody else's trust, affection, friendship, then it is indeed the star of Satan that has come to dominate a particular person's sky. There is an important distinction, too, between the agnostic or atheist existentialism of Camus or Sartre and Marcel's kind. The former two are concerned with man the disillusioned and pessimistic one — a survivor, in our times, of brutalities unknown to any other generation. The absurd nature of existence haunted Camus (his doomed Sisyphus) and prompted Sartre to alternate between savage contempt for the Western bourgeoisie, of which, of course, he was part, and a fierce and relatively eccentric Communism, not too removed in its personal, and arguably quixotic, character from the existentialist "positions" other troubled but searching men and women had found for themselves in the 1940s and 1950s. Marcel, in contrast, was less political — and also more preoccupied with a certain kind of psychology.

It is a psychology whose character has been especially well described by the American psychiatrist Harry Stack Sullivan. Sullivan was, in his own way, an existentialist. He wanted to get to each person he saw directly, openly, without the intervention of theoretical structures, which he believed to be potentially dangerous — because a given life history is unique as well as susceptible to generalizations that, often enough, even Freud's, amount to reifications. Sullivan kept on emphasizing that no one can see, hear, touch the Id, the Ego, the Superego. He warned repeatedly against the tendency we all have to confuse our ideas or formulations with biological or psychological reality — with what actually happens in a person's brain, mind, life. Theories can help us look at events, give us a way of seeing things; but Sullivan felt they also tend to remove the psychiatrist from the particularity of *a* patient, and worse, they become articles of faith in a field presumably meant to be investigative and therapeutic.

Sullivan had no mind for "stages," "periods," or even "complexes." His was a twentieth-century American, empirical mind. He could see his patients become anxious, and he reasoned that years ago they had begun to feel worried or hurt because things were not going well between them and *someone else*. Sullivan's "interpersonal" psychiatry rests on the assumption that each of us learned to get along with significant "others" — but at varying costs. Anxiety, for him as for Marcel, is connected to a person's vulnerability — his or her sense of being alone, uncertain, all too insignificant. More than any other psychiatric observer and writer, Sullivan emphasized loneliness as a major developmental issue — not a "symptom," not the result of various conflicts exerting their toll, but a state of mind that is a major influence in the lives of person after person, the so-called normal as well as the psychiatrically ill. He was critical of Freudian constructs, insisted that their reductionist tendency be acknowledged. He was not afraid of plain words like *hope* or *despair*, or again, *loneliness*, though he also could be rather dense, some would say murky. Again, one thinks of Marcel, who struggled in complicated and often impenetrable prose for a view of man that would, in all directness and simplicity, acknowledge his strivings for meaning, for purpose, for self-respect, and the affirmation that goes with the relatively consistent affection and love of others.

Both Marcel and Sullivan took up matters of the heart without succumbing to sentiment or piety. In an ironic way, each was saved from that fate by a capacity for the abstract, by the achievement of scholarly competence, by membership in an intellectual tradition. At times Sullivan reminds one of Kierkegaard as well as Marcel. The notion of "security" and "security operations," an important element in Sullivanian "interpersonal psychiatry," emphasizes the restless, searching side of mental life. Moreover, Sullivan was no stranger to irony or paradox. He knew that each of us looks for what we never really get in full — a lasting state of ease and comfort, a condition of satisfaction with ourselves that does not yield to the corrosions of time and circumstance. As a clinician he knew how determined and devious a person can be in the course of pursuing a given "security operation" — a maneuver involving others that presumably is meant to purchase serenity, but often buys only temporary solace.

Freud's "ego mechanisms of defense" are largely "internal,"

and often executed within the unconscious. Sullivan was more interested in the observable dealings each of us has with one another. They may have purposes other than we realize, but they take place in the world, have to do with people, places, things. No one, really, can directly observe a "projection" or "introjection"; they are matters of inference and interpretation. Sullivan's "security operations," in contrast, are the stuff of novels, short stories, plays — and of the existentialist literature. When he referred to "selective inattention," for instance, he had in mind daily events in the lives of all of us such as Kierkegaard and Marcel, for their own quite different purposes, also remarked upon. Sullivan had in mind everything from the most ordinary to the extremely bizarre. He wanted to make sense of human activity as it could be seen and heard — even as he believed that the most disturbed of psychotics, emitting apparent babble in a mental hospital, is really behaving in a quite understandable fashion, given the observer's willingness to learn patiently why, in fact, effusive incoherence may suit a particular person's purposes (as a "security operation") quite well.

There is an earthy, empirical side to Sullivanian psychiatry — an insistence on tethering ideas to things — that is, perhaps, American, and yet connects rather well, ironically, with the European, existentialist philosophical tradition. Sullivan tried to inspire others, reached out for colleagues like Marcel, was no loner like Kierkegaard. He headed the William Alanson White Foundation and the Washington School of Psychiatry, and for years was an important contributing editor of its journal, *Psychiatry*, which became (and still is) a major instrument for the explication of his kind of psychological thought. Although he was anything but a felicitous writer, he was, like Walker Percy, obsessed with the problem of language: how to understand and respond to the exceedingly various communications that patients present to their doctors. The bulkiness and awkwardness of his writing, actually, is not simply the result of literary incompetence or insensitivity. Like Heidegger, Harry Stack Sullivan tried hard to cram into his phrases and expressions as much as possible of the world's complexities, and of the nature of man's predicament — as the one who can fathom some of those complexities and speak about them.

Speaking, for Sullivan, was no mere avenue to another's unconscious; he regarded conversations as an active, energetic response to the world, quite worthy of being regarded on its own (descriptive, analytic) merits. Speaking not only affords the listener (if he is inclined to be interested) elements of unconscious symbolism and conflict, or evidence of defensive postures of various sorts; speaking is a means by which one joins hands with another (Marcel), or enters the world of Being (Heidegger), or takes risks with one's pride, one's integrity, one's "situation" (Kierkegaard). The "security" Sullivan mentions so often is both jeopardized and enhanced by an utterance — especially so, he knew, because the listener (including a psychiatrist) risked his own "security," often unwittingly, of course. And that "security" has a religious character; it is sought, it is ineffable and elusive, it is affirmed by others, yet only "through a glass darkly"; Sullivan's view provides no utopia, is distinctly post-Eden in character, and emphasizes (as did Christ's teachings) the significance of a community of suffering, searching individuals, all too aware of how little they have on their own.

The contrast of such a mode of psychological portrayal with the philosophical implications of traditional psychoanalytic theory is instructive. Freud had no vision of permanent harmony in mind for his patients — at least for the most part. In his *New Introductory Lectures* he did succumb slightly to the temptations of messianic sectarianism — with broad hints that various social and personal ills (war, poverty, greed, hostility) might yield to a growing cadre of the psychoanalyzed. But in the main he was guarded if not pessimistic; he held out only the conviction that through psychoanalysis, and even then only in the case of the relative handful who, for one reason or another, could avail themselves of it, the irrational would retreat in the face of persistent clarifications and interpretations: the stuff of insight. It is true, he did look at what went on between people like himself and patients — the phenomena of "transference" and "countertransference." Yet they are terms meant to describe irrational responses, based on events that have taken place in two people long before they have ever met each other.

Even in the contemporary literature that is generated by the membership of the International Psychoanalytic Association, one does not find the full acknowledgment that Sullivanians have made all along as a matter of course — that the so-called therapeutic process is very much, and not incidentally or peripherally, a matter of two human beings going beyond labels and categories, even those like "doctor" or "patient," and coming to affectionate, trusting terms with each other. As recently as the 1940s an *ego* psychologist like Heinz Hartmann could write of a "value-free" kind of "position" as ideal for the psychoanalyst; could advocate a "neutrality" with respect to the patient's ideas and ideals; and could refer to the world of money and power, of class and caste, of kith and kin, of culture and religious faith, as an "average expectable environment" — something one more or less sets aside in the semidarkness of the psychoanalytic office, wherein the doctor removes himself from the patient's range of vision, keeps even social amenities to a minimum, and yet becomes privy to the innermost (and he hopes, uncensored, unrestrained) thoughts and feelings of another person, who has, meanwhile, found himself or herself enfolded in one more abstract category, as if there weren't in this modern life of ours rather too many for our good: that of "analysand" — one who is an object of analysis.

Though sharply critical of psychiatry and the social sciences, Gabriel Marcel would not turn his back on the need for rational, analytic thinking of Sullivan's kind — directed inward as well as toward the "conquest" of nature's "secrets." There are outrageous moments in Kierkegaard, when he seems to scorn reason, and make demands on "mystery" that defy anyone's comprehension; and in fact, make the reader confused, angry, or ready to laugh. Marcel is less given to verbal display; he put his dramatic inclinations into the writing of plays. He was, too, a twentieth-century man, and so had a chance to see the full-fledged emergence of psychology, sociology, and psychiatry as disciplines — but also, he knew, as objects of faith. He saw the aggressive, manipulative side of contemporary science; and was especially aghast at the willingness of those who study man to treat him as if he, too, were something to be plundered.

Less emotionally than Marcel, and less explicitly, but with enormous intellectual resources, Martin Heidegger, the twentieth-century German philosopher, also gave his attention to modern man's psychological side, of such consuming interest, he knew, to the bourgeois class of the Western industrial states. Heidegger was personally more aloof than Freud, and his writing hardly offers the clarity of exposition to be found in, say, *Civilization and Its Discontents*. Moreover, he insisted, coldly it seems, that he was not trying, like Marcel or Kierkegaard, to figure out how men and women ought to live in the brief time allotted them. Austerely, intricately, he wanted to comprehend "Being." Self-aware, he knew that it was precisely the capacity and intention to be so that distinguishes not only him but all the rest of us — hence his use of the rather ironic abstraction (for a so-called existentialist philosopher) of *Dasein* as a designation for the essence of human beings — the ones who are open, through awareness, to Being.

Nevertheless, for all his relentless and often thickly worded efforts to detach himself from man and understand him, Heidegger effectively and emphatically shirked analytic reductionism. When he wrote about anxiety and its place in the mind's life, he joined hands with Kierkegaard rather than the psychopathologists — by regarding anxiety as more than disease, and as nothing less than an essential part of our inheritance as human beings, a means by which we may come closer in touch with ourselves. For Heidegger anxiety is not an expression of "intrapsychic conflict," or irrational impulses coming up against the strictures of a conscience or the good judgment of one's socially minded "ego," but rather the only real instrument of self-discovery we have. Someone who is without anxiety, who has, perhaps, finished a long analysis and feels able to work effectively and love comfortably, ecstatically (and these days, some would demand, efficiently), may well be a person in the greatest jeopardy. One thinks of a psychiatrist who sees patient after patient: fifty minutes, and another fifty minutes, and still another fifty minutes. The patients learn what the psychiatrist may never dare acknowledge to himself, for all the insight he has with respect to himself, for all his competence at analysis of the "countertransference reactions" he experiences — learn that there is a coldness, a mechanical quality, a deadness to life that permeates even psychotherapy or psychoanalysis.

Freud was no philosopher; he had a certain disdain for the field, perhaps because he appreciated the dangers of endless rumination, perhaps out of his doctor's desire to *do* as well as *think*, perhaps in response to a given age's scientific optimism. It is no small irony that today many of us who practice psychoanalysis have come to realize how philosophical in nature many of our patients' problems or complaints turn out to be. Ralph Greenson has observed that his patients, rather often, don't come because they have a specific symptom, don't even have a definable psychiatric disorder, but suffer from vague unease, from boredom, from a feeling of dissatisfaction with "life," from a surfeit of honey and a rather short supply of purpose — other than to keep on making bucks, having sex, watching children grow up, going to parties, taking vacations, having new adventures, developing new interests or hobbies. And, of course, a trip to the analyst's office can be one of the last category — a thing to do for a while, a response to a social or cultural imperative of sorts, if not, even more sadly, a mere faddish indulgence.

Still, the desperation of the well-to-do is not to be dismissed; ought not, either, to be mocked, caricatured, or even compared pejoratively with the terrible, undermining, exhausting, humiliating experience of the world's overwhelming majority: impoverished and hungry men, women, children. No one at the edge of starvation is likely to be in a physical or mental position to appreciate the particular "malaise" Walker Percy, drawing on the existentialist philosophers, keeps portraying in

his novels. Maybe, though, someone about to die of malnutrition can turn meditative, can smile at fate, can welcome the
stars as brothers and sisters, can surrender to the sun's en-
abling inferno, can embrace the moon's cold light. Maybe there
are indeed cries of Kierkegaard's "infinite resignation" in our
ghettoes, in our migrant farm camps, not to mention the sub-
Saharan nations of Africa, wherein live millions of the apparently doomed. I have at times thought such to be the case. I
recall the shrug of a mother I knew in rural Alabama, and I
recall her words, not so out of keeping with Kierkegaard's: "I
didn't ask to be put here. I *was* put here. I didn't ask to leave;
I'll leave by His will. My will isn't what matters; it's His. If He
wants me to suffer like this, I guess He has His reasons. You're
here to prove your trust in Him. If someone offered me a million dollars, and said I could have all I want to eat for myself
and my children, but I'd have to stop thinking about Him and
start thinking of myself only, then I'd know I was in real trouble. I'd start worrying a lot about myself. I *hope* I would. I hope
I'd remember Jesus. He warned us about thinking about ourselves and not Him. He asked a lot of us."

Another time she was less sure of herself — and, alas, nearer
to death. She was all too willing to accept anyone's porridge,
handout, welfare sum, however slim. She was ready in an instant to move into a Beverly Hills mansion, a Park Avenue
duplex, even a modest old clapboard home near Harvard
Square. In exchange for bread, she would risk a certain grim
kind of eternity. She would consign herself by her own description to Hell, where she expected to see a lot of others like herself — the tempted poor. Better a life of alienation, better
aesthetic ramblings, better the inauthentic, better the endless
summers of the sated, psychoanalyzed bourgeoisie, than the
glimmer of a divine presence, the suspicion of a redemptive
promise, she occasionally clung to — while holding her bloated
belly and wondering whether it could take any food, even were
it miraculously to arrive.

Let Kierkegaard point his finger at the smug Danish burghers. Let Heidegger worry that his fellow German intellectuals had become in dozens of observable ways "inauthen-

tic" — strangers to themselves and fools, really, *sub specie aeternitatis*. Let Marcel be saddened that so many who own so much feel alone, trust no one, really, least of all themselves; and spend lifetimes craving people or possessions, which in turn become set aside in favor of other people, other possessions. For a woman dying of a mixture of malnutrition, diabetes, and congestive heart disease, at thirty-two, those lives, those journeys so despised by various existentialists, seem oddly dazzling, the stuff of a moment's daydream: "I'd like to try the bad, sinful things our minister talks about. I'd like to be fat and sassy, and have a lot of clothes and a big car and ten refrigerators full of food. I'd like to be *tempted*. I'd like to behave in a real sorry way. I'd like to be ungrateful for all I have. I'd like to be sitting in some mansion, and wondering what to do with myself. Boy, would I like that! I wouldn't care if I was all alone — if God had written me off, and the minister, and everyone else. Let me tell you, there are days that I sit here and I wish I was a lazy, rich, white one, like that lady I once worked for, before she went and died on me, and it's been bad for us ever since."

So it goes, the convergence of the fantasies of the benighted, wretched poor and the realities experienced by the knowing, spoiled rich. And so it goes, the class-connected nature of human thought and desire. Had Kierkegaard found access to another kind of dialectic than Hegel's — that of Karl Marx — the Copenhagen middle-class pieties might have seemed more pitiable than execrable. Even Jesus Christ, prototypically poor and persecuted, wondered aloud for a few seconds, at the very end, whether "infinite resignation," with all its suffering and ignominy, is quite to the point. Even Jesus Christ, who took unto Himself the disciples as a community of trust and love, found hesitation and doubt endemic, and a fatal kind of betrayal apparently inevitable. Even Jesus Christ, who challenged all "powers and principalities," who reviled the idolatry of the temple, who used parables and ironies and paradoxes in the service of Being, who asked that everyone be open to its mysteries, who tried to show, again and again, that the anxious can become the secure, that the hurt can become

25

the joyful, that those who have deceived themselves and others are headed nowhere fast — even He seemed for a while oblivious to God, self-absorbed and, in Heidegger's word, "fallen": so dependent, it seemed, on what was happening to Him, that He appeared, at least, to have lost sight of His "true self," or, perhaps, the destiny His particular sphere of Being had in store for Him, and peculiarly, for us.

If none of the major existentialist philosophers, except for Sartre, is explicitly "class-conscious," they all are anxious, indeed, to see the connections between private or idiosyncratic thinking and the everyday events of the world — not only to examine particular instances of human relatedness, but show how words like *history, society, culture* become for each of us all too much taken for granted, even though they are determinants of our lives rather than occasional sources of apprehension, wonder, awareness, concern, and so on. If existentialists risk naïveté or worse, insofar as they tend (Sartre apart, once again) to talk of "freedom" without referring to the specific curbs exerted by various economic systems, then materialists (Marxists or capitalists, but also any number of natural or social scientists) have their own risks to face. *Transcendence* is a hard word for many of us brought up in the twentieth century to understand. It is not something a biologist or neurophysiologist or psychiatrist is apt to recognize as familiar, or easy to explain. Many would sneer at its implication — or insist that one day, given more "research," we will know the anatomy, the psychopharmacology of the "phenomenon." But for existentialist philosophers Kierkegaard's "leap" is but one of various kinds of transcendence; and as a matter of fact, when discussing man's nature those philosophers constantly refer to the potentiality each of us has for going beyond what seem not only our usual selves, but what we imagine as possible.

The whole is greater than the sum of its parts, bored students learn in high school — another vaguely mathematical, vaguely and maybe suggestively philosophical comment, handed down as a once-original idea, now a cliché. Yet Jaspers knew we surpass every expectation of ourselves in mysterious ways, in ways impossible to "define" or "explain"; and Heidegger insisted that it is in our very nature (an extraordinary privilege of ours) to move beyond our particular being and toward Being itself — toward the achievement of ourselves, toward the Is of what is, toward a moment of affirmation at once ineffable and utterly apparent; and an old migrant farmworker, a tired mother and grandmother can "allow as how" there are moments, oh yes, there are those rare and special and eye-opening and unforgettable and hard-to-talk-about moments: "I will feel tired and sick. I will feel mean. I don't like anyone, even my own children. I've been out picking. I have no strength left. I won't last the night. My lungs are bad, and I can't catch the air very good. Suddenly I'll see my youngest child, and she'll be coming to me, and I'll be different. It's not a second breath of air. I'm still struggling for the first breath! It's God, giving me His strength. It's me becoming a different me; I'm free of my old, weary self.

"I asked the minister how it happens. It doesn't always happen; just sometimes. It happens when I'll see a certain look in my child's face; she needs me bad, and I want so bad to be good to her, even if I've been out all day under that sun, on my knees, picking the beans. She's my last, you know. I've made a lot of mistakes with the others. Some of them have turned out real bad. Don't ask. I wish I could have been a better mother. I wish I could have offered my children a better life. I wish I'd married a better man. He would walk out and leave me and come back and leave me bearing a child. He's been married to the wine bottle all his life, to tell the truth. The minister talks of the devil; well, that devil must be the one who makes all that wine, and sells it. The crew leader is the devil, too. He's a wicked man.

"There are a lot of times, though, that it's been *me* who's been wicked. You mustn't always try to excuse yourself by pointing the finger at someone else. In church I look at myself, and I know I've sinned. I don't stand up for what I believe. I let the crew leader push me around. I just do what everyone else does; and I fight to breathe. But when I see my little child, the last one I'll ever have, smiling and coming toward me, and the sun is going down, then I'm another person, and I'm free, and I

27

feel like I could hold the whole world in my hand, like we say in church, and there she is, my child, and I lift her up, and let me tell you, I've forgotten about my troubles breathing, and I've forgotten about my other troubles, and I'm a new person, tired as I was, and late in the day though it is — a new person. For a few minutes I'm almost a stranger to myself, that's what, because I feel like this new person — almost as if God had breathed His strength into me, and I'd said yes, I'll use His strength, yes, I will."

What is to be said in response to such an outpouring — itself a remarkable affirmation of self, if not a moment of personal transcendence? (One has to spend time, perhaps, with migrants such as she to realize how utterly silent, shut off, and grimly withdrawn they often can be.) How does one explain even her physical capacity, given severe cardiovascular disease, to talk so much, to be, suddenly, so active and energetic and responsive not only to a child but to "life" itself — her ability to find hope of a kind in the midst of such sad, confining, unrelenting, and overwhelming poverty? Does she have reserves of physical strength not ordinarily apparent, but set in motion by a series of neurophysiological (and neurohormonal) reflexes? As for her mental state, is her temporary exuberance and optimism also a matter of reflexes — or of the resolution, so called, of intrapsychic conflict, so called? Has she, for an interlude, mastered a chronic depression, or entered a manic ascension, or found "denial" and "reaction-formation" useful "mechanisms of defense"?

At the very least is she not resorting to illusions, turning her child into much too vivid and redemptive a figure, merging the appearance of the child with a religious tradition and a certain naïveté of outlook — all into a moment's psychological excess? The "reality" of her situation is, after all, not about to yield to any prayers, exclamations, annunciations. She is fated for a relatively early death, and the time left her will be no better than the time already spent in the course of a life's unfolding. As for her much-loved last child, the prospects are not all that good, despite the mother's occasional conviction, or, for that matter, a minister's prayers, a social worker's earnest efforts, a

28

teacher's estimate that this child is bright and able in school. The mother herself, at other moments, and tersely and right to the point of things, has described what will "really" take place: "It'll go on and on; she'll live like all of us, she'll be like all of us."

Realism can be skirted or shunned by the well-to-do; it is an utter, daily necessity for the poor. But realistic analysis and description tell only so much about anyone's life, whoever he or she is. The woman just quoted both knows that and doesn't know that, even as transcendence is not a lasting "state," but a thrust of resolve, an assertion of spirit — at once momentary and timeless. One can live by every statistic a desperate if not doomed life, one can be a nobody in everyone's eyes, including one's own — and yet say yes to a child, to oneself in such a way that all realism is abandoned. Instead, one submits to hope, claims it as an inheritance, a privilege of one's humanity, all of a given temporal world's "principalities and powers" notwithstanding.

The woman who realizes she has no prospects at all is also the woman who finds herself graced with a child's look, and her own response to it; they fall in each other's arms, become at a remove from various others — the crowd of migrants, the band of crew leaders, sheriffs, growers: those who, in sum, remind her to whisper, cringe, give up, lose faith in herself or conviction about life's worth. She and her child become an island of sorts — not in self-righteous or arrogant smugness, or in contempt for others, but because, of a sudden, they have chosen not only each other, but themselves. They *are;* they are "free," as the mother herself both implies and at one point says outright — though not politically free, and not free from social exclusion or virtual economic peonage, and not even psychologically "free," in the way so many of us have come to think possible or desirable: swinging with awareness, insight, and blessed by reduced "conflict," or an absence of it, and by an ability to "cope," and by the achievement for ourselves of something called "the whole person."

That mother's freedom is abruptly won, startles her, vexes her, leaves her — only to reassert itself at other times. If one wanted to be categorical and faithful to Heidegger's phenomenological thought, one would observe that initially the woman felt herself to be but one of a crowd of hurt, suffering, badly put-upon migrant farm workers, and so walked bent, joyless among others. When she saw her child, her body straightened, she moved away from the others. She was, of course, reaching out for someone, hurrying toward her. But she cast a sidelong glance as she did so; for an instant she not only felt apart from some people, but she took notice of so very much — had caught sight of herself as well as the child to whom she is drawn so strongly. She has no answers for her life. She sees no likelihood of a different tomorrow. But she briefly felt, by her own description, "peculiar" — wrested from all that she ordinarily takes for granted, thinks not at all about, goes along with, questions in no way. She defined her peculiarity rather briefly, but with a knowing assertiveness, the result of a decisiveness she had found within herself — "out of the depths," as it has been put.

She had stopped being herself, had for a while found herself to be "someone else." The "someone else," for Heidegger, would be her "authentic" self, which had emerged — which she allowed to overcome her or, put differently, which she chose. For a time she ceased being a migrant peon. She was racing to a child — and had God on her mind. He was urging her on, giving her energy, summoning her. As she left a crowd of migrants, she left in her mind the confines of a given life, including its psychological and spiritual consequences. Just as Kierkegaard's bourgeois contemporaries had become lost to themselves, had become absorbed in the crowd's tyranny, in the complacency and petty self-justifications of "everydayness," then a migrant woman, or any one of millions of working-class individuals, can also lose themselves, so to speak — every day and quite thoroughly. One doesn't have to wear a gray flannel suit, and carry an attaché case, to be a member of a regimented world that bears down hard but, ironically, offers relief, pleasure, satisfaction, even exhilaration and drama to fool oneself. Among the poor or the marginally well-off, as with the quite well-to-do, there are stratagems of guile and bluff, illusion and self-deception — tricks of the mind that put the already suffering person even more in jeopardy; and, as the migrant woman knows in her bones, the stakes are even higher than they may seem.

Philosophers like Heidegger and Marcel, and before them Kierkegaard, and, from a different tradition, Wittgenstein, have known the enduring challenge of analytic assertion — the continuing danger of self-delusion: mere concepts become endowed with "life." On the one hand, a thinker wants to develop his ideas as fully, and maybe as elegantly and persuasively, as possible. Thousands of words stand in the aisle, waiting to be given a curtain call. The use of them is itself an affirmation of one's nature. Yet the phenomenon of transcendence defies words, as does, really, that of "resignation" in consequence of a "teleological suspension of the ethical" — Abraham's decision to trust the Lord against (paradoxically) every God-given moral instinct in his aged but persevering mind and soul. What is one to do — retreat into mute murkiness of thought, or into a silent scorn for anyone who has anything to say? In order to acknowledge one's "finitude," need one deny one's "humanity" — the craving to come forth and *declare*, for all the risk of self-importance, condescension, self-delusion, plain foolishness, and, not least, sinfulness?

The sin of pride, that sin of sins, curses not only businessmen bloated with money and power, or ignorant, prejudiced yeomen, or factory workers, sadly anxious to mouth banalities or utter hateful curses in every direction. Kierkegaard knew the devilishness of his own brilliance. Wittgenstein had his own reasons to suggest "silence" for himself, and maybe, the rest of us. He made his suggestion at a certain point in his life, and in his career as a philosopher who wrote for others. (Presumably there are some philosophers who never write — as a matter of principle rather than of psychological inclination or "need"; rather in the tradition, perhaps, of the Chinese poet who tore up all his poems and sent them floating down the Yangtze River.) As for Martin Heidegger, one feels him straining mightily with words — even in a language that lends itself well to his purposes as a philosopher determined to build a very special and inclusive (world-embracing) point of view. At a certain point he, too, has to pull back and acknowledge the inadequacy of words, though language lies so close to the heart of our "nature."

Heidegger realized that no one, including even the extraordinary author of *Sein und Zeit*, can offer a final determination of Being, or of the diverse ways particular individuals might just possibly come to experience it — radically open themselves to its presence and mysteries. For Heidegger, anxiety was a way, maybe *the* way. Kierkegaard, having renounced the possibility of marriage with Regina, also dwelled on anxiety. It can be maintained that Abraham's "resignation" is, in fact, anxiety raised to the ultimate: anxiety become so strong and pervasive that it dissolved itself as well as its container of sorts, a merely human and inevitably anxious person. Marcel was not unaware of anxiety as a great influence upon all of us, but he chose to stress friendship and love as other vehicles by which we can move toward a "radical openness to Being." The migrant mother whose utterly unpretentious words I have quoted above knows anxiety all the time — of a kind so "basic," so compelling and, alas, devastating, as to make even a psychologically hurt or troubled theorist who writes about anxiety analytically or philosophically or theologically seem a bit sheltered, provincial, even spoiled. Nevertheless, she finds rather a lot in the sight of one of her children (though, at certain times only) and for "reasons" she would be the last one in the world to care to mobilize or parade before any viewer (or reader). Who is to say — she may find an avenue to Being in those moments. Heidegger never wanted to set himself up as a judge — as an "expert" who knew who was becoming "open to Being" and who was not, who was saved, who damned, who had a chance, who needed advice, a book to read, an exegetical summary of *Sein und Zeit* maybe, with a few "applied" suggestions. Perhaps that migrant woman might indeed have aroused his interest, even confused him. He often acknowledged a certain perplexity about his existentialist analysis: how to know which person, in concrete example, has actually moved "closer to Being"?

As a migrant, the woman has something in common with others who are far luckier in most respects. She wanders from town to town, county to county, state to state, in search of work, money, food, a chance for survival. Others wander because they feel detached, restless, out of sorts, unable or unwilling to settle down, settle into a conventional life. Movies like *Easy Rider* or *Five Easy Pieces* give voice to such migrants: spiritually dispossessed youth, many of them — though well-off older people by the many thousands have their own habits of overworked if not desperate mobility. Jack Kerouac's *On the Road* preceded Jack Nicholson's sad, lonely, tough, embittered trek, apparently ceaseless and uncompromising. The latter's well-to-do and well-educated background struck no one who appears in *Five Easy Pieces* as improbable elements in the life of a determined, restless outsider.

When Walt Whitman roamed over the American land he was full of hope and appreciative love. Not that many of his countrymen at the time, had they known him or cared to read him or been able to fathom him, wouldn't have laughed, scowled, or moved on quickly to some other concern. But Whitman loved a nation and a people, loved life as he happened to observe and experience it, felt not so much removed from others, isolated, adrift, cut off, and estranged, as a fortunate singer, privileged to see a lot, which he then could put into music. Kerouac was less hopeful; he was running away from so very much, though the open road, the inviting West, the possibilities of a vast continent, did at least temper his youthful pessimism, cynicism, self-imposed social ostracism. In contrast, Jack Nicholson as Bobby Dupea seems terribly alone (despite the efforts of his girlfriend); he has turned away from his cultivated and sensitive family, from the artistic and committed life he was brought up to consider his own. He has not only sought voluntarily the company of relatively hard-pressed, fearful, sullen, or hurt people; he has become, among them, the most cynical, morose, truculent. If they are confused, at a loss, the blind leading the blind or submitting en masse to the imperatives of a crudely materialistic, shrill, opportunistic world, he is brazenly willing to join them, dazzle them, even, with his presentation (it could be called) of their apprehensions and confusions. They live better than migrant farm workers, possess a certain tough independence, but are in obvious psychological, spiritual jeopardy.

All over America men and women keep relentlessly on the move — out of personal dissatisfaction, out of various disappointments and disenchantments — on the hunt for something different, something better. For what? More money, a nicer climate, a job with good prospects for advancement? Even those who *do* come up with such explanations will admit on occasion that their search is more complicated, and more desperate, too. A man who has never been anything but comfortable, socially and economically, a born Southerner who has moved from region to region in the United States, and tried a stint or two abroad, as a business executive, told me in the course of our talks quite clearly why he doesn't mind moving, and moving again: "I could stay in one place. I could dig in. I've tried doing that. But I get bored. So does my wife. So do our kids. We like to see different places. We like to travel. I get tired of the same old people. I don't know why; I just do. There's no place that's ever claimed me one hundred percent. Maybe, before I die, I'll put down some roots. People say you should. But we keep on meeting a lot of people who think like us. They're only here on this earth once, and they want to see all they can. I never get tired of exploring. My kids don't, either. One of them wants to be an astronaut. The other wants to be a scuba diver. Two explorers! I have a daughter, and she's grown, and she's moved across the country, and her husband is in the service.

"My wife gets angry sometimes; she says we're running from something. So is everyone! From bill collectors, mostly! I can't stand those ministers, who try to tell you that you're in trouble, or you have something wrong with you, or you're 'unhappy.' They want you to be 'unhappy'; that's how they make themselves a bundle — they win you over to their church, and start collecting your money on Sundays. I'm not 'unhappy'; I just want to live my life out, and have some fun, and enjoy the world. I've seen a lot of it, and I'm glad. I may have my bad moments, like everyone does. But I know how to snap out of it. I'm never really in trouble when I'm on a plane. Stay ahead of your worries. Move faster than they do — that's what I say!"

It is all too easy to call him "troubled." If he is, then a whole culture, social system, and economy give his habits, preferences, modes of living, a good deal of sanction. Is he to be called a foreigner in his own country, a spiritual exile, an "alienated" fugitive of sorts? Or is he quite adequately and thoroughly integrated into a nation which, actually, has for a long time encouraged its citizens to express their various discontents through moving out, moving on, moving ahead — getting someplace, getting by, getting? And what do the dreary or unhappy or insistently self-satisfied or energetically mobile lives of America's migrant farm workers or its migrant businessmen and salesmen and members of the military have to do with "existentialism," with Heidegger's elusive "Being," with Marcel's passion for "fidelity," with Kierkegaard's "stages"? Are we to say that Bobby Dupea or various "easy" motorcycle riders are quirky individuals, men and women who belong nowhere, drifters and adventurers who may please romantic moviegoers (or clever, money-hungry scriptwriters, producers, directors) but bear no real relation to (in Agee's phrase) "human actuality" as it is to be found in thousands of American communities over the breadth of the land?

In fact, Bobby Dupea says what one hears others say again and again in the course of doing "fieldwork"; in a moment of exasperated introspection he observes: "I move around a lot, not because I'm looking for anything, but to get away from things that go bad if I stay." But such an assertion is a backdoor way of getting at one's pessimism, fearfulness — one's frantic conviction, underneath it all, that nothing really means much in the long run. Once the businessman quoted above asked: "What does life mean?" It was a defiantly rhetorical question. "Hell," he answered himself, and paused a little too long — as if he may have felt, somewhere deep down, that there was no need to go on. But he did: "Hell," he repeated, "life doesn't *mean* anything. It just comes to you, and it leaves you. You're you when it's with you, and you're no one when it's gone. I can't think too much about 'life.' I get sick. I want to go in my car and take a drive and get a beer."

A man in flight. A man uninterested in facing up to his "condition" — and maybe, on a more personal or microcosmic level, afraid to get tied down to any situation in the least demanding ethically. A man hostage to his self-centeredness or greed. A man whose masks have long ago become part and parcel of "life" — from each morning's moment of awakening to the last second, every night, before dreams take over. Or the next to the last: "When you're in bed, and trying to catch a few hours of sleep, you have these thoughts. You wonder if there's anything bigger than you. Is there a God? How do I know? What should you do with your time here? I don't know. If you had another chance, how would you live your life? I don't know the answer to that one, either — but it bothers me more than the other questions. Maybe some people know how to do things better than I do. I don't claim to know any secrets about life. Those ministers do, but I don't listen to them. I just try to get through the day. Is there anything else to do? In the middle of the night, when you can't sleep, maybe you think there might be a better way to live a life. But in the morning, there's no time for that kind of thinking. I have to get up and go to work. If I don't, we'll all be wondering about a lot of things — where the next meal is coming from, for instance."

In the morning he shivers, literally. At forty he has "thin blood," so he believes. He puts on a bathrobe and feels better. He drinks hot coffee and feels better. He gets in his car, puts on the heater, listens to the radio, and feels better. He is a "hot weather" man. He likes to sweat. He likes to exercise, to work up a sweat. He also likes to keep his distance from others — and wants his children to do so. They should be wary of commitments, be scornful of a lot of slogans, enticements, obligations. The world is dangerous, and each person is subjected daily to various crooked schemes. People are generally not to be trusted: "Only a few, there are only a few you can really rely on. Most people are out for themselves." "It's too bad," he says, a little later, but he is angry rather than sorry when he makes

that remark. Nevertheless, he is not downcast when con-
templating his country and its people. In the abstract he loves
America. In the concrete, he watches everyone warily. He can
even be rather brusque and crude when talking about his wife
and children. He is a comfortable drifter, a middle-class red-
neck, and sometimes, a pathetic shadow of a boy he still can't
quite forget: "I used to be worried about people — when I was
a kid of eight or nine. A boy I played with, he was my age, died
of a blood disease. I cried for him. I felt sorry for his mother and
father. But my dad told me the boy's father was no good; he
owned a store and he cheated everyone, if he could get away
with it. Probably the boy would own the store now, if he'd have
lived; and he'd cheat me, if he had a chance. I used to be honest
when I was a kid.

"I was born in Arkansas. We were pretty well-off. My father
lost everything in the Depression. He was never the same. He
got a lot back, but he never got back his self-confidence. He
never really trusted anyone, again. Then my mother died. And
he found out she'd been cheating on him. So he just made
money and had a girlfriend a year for himself. He was a smart
man. He used to tell me not to be so nice to everyone, and I
finally learned my lesson. A kid stole some of my money and
my watch. A girl made up to me, then went for someone else
the day after she'd told me I was her 'only one.' My wife and I,
we have an understanding — don't ask too much of each other.
She goes her way; I go mine. We've stayed together for the kids.
We're not enemies. We have good times together. But if I have
to go out of town on business, I don't get any third degree
from her.

"I haven't been back to Arkansas in twenty years. I have
some property there, through my father's estate. A lawyer
handles everything for me. If you have a good lawyer, you're in
good shape. Without a lawyer, you're nothing. You're in trouble. You're at the mercy of everyone. You have to watch yourself. There are sharks everywhere, ready to eat you up alive. I
had a crazy dream after I saw that movie *Jaws;* I was driving
my car, and suddenly I saw the road end, and before I could do
anything, I was going off a cliff, and headed for the ocean

below. And would you believe it, I could see through the water, while I was sitting in the car, and there were sharks, lying there in wait for me! It must have been down South — maybe the Gulf of Mexico, because the water was green and like in the Caribbean. I hate those scary movies. I'll never go to one again. Life is bad enough, without being reminded of how really bad it can get!"

In a strange way, he is partially "free." A certain mindlessness enables in him a liberation of sorts. His gruff, pugnacious self-centeredness, his carelessness, which takes the form of political and social conservatism, allows him an ironic distance on others and himself — a distance necessary for his survival, he indicates. One wonders, as one listens to him — and thinks of others not unlike him in many respects — whether the social and political outlook precedes or is a consequence of a more personal, idiosyncratic "alienation," a sense of being "different," of being shy and wounded and rather open to the world's bruising assaults. Yet, like the migrant woman, he is no drifter in search of a redemptive or poetic experience. The romantic side of the existentialist philosophical and literary tradition becomes, on acquaintance, a flimsy and mocking caricature of life as it is actually lived by various men, women, and children. The outsider who mocks the superficialities of a given world, who throws aside various pieties and rides (on a horse, in a car, on a motorcycle) into some landscape's sunset or sunrise (or toward a low-hanging, beckoning, soft moon, or an aloof, cold one), is often himself or herself a rather inadequately rendered figure, at the very least.

It is simply not true, psychologically, that the people quoted here, or others like them, are any less complicated than, say, Bobby Dupea in *Five Easy Pieces* — even as his complexities of character and motivation are not altogether apparent. As a matter of fact, the romantic hero, or antihero, gets away with too much, even as the coarse, conventional braggart of our middle-class world, or the pitiably driven ghetto resident, or migrant farmer, doesn't often get away with anything — since, of course, their "narrowness" or their badly injured lives are constantly subjects of discussion among social scientists or social critics, some all too "existentialist" in their self-definition. The shoddy uses to which Western bourgeois high culture has put existentialism need no documentation. A philosophy meant to rescue individuals from one kind of abstract line of thinking, with all the dangers of loss of particularity, has itself become a means by which a host of stereotypes is foisted on thousands, if not millions, of people. The movies have not invented, though they have surely magnified, the existentialist mythology that still influences pervasively some American social criticism, thirty years after the end of the Second World War — at which time Camus emerged as an influential philosophical novelist, Sartre as a political philosopher without rival, and Kierkegaard as something more than a half-crazed, perversely elliptical, and persistently teasing and provocative theologian who wrote, of all things, in Danish. And if the restless wanderers with scorn in their hearts for brutal, mechanistic industrialism have been blown up into larger-than-life, lonely, courageous wise-ones, then others have paid the price, have been caricatured as stupid, greedy, thoughtless.

Who can do justice to the concreteness and particularity of human life — that of any person under any sun? How is even existentialism to be rescued from an intellectual version of the sin of pride? Who can portray *this* man, *that* woman at once precisely and broadly enough so that an individual's character is brought to life — so that, too, various political theories and social analyses are themselves qualified and only thereafter illuminated, rather than confidently and by rote confirmed? How to suggest, further, an alternative to the "malaise," the "sickness unto death," at once personal and cultural, that plagues us? We are rather accustomed, these days, to dire if not apocalyptic critiques — prophecies that leave little room for anyone to find much leeway, never mind hope. And yet. And yet, even those who make the inquiries, who come up with the predictions, have to make do, at the very least — and, maybe, find for themselves, in spite of their own words, a sense of purpose and conviction, a smile that is not always wan, a responsiveness that is not insistently begrudging or contemptuous.

In a *favella* just above and outside Rio de Janeiro, in 1974, a mother of ten children spoke to an American doctor and his family. She was so poor that the very word seemed elevating rather than descriptive, as the woman herself knew: "We have nothing. If we were better off, we'd be poor! We don't ask for anything, either — just for today, and tomorrow. We look up at the statue of Christ. He gives us the only thing we have — hope for today and hope that there will be a tomorrow. Don't ask us about next week. We try to forget yesterday. My oldest girl says there is no God. She sticks out her tongue at the statue of Christ. I think Jesus must smile at her and forgive her. He is angry at the people who live on the Copacabana, the rich ones. He will forgive a girl her bad time. He will pray for her. His arms are outstretched, praying for all of us. I get up in the morning, and watch the sun begin to touch Him; it is enough for me to see Him like that, early in the day. He shines. I feel able to match wits with the day. I have Him and the sun right here with me, closer than the mountain or the sky: He and the sun are in this plant.

"We were not put here, my children and I, to have a good time. My husband died with hope on his lips: 'I will see you in a second or two,' he said — his last words. He knew how to measure time. He never had a watch. We have no clock here. We have no electricity for electric clocks, and no money to buy the kind you wind. But there is the sun, the moon, the stars — and Christ over there, across the bay and high up, giving us the once-over! He teaches us time; but it may not be the kind of time the teachers make our children learn. As for the plant, it grows by day and rests by night. The plant has its own time to keep. One day it seems to be near death, the next day it shows a new life to us. We say hurrah. We look at our Lord, and He seems to have a smile on His face. It is true: that face changes. I am grateful for the days when the smile is there. On some days He seems very sad. I'm not sure whether He is crying, or I am! It is important to know the difference!"

The poor, benighted, superstitious lady — surely beyond the helping reach of anyone very important. And the three of us standing in that shack and trying to make conversation —

Yanqui visitors so privileged as well as earnest, so embarrassed and humiliated by what we saw, and realized to be connected in various ways to our own pleasant and comfortable lives. We could not forget what we had been told earlier, that the entire *favella* would soon be leveled, to make way for high-rise condominiums and a shopping plaza, in the name of "progress" and "civilization." That woman and her children were to be moved abruptly, arbitrarily, and without consultation — to another, even more crowded and desolate *favella*. Eventually there would be a "project" built for them, or so the "authorities" promised — the planners, the bureaucrats, the social technocrats, the educated and conscientious and proudly "aware" officials, with their slogans and social science talk and their fantasies of a better world.

Eventually the three of us began to realize not only how awkward our presence was for everyone — ourselves and those we were "observing" — but that we were "outsiders" in more than the obvious sense of the word. We were cut off existentially as well as at a remove socially, economically, culturally; we were caught in the limitations and consequent blindness of our particular lives, and so tempted to do our own kind of harm to those lived by others. A day later we went to speak with an expert on urban affairs, an "activist scholar," he called himself. As we listened to him, we began to hear ourselves — maybe not literally or ideologically, but existentially, in the sense that his world was ours, whereas in that shack, again, we were "outsiders." He began emphatically: "We have to do something for those people." Then he became the educator: "They are the poorest of the poor; they come here to our city from all over. They want something better. When *you* look at them, they seem in a bad condition. But do you take the time to see what they have left to come here, to Rio de Janeiro? We are poor; we are not the United States. We are growing, building — so now everyone looks at our modern skyscrapers, our hotels and apartment houses and office buildings, and compares them to the *favellas*. We are called cruel and selfish, because we don't get rid of every *favella*, don't abolish poverty. Have you done so in the United States? Where is there a country without slums?

England or France or Italy? I have visited them; and they have had a lot longer time, and more money, to do what people ask us to do right away!

"We are trying to build up a capital base. We are trying to get more investments from abroad — and more tourists, too. Slowly we will develop a middle class, and slowly the money will filter down to the poor. We will improve their education and their health facilities. We will build settlements for them. The smarter ones will rise up; and they will then help their own kind. All of that takes time. There is no other way. As for revolutions, they end up destroying everything, and the poor are no better off. They become cannon fodder for the Communist generals. At least here we leave the poor alone. We don't interfere with their thoughts. We don't try to brainwash them. They are free to go to the Copacabana and swim, as a matter of fact, just like the rich do — side by side with them. We have a democracy here! The poor are always a burden, though. I know that. It's up to us to make them less of a burden. That's our job."

It is not an altogether forced or gratuitous step from the two Brazilians to Hegel and Kierkegaard, the latter pair locked to this day, through their readers and interpreters, in a confrontation. Nor are the Brazilians strangers to the worries and strivings that have prompted twentieth-century philosophers like Marcel and Heidegger. The Being Heidegger tried unremittingly to explore is the Being a hard-pressed woman of a Latin American *favella* seeks in those spare moments she somehow manages to find — amid a life's flux, to use a hallowed and ancient philosophical word. It is a flux she can't define; it is *hers*, no one else's — though, of course, she shares assumptions, hopes, fears with others. One does not see women en masse rushing for a glance at Rio de Janeiro's statue of Christ. And each person who looks upward at Him does so with particular eyes. This woman finds, through the effort of her mind and heart, at least a touch of transcendence, which she then makes astonishingly, boldly, instructively concrete: one flowering plant. A curse of the intellectual life — a class-connected curse, it must be emphasized — is the condescension or patronization toward the poor and the uneducated that not rarely wells up, unwittingly in some, against the will in others, gratuitously and smugly in still others — as if that Brazilian mother's search, and yes, the symbolization she manages for herself and others, utterly connected to the immediacy and singularity of her one, given stretch of time on this earth, is altogether different from, say, Kierkegaard's or Heidegger's.

It was a novelist, Dostoevski — so appropriated by upper-middle-class, Western, agnostic intellectuals — who knew in his bones and in his heart and cried to high heaven, and to his chosen Lord, Jesus Christ, that if something called "existentialism" were ever to mean something, it would have to come to terms with a woman of the *favella* as much as a scholar who has written articles and books on "alienation," or "estrangement," or "despair," or "authenticity," or yes, "existentialism." Not that Dostoevski was a constant anti-intellectual; he did have his moments — provoked by the spontaneous expressions of a heart that could be cold and ungenerous as well as offer us a Sonia, a Raskolnikov, a Mishkin, an Alyosha, and enable us to see them through so much that is spiritually edifying, touching, shattering.

However, Dostoevski also wrote letters, essays, book reviews, and in his novels carried on lines of discussion, reflection, argument. He is regarded by some today as a political conservative, an abject royalist of sorts — willing, even anxious, to submit to the Romanovs. It can be argued, even so, that he was the most radical of thinkers; he may not have wanted to work for political revolution and a thorough redistribution of Russia's land and wealth, but he did not set himself above the poor, the ordinary men and women of the world. His "concern" for them never smacked of *noblesse oblige;* if anything, he thought and wrote as a fellow sufferer of theirs, no less limited, vexed, and flawed than any of them. And his vision of their lives was redemptive in the religious rather than sectarian sense; that is, he allowed for transcendental possibilities, and knew that even a storyteller could only hint at how those possibilities came into being — Sonia and Raskolnikov touched by grace, and destined not for a royal road of romance, but further struggles, which, however, have a significant direction to them, based on a spiritual and psychological commitment made by one or another person.

Dostoevski's "existentialism" was sometimes implied, sometimes shouted, but it was not the stuff of a creed. How can one speak dogmatically for the millions of individuals who have found themselves asking unanswerable questions? The Brazilian mother knows the risks of speaking even for her next-door neighbor, for her own children, for her beloved husband, now gone. The Brazilian city planner, on the other hand, ignores such risks. There is no small contrast between their two modes of thought or analysis. They are enemies of sorts, and know that about each other. And yet — again one adds that necessary modifying phrase. There are links that connect those two, ties of concern; there are currents of hope they both ride. The woman would welcome a new, modern apartment house — all that goes with it that she now lacks, like electricity, running water, some protection against the elements, against rats and floods and a sudden seizure of cold. The planner would welcome a kinder life for her; underneath his brusque, evangelical materialism and militant economic practicality, there is a hardworking man of compassion, responsive to the wretchedness it is, actually, his chosen job to struggle against. The woman has her cool, collected, calculating moments; the man has his emotional, moody, sentimental, even religious side, which he may dismiss or attempt to rid himself of, but which is there, nevertheless.

In one aside he almost cried out, however self-servingly, for the kind of comprehension a novelist would offer: uncategorical, ironic, in keeping with his inconsistencies and ambiguities — in George Eliot's word, "indefinite," meaning as inconsistent and even contradictory as he, in real life, in his speech and actions, turns out to be. "I am only a mile or two away from a *favella* myself," he said in the course of the same conversation already drawn from. Then he explained the distance and its significance to him: "My father begged for a living. I was born in a hut, no more than that. Please don't forget that a man is not all he appears to be. I am usually myself. (What is myself? No point asking! I could talk for a week and not answer such a question!) But when I go to a *favella,* and make the mistake of talking with a mother and a father and their children, I dissolve into tearful memories — memories that make me feel eight years old, memories that have me pleading with my mother for food, for a toy, and getting no, no, no for an answer.

"My father was lucky; we all became successful because he did — suddenly. He got a job for a rich family, to work on their land. They owned a house, an estate, on the hill where the statue of Christ stands. My father had a green thumb. He worked long hours. He almost killed himself working. We never saw him. He left as the sun was rising, and he came home when it was dark. He owned no watch. He collapsed one day; he was on his hands and knees in the large garden, and it was hot, *very* hot, and sticky, and no one but my father would work so hard under such conditions. The owner of the estate happened to be leaving the house; he was going to his office. He was a strange and wonderful man. We have terrible traffic jams here in this city; they can last for hours. There is no getting around them — except if one is like my father's boss, his patron saint, *my* patron saint. He bought an ambulance, and he went to his office. He was driven to it, that way. It would be like in a movie — the red lights whirling, the screech of the siren, and all the cars moving out of the way, or the driver going on the sidewalks or the other side of the street!

"Well, that morning the ambulance was used for its proper purpose! The boss saw some of his servants carrying my father, and asked what was wrong, and they were afraid to tell him, the staff, for fear he'd fire my father. It is awful, the way we misunderstand people — see them as they are *not.* A rich man can be victimized by prejudice as well as a poor man — or a city planner, a bureaucrat! Anyway, the boss stopped everything; he went over and ignored everyone except my father. Maybe he knew that he had to find out for himself about my father. He did, too. He told the staff to leave, and he kneeled down and asked my father how he was. My father was dizzy; he had fainted because of the sun. He was just waking up. When he saw the boss's face, he started crying. My father was afraid.

45

He couldn't answer any of the man's questions. He just asked for forgiveness. He remembers pleading for his job — his *life!* But the boss was worried about my father. Do you know what? He started crying himself! He was Hungarian, I believe. He was an emotional man. He was a kind man. He had suffered. He had fled the Nazis, come to our Brazil, made a fortune. He gave a lot of money away to charity. He leaned over and told my father that the ambulance was there, and they would both go for a ride! He lifted my father up. The ambulance was air-conditioned. He took my father to a doctor, and the doctor said my father needed good food, and should protect himself from the sun in the middle of the day. Later the boss asked my father about us. My father told him the teacher had said I was a smart boy, so the boss asked to see me.

"That was when my life changed; that was when it began — this life I lead. It's not only the money he gave us. People always mention that — the money. I do so myself! But there was more, much more — a person's faith in me, his loyalty to my life. I don't know how else to put it. When someone shows trust in you, then you find trust for yourself, and you become someone else — you're different, a new person. For years later my mother and father used to look back to that day when my father collapsed. They were happy that their lives had changed. But mostly, they would talk about me — how I have *two* birthdays, how I was born *twice.* Now that is foolish; but I see their point. I hope I remember my first life all during this second one. I hope I'm doing what is right. I can't give a lot of money to the poor; but I hope Brazil will be a better country when I am old, and that children like I was will have a chance to improve themselves."

At the end of the conversation he begins to talk like his usual, managerial self; he begins, it can be said, a return to himself — as he is, for the most part. But exactly who is he? To use Heidegger's language, the man lives on the "ontic level" — the level of daily observable life — as a rather lucky member of Brazil's expanding but still small bourgeoisie. He is a sincere, hardworking reformer; he is married, has two sons, wants no more children, assumes they, too, will go to college, as he did. (He was, of course, subsidized by his father's benefactor. As for the father, he became a chauffeur, drove that ambulance every morning over many years.) But ontologically — spiritually, symbolically — the urban planner was, at least for some moments, a man quietly mindful of his past. He was at moments put on edge by the memories, even haunted by them. He is a man who has worried about the meaning of his work, the purpose of his life — has done so, especially, in the car, as he, too, has struggled with Rio de Janeiro's traffic jams. The streets are, in a strange way, for one man, at least, thoroughfares between the ontic and the ontological, a means by which a hurried, occasionally self-important and autocratic, high-level bureaucrat can without design or presumptuousness move away, for a moment at least, from the tangibles of "everydayness" toward a brief examination of what he lives by and for.

Not that the self-scrutiny is dramatic, or produces an "existential hero." The planner has never in the least been tempted to turn his car around, head for the open road — toward the jungles of the Amazon, maybe, or toward a deserted beach up the coast, as compared to the Copacabana. But he does occasionally stare a bit long at the statue of Jesus Christ. Sometimes he even goes out of his way — missing, thereby, fifteen minutes at the office — to catch a clearer, more startling and immediate view of the statue. And he does think of his father — on the ground, suffering, frightened and mute — when the statue looms near and high; thinks of him as a loving, dutiful son would, but also as a father of his own sons ought to, and as a man who wields power over many families ought, and as a doubting, uneasy, fearful person might — even though this particular city planner is known to everyone in the office and other offices nearby as bold, strong-minded, all too sure of himself.

A novelist is, again, best equipped to portray and comprehend such a life. And there are, of course, other lives — millions upon millions of them, each in certain respects, at least, *sui generis*. There are, naturally, things that connect us, one to another: shared antecedents, experiences, expectations — which also, however, require the proper connections to the lives of individuals. An American's "angst," for instance, is not a Russian's; and it makes a difference, in both cases, whether the given man or woman is living in the nineteenth or twentieth century, in a city or town or rural community, and, for that matter, *is* a man or a woman. It makes a difference (if he or she is an American alive today) whether "home" is Covington, Louisiana, where Walker Percy lives, or Chicago, Illinois, where Saul Bellow lives, or north of Boston, where John Updike lives. It makes a difference if the person is a doctor, a writer, an academic philosopher, or theologian, and if he sees the world through the eyes of a storyteller of somewhat comic sensibility, or is factual and analytic in mind.

If such observations are the banalities of today's social science literature, they have yet to be worked into the grain of this century's various existentialist writings, perhaps because those writings have often been, by conviction, personal expressions. Once someone starts doing a study of existentialist writers or thinkers, starts figuring out and making explicit the various "influences" at work in their lives, starts connecting those influences to "content," then (at the very least) the person is skirting irony in the pursuit of knowledge. Yet life and art, the factual and symbolic, are related. The tension between Heidegger's "ontic" and "ontological" does not mean that those two "levels" do not connect. They are not utterly separate and distinct spheres of existence, despite Kierkegaard's image of the "leap."

The meaning of "Being" — a lifelong search, with no final answer — is pursued by one person, or another person, each through the given chance (it can be called), so mysterious in its arrival "upon" us, of a life. A distinct, growing consciousness, a sensibility, is grounded in a body, with its relentless humdrum requirements. And our minds have, of necessity, dozens of all too routine but utterly essential obligations to remember. The special cries of wonder and sadness, of angst, of fear and trembling, which one hears in a migrant labor camp of central Florida or eastern North Carolina, or in a *favella* of Rio de Janeiro, as well as in the salons of the upper-middle-class world of Paris, New York, or the two Cambridges, are not part of an existentialist "questioning," an exploration of Being, that has little to do with, that proceeds apart from the "ontic" —

and the antic, the wistful, sadly comic, quite hilarious, or the terribly grim, unnerving, and plain wretched "facts of life." It is those "facts," of course, that novelists pay such close heed to — the incidents which, one by one, come our way on this journey of ours. Some novelists are only too glad to let that portrayal be enough — the imaginative, suggestive, dramatic evocation of everyday life that a story affords. Others are themselves all taken up with various reflections, if not obsessed or haunted by them; and are unable or unwilling to separate their "ultimate concerns" (in Paul Tillich's phrase) from their lived-out version of the "ontic" — the walk to the desk, the relentless movement of the pen, the working of the typewriter's keys, the filling up of paper, page after page.

It is another irony of this life that existentialists, presumably more aware than many others of the pride and arrogance and, alas, self-deception that get worked into various sociological, psychological, and philosophical categorizations or generalizations, nevertheless themselves are moved to find order in the universe — to fight the seeming chaos of things — and so, soon enough become at least tempted by, if not trapped in, the constructs and distinctions and classifications that as a consequence come about. No wonder Kierkegaard turned to brief stories, to allegories, to writing that made him "a kind of poet." No wonder Gabriel Marcel and Sartre wrote plays. No wonder Walker Percy, after years of writing articles, turned his attention and energies to the novel, to its possibilities as a means of remaining true to the particular, while conveying elements of philosophical discussion. Perhaps the change in interest or medium is itself an "existential" act — even "a leap of faith." The departure is from statements, interpretations — the fixed, static, asserted, and defined. The voyage is toward the ambiguous, the imaginary — the concrete, yet metaphorical and "merely" entertaining or "only" suggestive. Whatever the motives, or the philosophical justifications, the consequence for a Marcel or a Percy has, no doubt, been a mixture of emotions: apprehension and self-doubt, but also relief, a sense of satisfaction, of fulfillment — maybe, even, of liberation.

TWO

The Essays

WHEN WALKER PERCY'S first novel, *The Moviegoer*, was published in the spring of 1961, no rush of attention followed. The book was ignored, or reviewed only briefly, by most magazines or quarterlies. *The New York Times Book Review*, however, published a short but admiring review by Southern-born critic Robert Massie, and *Time*'s anonymous reviewer was equally impressed. *Commonweal* offered the longest and most detailed consideration — and for good reason: Walker Percy had contributed a number of articles to that magazine in the 1950s, so its editors were no doubt both surprised and interested to see a man they had known as a physician of broad sensibility — he had written on matters literary, philosophical, and theological — suddenly emerge as a novelist. *Commonweal*'s review, written by John Kennebeck, was titled "The Search," perhaps because he had in mind a quotation from Dr. Percy's novel. Binx Bolling is the twenty-nine-year-old New Orleans stockbroker who narrates *The Moviegoer*, and early on in the story he says what in many ways he will keep on repeating: "The search is what anyone would undertake if he were not sunk in the everydayness of his own life. To become aware of the possibility of the search is to be onto something. Not to be onto something is to be in despair."

These few favorable reviews were not enough to make *The Moviegoer* a bestseller. For one thing, it was obviously a philosophical novel, a novel of ideas — with no episodes of violence and no explicit sex. Nor was the book's publisher, Alfred Knopf, all that anxious to press it upon the public. (Walker Percy's second, third, and fourth novels, *The Last*

Gentleman, Love in the Ruins, and *Lancelot,* were published by Farrar, Straus and Giroux.) Moveover, the author was forty-four when the novel was published, and had been a physician for some twenty years. He did not strike his limited number of reviewers, however sympathetic, as a promising writer who deserved careful scrutiny, but rather as a thoughtful Southern doctor who had happened to write a good novel in the midst of pursuing other concerns. For some novelists the first novel turns out to be the last, and when the writer is a middle-aged doctor, interested in linguistics and given to quotations from Kierkegaard (one of which, "The specific character of despair is precisely this: it is unaware of being despair," is the novel's epigraph), it is not hard to imagine yet another sensitive, intro-spective Southerner who has had a particular story to tell, but is certainly no Faulkner or Thomas Wolfe: prolific, driven, ready to invoke for readers a torrent of words, images, charac-terizations — and so, worthy of extended critical analysis.

Percy's editor at Knopf was Stanley Kauffmann, now film critic for *The New Republic.* He recalls a lunch with Dr. Percy in New York a few months after *The Moviegoer* was published. The author was not in despair, if Kierkegaard's definition of it be accepted, because he couldn't help but be aware of his mind's natural sense of regret: he had worked hard on a novel which was meant to be not only well constructed and enter-taining, but a message of sorts from himself to the many others who share his fate — seekers, though not always sure of what — the effort had been consuming and persistent, had even been declared a success by a few critics; yet soon enough *The Moviegoer* had disappeared from just about everyone's sight, one more flicker of light quickly extinguished. What was the point of it all — trying to write a serious novel which in a sly, comic, and disarming way brings philosophers like Kier-kegaard and Gabriel Marcel face to face with those many thousands whose "everydayness" Binx Bolling evokes and ul-timately analyzes so powerfully? Kauffmann remembers reas-suring the good doctor, whom he had then met for the first time, after their considerable correspondence, that the novel was fine, was exceptional, and no one or nothing could take that away from the author. Months later, in the spring of 1962, three others associated themselves with Kauffmann's estimate. In the citation they wrote about the winner of the 1962 National Book Award for fiction Lewis Gannett, Herbert Gold, and Jean Stafford said: "*The Moviegoer*, an intimation rather than a statement of mortality and the inevitability of that condition, is a truthful novel with shocks of recognition and spasms of nostalgia for every — or nearly every — American. Mr. Percy, with compassion and without sentimentality or the mannerisms of the clinic, examines the delusions and hallucinations and the daydreams and the dreads that afflict those who abstain from the customary ways of making do."

The selection was a surprise — to the book's author and editor, and especially to its publisher. Sales suddenly increased, perhaps out of curiosity at first, but soon enough because "shocks of recognition" were felt and acknowledged to others. Sometimes the author was told what he had prompted, or asked with desperation for help. His mail increased markedly, and his phone more and more became a source of anxiety: who would call next, asking what weighty or dramatic question? And a number of people, among them literary critics, began to direct their questions at him and his life. He was interviewed repeatedly in the literary quarterlies. Newspapers did feature stories on him. Candidates for the degree Doctor of Philosophy began to examine *The Moviegoer*. In 1966, a second novel of Dr. Percy's, *The Last Gentleman*, was greeted with wide and enthusiastic applause; it was nominated for another National Book Award. In 1973, a year after *Love in the Ruins* was published, the author of only three novels was the subject of a substantial, scholarly book, *The Sovereign Wayfarer;* its author, Martin Luschei, converted a Ph.D. thesis into a highly readable and suggestive series of essays on Dr. Percy's various writings. Luschei, too, wondered at the transition; a man self-described as a "failed physician" became in his middle forties the author of a literary surprise, then went on to consolidate his career as a highly original and sophisticated writer. One critic, writing in *Texas Studies in Literature and Language,* put the question rather briefly and pointedly: "How does it happen that a mid-

dle-aged doctor with such an unlikely background for literature has achieved so much success as a novelist?"

Dr. Percy's background is actually rather consistent with the
outcome of his life. *The Moviegoer* is dedicated "in gratitude to
W. A. P.," who was William Alexander Percy, a first cousin of
the author's father. Will Percy, as he was known, had many
sides to him. He was a planter who lived in Greenville, Mississippi. He was a lawyer. He had been a brave, decorated soldier
during the First World War. He served with Herbert Hoover in
Belgium when that country desperately needed food and
clothing. He fought the Ku Klux Klan long, hard, and successfully. After the great flood of 1927, he led his people, black and
white alike, in their difficult effort to win back land and,
equally important, make sure that the Mississippi River would
never again lay claim to so much territory. But more than
anything else, Will Percy was a writer. His first book of poems,
Sappho in Levkas, was published in 1915, when he was about
Binx Bolling's age, and (one gathers from what he has written
about himself) similarly introspective, solitary, unable or unwilling to "fit in," "adjust," go along with the various "norms"
which press upon all of us. Three other volumes of poetry followed, and finally in 1942, just after his death, *The Collected
Poems* appeared. A year earlier Knopf had published *Lanterns
on the Levee*, a series of autobiographical essays which ranged
widely over social and political issues, the South's ever-present
race problem, and, not least, the author's struggle to reconcile
his worldliness, his cosmopolitan interests, with his sense of
obligation to and affection for the rural and somewhat removed people of Mississippi's Delta. At one point Will Percy
characterizes the kind of library he would see while growing
up: "leather-bound sets of the *Spectator*, the *Edinburgh Review*,
the works of Mr. Goldsmith and Mr. Pope, *Tom Jones* and *A
Sentimental Journey*, translations of Plutarch and Homer,
amazing poems about plants and flowers by the grandfather of
Darwin, *The Faerie Queene* and Bobbie Burns." Moreover, there
were men to hear — like his father, LeRoy Percy, who was also
a lawyer and planter, not to mention a United States Senator
who fought bitterly the racist, but also populist, Mississippi

Governor James K. Vardaman. LeRoy Percy's father was the first William Alexander Percy, known as "the Gray Eagle of the Delta"; he fought hard against secession, and was a man of considerable education and cultivation.

Ultimately the Percy family of Louisiana and Mississippi traces itself back to Charles Percy, a man married three times, an adventurer and entrepreneur. In 1776 he settled in what is now Wilkinson County, Mississippi. "He blew in," Will Percy writes in *Lanterns on the Levee*, "from the gray or blue sea-ways with a ship of his own, a cargo of slaves, and a Spanish grant to lands in the buffalo country south of Natchez." The Spanish both honored and liked him; though he was an Englishman by birth (his house was called Northumberland Place), they called him Don Carlos and made him an *alcalde,* a sort of mayor and judge. Will Percy writes of that mysterious and tempestuous ancestor — and his various descendents — with wry amusement and detachment rather than self-conscious pride, but he makes clear his delight that the Percys from the beginning were somewhat offbeat leaders. They had money. They wielded political influence. They were educated. And, perhaps most important of all, they thought for themselves. From generation to generation they produced nonconformists, men who challenged prevailing orthodoxies, often at a considerable risk. They possessed a certain stoic *noblesse oblige.* One feels sure enough socially and intellectually to stand above the cruder passions of the day. One gives of oneself unstintingly. There are values to be maintained, and a lifetime is spent in their defense, no matter how few are willing to do the same. In the nineteenth century there were Percys who went to the leading Southern and Northern universities, Percys who became lawyers, doctors, and public officials. Again and again they not only charted their own course, but insisted on explaining why. They were literate, and they wanted others to know what ideas and beliefs crossed their minds. Will Percy's father wrote letters to newspapers, to *The New Republic;* in July, 1922, he wrote a compelling and influential piece, "The Modern Ku Klux Klan," for *The Atlantic Monthly.* Thereafter he was virtually the leader of those who dared fight the Klan in a decade when that organization, as he pointed out in his article, was making strong gains among Northerners.

As for Will himself, his home was a mecca for writers, artists, and scholars. Faulkner came to play tennis, and young sociologists or anthropologists from Chapel Hill or points north came to study the Delta, as did Hortense Powdermaker and Harry Stack Sullivan. Carl Sandburg and Stark Young were guests; so were Stephen Vincent Benét, Jonathan Daniels, and Langston Hughes. Raymond Gram Swing and Dorothy Thompson arrived and lingered. Prominent Europeans had been told to look up Mr. Percy, and did. His friend David L. Cohn, also a lawyer and writer, called him affectionately and discerningly an "eighteenth-century chevalier" — a shy, even aloof man who at the same time could be open, generous, and, above all, responsive with words to what he sensed others were experiencing. He traveled widely, and brought home to Greenville stories, anecdotes, and viewpoints he had heard abroad: in Polynesia, Japan, Greece, Italy, North Africa, Egypt, Turkey, as well as more conventional countries (for an American tourist of the first decades of this century) like Britain, France, or Canada. He also put into images experiences he had in those distant lands, Greece especially. Early on, he found conventional Christian religious practice uncongenial; the Greek poets and philosophers were his gods, and as one reads his prose and poetry one feels them close to him, telling him that in a way he is a kindred spirit, standing strong and faithful at his own kind of Thermopylae. But there were others he found congenial. "He admired Donne," David Cohn tells us. "He loved Keats. Yet the symbolists were not alien to him and he made translations from Verlaine and Mallarmé."

Will Percy was a lifelong bachelor, yet in 1929, after a cousin, LeRoy Percy, Walker Percy's father, a Birmingham, Alabama, lawyer, committed suicide, his wife and three sons came to live with "Uncle Will," as he became known. Two years later the mother was killed in an automobile accident, and Uncle Will became the father (and friend and counselor) of three orphan boys: Walker, his brother LeRoy, and their younger brother Phinizy, to all of whom *Lanterns on the Levee* is dedicated.

Walker was the oldest, born on May 28, 1916. He was twelve when made fatherless and fourteen when adopted. At Uncle Will's an enormous library was at the disposal of Walker and his brothers, as well as a vast record collection, fed to an enormous Capehart, the first one in Mississippi, legend has it. The boys, of course, went to school: Walker to Greenville High School. Among his friends there were Shelby Foote, later a novelist, to whom *Love in the Ruins* would be dedicated, and Charles Bell, who would publish several volumes of poetry and two novels. Walker took to writing poems, some of which appeared in the high school annual. He remembers selling some for a quarter or a half-dollar. He remembers writing a story for *Liberty* magazine. The editors, unfortunately, did not dignify him with a rejection slip. He remembers riding with his friend Shelby Foote up to Oxford, Mississippi, to visit Mr. Faulkner. "It was Shelby's idea; even in high school and college he knew he wanted to be a writer. But I guess I wasn't completely uninterested in writers and writing myself."

If anything, then, Dr. Percy's "background" was what some would call "literary." (Needless to say, many of our finest writers have no unusually rich cultural "background" — apart from what they themselves have managed to build up.) Uncle Will, who himself had gone to Sewanee, then Harvard Law School, encouraged Walker and his brothers to leave Mississippi for college. Their father had gone to Princeton and Harvard Law School, where he was an editor of the *Law Review*. Walker went to the University of North Carolina, then to Columbia's College of Physicians and Surgeons. At Chapel Hill he became intensely interested in science. He majored in chemistry, studied biology and physics: no more poems or stories for *Liberty* or any other national magazine. But he did not stop writing altogether. In November of 1934 he published in the *Carolina Magazine* an essay titled "The Willard Huntington Wright Murder Case," a shrewd and well-written psychological analysis of why a well-known music critic and literary editor began writing mystery stories and did so under a carefully concealed nom de plume: "For fifteen months after the enthusiastic reception of *The Benson Murder Case* the identity of

Van Dine remained a mystery. It was," the young Percy pointed out, "figuratively a premeditated murder of Willard Huntington Wright by S. S. Van Dine, as skillfully executed as one of the murders confronting the inimitable Philo Vance.

"For almost a year and a half," the essay continued, "a nation of detective story readers, writers, and critics speculated on his identity. But so baffling was the conspiracy between author and publisher, that Wright was even asked to review one of his own books. Many guesses were made, most of which were backed by convincing evidence. Van Dine was conclusively proved to be John Galsworthy, H. L. Mencken, Pola Negri, and 'Ma' Ferguson. Only when Wright, weary of the intricacies of a double life and probably impatient to bathe in the amazing success of his 'cases,' submitted a caricature of himself to a Chicago paper was the mystery cleared. But even then, when S. S. Van Dine was identified irrevocably with Willard Huntington Wright, most of Van Dine's readers remained in the dark."

Percy goes on to furnish details of Wright's life, and shows how a prolonged illness proved to be a decisive turning point. A man preoccupied with aesthetics found in "practically every detective story" he read certain principles, which he then decided to work into stories of his own. (Some seven years later Percy himself would fall sick, and be moved to consider leaving one career for another.) But if Wright killed himself, his grave was frequently robbed by S. S. Van Dine. Percy shows how many of the former's earlier tastes and achievements come across in the latter's stories: "The scientific precision of style and the Byronic tendency in fiction which distinguished his former works were put to good use in creating Philo Vance." Nor was the "murder" unregretted. Percy uses not one psychoanalytic word, but he had read the words of both the murderer and his victim rather carefully, and so could show how embarrassed Wright was by his own rather popular success, even as he enjoyed it enormously. For Percy such mixed feelings were not surprising; nor does he want to use the occasion of psychological analysis as an excuse for one or another kind of thinly veiled moral judgment. Wright may have felt apologetic about S. S. Van Dine's writing, but young Percy was interested and delighted that one kind of person, seemingly quite decided in his preferences and interests, could all of a sudden, well along in life, go through an abrupt and difficult crisis, then emerge as rather different — not just older and a bit wiser, but drawn to pursuits altogether new and quite refreshing. His interests prefigured the course his own life would take.

In March of 1935 the *Carolina Magazine* published another piece by Walker Percy, this one called "The Movie Magazine: A Low 'Slick.' " The author knew his movies, knew a good deal about Hollywood's actors and actresses, and had obviously been reading every movie magazine he could get his hands on. He knew the difference in style between a 1929 *Silver Screen* and a 1935 *Picture Play.* He knew where Ruth Chatterton's first divorce was discussed, where Bing Crosby's wife and her twins had been pictured. At one point he allows himself the following generalization: "Every movie interview and feature embodies one or all of three motives: to reconcile the peculiarities and weaknesses of a movie star to the ideal held by the fans, to trace the star from his honky-tonk days to his Hollywood pinnacle, and to give the world the star's philosophy of life. The first device is unadulterated hooey, the second is a dramatized rise-to-fame yarn with a small element of truth, and the third is a stock series of common sense platitudes which apparently guide the lives of all the stars."

This article is no prelude to a later novel, though at one point the author does talk about "Chapel Hill moviegoers," of which he certainly was one. (His class yearbook even shows him standing in line before the Carolina Theatre.) But the author of the article did demonstrate certain qualities of mind that a later novelist would also possess: a sense of humor about people and their foibles, be they movie stars or moviegoers; a capacity for social satire; an offbeat side — an interest in taking seriously what others take for granted or ignore. Perhaps most important, the article was written by a shrewd observer of the human scene who could write an old-fashioned, literate essay — no sociological jargon, no pretentious effort to prove something, only a desire to render certain observations and state them well.

One gathers from talking with him and his brothers and friends like Shelby Foote that the author of those two articles was not unlike his Uncle Will — a friendly and amiable youth who at the same time was rather private, and always curious: what are people like, not only one's classmates in Chapel Hill — in the 1930s a fairly homogenous group, socially and economically — but the many others who live far from universities, and have their own ways of finding relaxation, their own heroes or demons? By his senior year the youth who had paid so much attention to S. S. Van Dine's mysteries and America's moviegoers was absorbed with science almost totally: "It was a religion for me; I believed that any problem, anything wrong, could be solved by one or another of the sciences." He especially wanted to know about the body: how does it work, and what goes wrong and why? He told his Uncle Will that he wanted to try medical school, and was encouraged to go to New York City — so much to see and do there. For Will Percy, Manhattan meant opera, the symphony, the theatre. For years he had made pilgrimages to Carnegie Hall or the Metropolitan Opera House. Besides, all Southerners, he was convinced, ought to spend some time away from home — both to obtain perspective on the flaws of their region and to gain an appreciation of its many virtues.

Columbia's medical school offered Walker Percy no such cultural sanctuary; he did not go on many musical forays, nor was he especially interested in comparing the North and the South. One gathers that he was an obliging but not inspired medical student; that he was never quite sure what kind of medicine — if indeed any at all — he might want someday to practice; that he once again went off, more than his classmates, to movies and more movies; and that every weekday afternoon he disappeared mysteriously into the subway, much to the bewilderment of his fellow medical students. He was, in fact, undertaking what few of his age then (the late 1930s) even knew about, let alone considered for themselves — the experience of psychoanalysis. Dr. Janet Rioch's office was on the East

Side, and in essence he was leaving the fairly cloistered life of Bard Hall, the student dormitory at the Columbia-Presbyterian Medical Center, for another world: "I had seen Harry Stack Sullivan, a friend of Uncle Will's. He suggested Dr. Rioch. He wasn't sure what ailed me, and I wasn't either. I must say that, after three years, five days a week, Dr. Rioch and I still weren't sure."

The remark can be interpreted as detached and amused, or as mischievous if not evasive; or it can amount to the completely candid statement of a genuinely puzzled man, who looks back at a certain effort, a certain commitment of time, energy, and money, with a nagging sense of uncertainty. Others seem to know what troubles them, he felt, and what to do about it, but he was evidently troubled in a way that seemed to escape his analyst's clarification, not to mention his own; and so, perhaps what troubled him was not a neurosis, but episodes of inertia or boredom or uneasiness or purposelessness.

And what have the movies to do with psychoanalysis? Walker Percy remembers being a medical student, so close to matters of life and death, and he remembers at the same time feeling a stronger desire than ever to attend movies whenever he had a chance: "I don't think it was an 'escape.' I wouldn't want to put it that way. I'd go all the time to movies up at Washington Heights. I think at the movies I was getting to know how people looked at the world, what they thought — just as a doctor does. The movies are not just fantasies; for a lot of people they provide important moments, maybe the only point in the day, or even the week, when someone (a cowboy, a detective, a crook) is heard asking what life is all about, asking what is worth fighting for — or asking if anything is worth fighting for. I would often look at the people as they were going into the movies and look at them coming out, and sometimes even stop and look at them while they were inside and watching. While staring at the screen, their faces somehow seemed more alive — not always, but rather often. And when they came outside, they weren't just walking down the street. They seemed as if they were going somewhere — a destination in mind. Or they seemed to be coming from someplace important.

Or they appeared to have mulled over a significant subject in their minds. But I'm afraid that's me: always looking at people looking at a movie, or looking at people walking down the street, or looking at people staring at a skyscraper." The state of mind that prompted many to go to the movies, he found, was a sense of absurdity or futility. They may not be philosophers, but they ask themselves those eternal and not easily answered questions which some dwell on, writing page after page, and others shrug off as beyond their ken.

Percy liked to do his own looking and asking, too. He was enthralled by what he saw under the microscope — not necessarily the evidence of pathology or the clues to tissue identification, but the beauty and elegance of cellular structure, the almost infinite complexity of something as apparently simple as a histological slide, made up of skin or muscle stained with a particular dye. As medical school came to an end, he decided to take a residency in pathology, and to stay in New York City, though he did return to Greenville after earning his degree, and spent a summer working in a clinic there. As a pathologist he could keep on asking questions of the most basic kind, in the hope of learning as much as was known about the workings of the body. He was still very much taken with science; he believed in it, wanted to obtain all it had to offer, was certain that then life would at last make sense.

The residency was at Bellevue, and started in September — the year, 1941. War had not yet broken out. Into Bellevue came the lame, the sick, the poor. Most likely they had for a long time ignored the various signs and symptoms which so often precede or announce a major illness. For a young pathologist there was more than enough to do; death was no stranger to Bellevue, and because the hospital served a heterogeneous population, there was a wide range of illnesses to be diagnosed — obscure tropical illnesses and vitamin deficiency diseases as well as the conventional ones. And there were patients on the "Chest Service," many of them: alcoholics, the impoverished, the weak and vulnerable of New York, all prone to tuberculosis, among other afflictions. Young Dr. Percy worked rather feverishly at Bellevue, came into constant touch with the tubercle bacillus, and no doubt on more than one occasion failed to observe the cautions one learns to observe in medical school: rubber gloves at all times when in danger of exposure; careful washing of hands; on certain occasions, a mask. Early in 1942, tired and overworked, he began to worry about his own health. He was coughing. He was experiencing chest pain. He lacked energy even after rest. Soon the diagnosis was made — tuberculosis. He left Bellevue for Lake Saranac in the Adirondacks, where a well-known sanitarium was so crowded he had to stay for a while in a boarding house.

The next five years of his life are the stuff of a novel — indeed there are resemblances to Thomas Mann's *Magic Mountain*. A young doctor, hitherto obsessed with rigorous scientific inquiry, becomes confined to bed, himself an object of constant scrutiny and evaluation. A man interested in watching others becomes cut off almost completely from the world.

Percy was hospitalized just before the war began; his brother LeRoy joined the air force, became a pilot, took part in America's assault on Nazi Germany, and his brother Phinizy joined the navy and ended up serving with John F. Kennedy on his well-known torpedo-boat mission in the Pacific. (As a result the two became friends, and in 1960 the Democratic presidential candidate asked the New Orleans lawyer Phinizy Percy to help organize and lead his campaign in Louisiana; but the lawyer was a Republican, and had to decline.) Meanwhile, their oldest brother could only sit or, very often, lie back and read; read about the slaughter going on, as the world's most "civilized" nations waged a war to the death against one another; read about the advances science had brought — faster planes with larger bomb loads, rocketry and radar, and, finally, the awesome and devastating nuclear bombs.

The questions Camus must have started asking himself while he fought in the Resistance were those Percy began to put to himself while he was for several years, on and off, a thoroughly inactive patient: "I was in bed so much, alone so much, that I had nothing to do but read and think. I began to question everything I had once believed. I began to ask why Europe, why the world had come to such a sorry state. I never turned my back on science. It would be a mistake to do so — throw out the baby with the bath water. I had wanted to find answers through an application of the scientific method. I had found that method a rather impressive and beautiful thing: the logic and precision of systematic inquiry; the mind's impressive ability to be clear-headed, to reason. But I gradually began to realize that as a scientist — a doctor, a pathologist — I knew so very much *about* man, but had little idea what man *is*."

The word *is* — existentialists use it that way. When Dr. Percy began to question himself and his assumptions, existentialism was by no means the vogue in America or, for that matter, Europe. A war was being fought, and, under such circumstances, one is inclined to act, not meditate, savor ironies, look askance at the slightest provocation. A good deal of Kierkegaard's writing had not been translated into English, Sartre had only several years earlier (1938) published *Nausea*. Camus had yet to begin his career as a novelist and philosopher. On his sickbed Percy read Thomas Mann, Kafka, Tolstoy, Dostoevski. The last of these especially moved him. He eventually came upon Kierkegaard's writing, and read him hungrily: "I lived a strange life then. For weeks I saw no one, except the person who brought me food, on a tray, three times a day, and occasionally a doctor. I read and read. Sometimes I listened to the radio — programs from Montreal. Then back to reading."

He was for a while quite ill. His friend Shelby Foote remembers visiting him, while on the way to war: "There he was, gaunt and pale. He was living the life of a hermit. I worried about him; I wanted him out in the world, near people. But he seemed happy where he was, flat on his back and holding on to those books for dear life." After two years of convalescence, he did seem to improve, so he was advised to resume cautiously a life outside the sanitarium. He went back to New York City, became an instructor in pathology at Columbia's medical school. But soon he had a relapse. Now he went to the Gaylord Farms sanitarium in Connecticut. There he was given the same bed Eugene O'Neill had occupied when he was a patient in 1912. After a year of further rest and treatment Percy was ready to go home, even as millions of others his age were soon to return from the war. But where was home? His Uncle Will had died in 1942, about the time Percy went up to Lake Saranac. His brother LeRoy had married soon after he came back from the war; LeRoy's wife, Sarah, was the daughter of Will Percy's law partner, Hazelwood Farish. LeRoy and his wife were living in the old Percy house, and he was running Trail Lake, the family plantation.

"I wanted to go home," Percy reminisces, "but I had no home. I went back to Greenville, visited various friends. The war was over. People wanted to settle down again; there had been too much excitement for too long. I guess I wanted to settle down, too — but at the time I didn't know that was what I wanted. I'd been alone in the woods so long, I was blinking at the strong sun, and all the people." When Shelby Foote came back, they agreed to go out West to New Mexico. They drove there, settled in Santa Fe: "But after several months Shelby headed back. I stayed. Don't ask me why. I didn't know why I was out there, and when I decided eventually to go back I didn't know why I was going back, either. I just decided I'd been away too long, after a year or so, from the grass and the trees and the bayous in Mississippi and Louisiana. But I loved being in New Mexico. While in the desert I just kept on reading, and looking around."

The mountain air was good for him; and Santa Fe is not only over seven thousand feet above sea level, but an interesting city with more than its fair share of writers, artists, photographers. Then, there were the spectacular sights, either a few miles up some road, or over in Arizona or Colorado; and too, there were the Indians. In Santa Fe Percy read Gabriel Marcel, Heidegger, Mounier, Jaspers, Sartre. He continued with his novels, more and more of them. He read about Indian religious customs and beliefs. He visited reservations, saw where D. H. Lawrence had lived, read him eagerly. Always, though, he was more than a little removed from others: "I liked the people I met out there. I slept in an old barn. I went to the Grand Canyon. I went to the reservations. I'm afraid at times I didn't see all I was meant to see. Instead of looking at the Canyon all the time, or the Indian dances all the time, I would watch people watching the Canyon or the dances. That's the way I've always been, I guess." He shrugs; and then he smiles — at himself. He is not boasting about an apparent idiosyncrasy which in fact he judges to be a mark of virtue or superiority. He is simply remarking upon a balance of sorts, uncanny at times for a visitor to experience: intense interest in people and a degree of distance from them.

When he came back to Greenville he still had no idea what he was going to do, or where he was going to live. The philosophical reading continued, especially Kierkegaard. I think it fair to say he went through an especially intense religious crisis. His parents were Protestants, but not actively involved with church life. His Uncle Will makes clear in *Lanterns on the Levee* that he forsook his mother's Catholicism (she was from a New Orleans French family) and never was drawn to the Episcopal Church his father had at least nominally been attached to. For the young physician there was no dramatic "conversion"; rather, a deeply introspective and somewhat withdrawn man gradually began to make commitments, and affiliation to a particular faith was one of them. On November 7, 1946, in a Baptist church in New Orleans, with Shelby Foote on hand as best friend and best man, Dr. Percy married Mary Bernice Townsend, who comes from Doddsville, in Sunflower County, Mississippi, the heart of the Delta. He had first met her five years before, when he worked briefly in a Greenville clinic. She had worked there, too, as a medical technician, having gone to Millsaps College, in Jackson. They had intermittently kept in touch, but only a few months before their marriage did the man feel in any way inclined to propose. Next they had to find a place to live. Uncle Will had owned a country house, a lovely but unpretentious place up in the hills near Sewanee, Tennessee. They went there and lived a quiet, rural life. The reading continued. There were walks, and occasional trips back to Greenville or into nearby Nashville. There were also religious discussions — eventually culminating in a decision to take instruction in the Catholic faith. Six months after they were married they became Catholics, and have remained so, believing ones, to this day.

Winters are not easy in the Tennessee hills, and anyway, the couple wanted to live in New Orleans. They went there in 1947, living at first in the Pontchartrain Hotel. Soon they found a house to rent. Percy was not wealthy, but he had enough money to get by, and it seemed that he had no inclination to practice the medicine he had only recently learned. He gave himself to a contemplative life. To live as he did from the time of his marriage to 1954, when his first philosophical article appeared, must have required determination — perhaps, a stubborn sense of one's purpose on this earth, mixed with a certain indifference toward the social conventions that press upon all of us: find a job, take up a profession, leave in the morning and go to work for someone, or if you stay at home, prove to the world that you have some justification — as a writer, a craftsman, an artist. Here was a man called Dr. Percy, who no longer had the slightest connection to a profession which requires the lengthiest of training. Here was a man rather wrapped up in himself, from a family which had always insisted upon the obligations of service to the community. Here was a man whose brothers and friends were working quite hard, and who himself had by 1946 fully recovered from tuberculosis; yet he read — not as a hobby, not casually or in fits of preoccupation, but steadily, almost as if he had been told to work at educating himself in certain subjects, and had found that effort to be a full-time job.

The subjects: philosophy, broadly speaking, with special attention to the nature of symbols; the question of language — its origins and structure — and a range of ethical and psychological concerns which in the late 1940s came to be characterized, perhaps a little too glibly at times, as "existentialist."

By coincidence, Percy's landlord in New Orleans turned out to be a philosopher, Julius Friend, whose library was available to his tenant, who read avidly. Friend himself had written a number of books and articles, perhaps the best known of which were co-authored with James Feibleman: *Science and the Spirit of Man* and *The Unlimited Community*. Both books had come out in the 1930s, and neither exactly rode a fashionable wave. In fact, Friend and Feibleman were bucking a strong tide of Marxist and Freudian influence among America's intelligentsia when they wrote as they did. They were openly admiring, though with discrimination, of the Thomist tradition and, before it, of elements of both Platonic and Aristotelian theory. They were skeptical of large-scale historical generalizations, especially Hegel's effort to submit all history to a series of formulations; insistent upon the value of the concrete, the particular, and, yes, the accidental or contingent, in any appraisal of human psychology; and responsive to certain idiosyncratic espousals. They drew on the ideas of a relatively obscure nineteenth-century American scientist and philosopher, Charles Sanders Peirce, who set forth the principles of a unique kind of scientific empiricism in language not always easy to understand. Peirce, like Freud and Feibleman, stressed the immediately mysterious if ultimately understandable nature of things.

In a posthumously published book of essays with the somewhat unusual title of *Chance, Love and Logic* (1923), Peirce straddles delicately the world of faith and the world of precise scientific observation. He has a high regard for what the philosopher Morris K. Cohen called "the actual diversity and spontaneity of things," but he was not one to ignore the order he saw, the coherence he believed man quite able to find. Laws emerge slowly and fitfully, he pointed out; a host of particularities finally reveal themselves to be related in some way. He was not as impressed with any given scientific operation, however exact and verifiable, as many other pragmatists are; and he was cautious about embracing large-scale principles, however much he wanted to avoid that fussy aversion to philosophical speculation acquired by many practical, insistently "rational" and "scientific" men almost inadvertently, and quite understandably. He held on to his eyes and ears, his eminently clearheaded way of looking at the world — but he was prepared to acknowledge his limitations as one man, alive in the nineteenth century and limited thereby to a given vocabulary, a given range of experiences.

Most important, he ventured into the realm of religion without shame, without pretense or show, either. The "unlimited community" Friend and Feibleman refer to in their book is

Peirce's: words we use or deeds we perform can have a life of their own; we die, but the import of our remarks, the thrust of our actions, have touched one person, then another, then another, and on and on. One ought not to try to declare precisely how all that happens. Nor is the lack of precision any cause for dismay or apology. In fact, "chance" is crucial; a nod here, a touch there, a word back then, can unexpectedly and unintentionally have momentous consequences. One generation's astonishing accident becomes in retrospect another's clearly comprehended chain of events or circumstances. And in the end "all human affairs," he said, rest upon probabilities rather than certainties: "If man were immortal he could be perfectly sure of seeing the day when everything in which he had trusted should betray his trust. He would break down, at last, as every great fortune, as every dynasty, as every civilization does. In place of this we have death." Peirce comes perilously close to accepting in his own way God's judgment on Adam and Eve — the death He decreed as theirs, to be handed down, as well, to their progeny; and when he uses the phrase "in place of" he skirts faith by daring to allow himself, brilliant experimental scientist and logician that he was, to wonder about larger, more conjectural issues, as well as specific explanations of discrete and well-regulated moments of "reality" — those experiments in the laboratory, those hypotheses, based on one or another observation, which we in the twentieth century know so well.

In a nice old house at the edge of New Orleans' Garden District, rather than in a Paris cafe, and through an American philosopher, Charles Peirce, Dr. Percy began to grapple with the same doubts and misgivings that had plagued Europe's postwar generation of intellectuals: what has the god Science wrought, and if after the near-apocalypse of the Second World War we can no longer worship that god — or, indeed, believe in anyone or anything — then what is the point of living? Kierkegaard continued to help him enormously, and Gabriel Marcel, who like Sartre and Camus felt the need of fitting ideas into stories, as well as a number of plays. Percy also read Jacques Maritain carefully. Susanne Langer's *Philosophy in a New Key* meant a lot to him. And there were those old friends from Lake Saranac, to whom he kept going back — Tolstoy, Dostoevski, and Kafka: "I'm afraid I've never been much drawn to the English novel. I only recently [1972] read *Middlemarch*, even though my friend Shelby Foote has been urging it on me for years. After the war, when I guess I made reading a full-time occupation, I kept asking myself what is *believable* these days, not just for me, but for others: my family, my friends, the people I knew. Dostoevski knew how hungry we all are for faith, but how hard it is to find — and to keep."

For almost a decade he must have struggled hard to keep faith in the value, the significance of his kind of life. His wife recalls those brief but all too charged moments: "The children would be asked what their daddy does, and they would ask me, and of course, I wasn't always sure what to tell them. I would say your daddy is a doctor, and he does a lot of thinking about what's happening in the world. Well, that's not so easy to put down in a form, as an answer to a question, or to tell your curious friends." They had two daughters, Mary Pratt and Ann Boyd, the second born deaf. The child's handicap stimulated in her father an even greater interest in language: how do we acquire it and do our attempts to describe the "process" actually convey what anyone might hear with his own ears, if only he were willing to listen to children?

Shelby Foote describes how his friend learned that the younger girl, Ann, could not hear, and what effect that discovery and its consequences had on his friend: "I believe Ann was six months old, nine months old, I don't know exactly. She seemed in every way normal. One day they were walking with her outside, and Walker saw a rather large snake, one of the more dangerous Louisiana ones, probably. He gave Ann over to her mother, so that he could get a rifle. He came back and shot the snake. Ann didn't move, didn't look toward the noise. She seemed as quiet and calm as can be. He was puzzled. He shot again, and still no response from the baby. He knew then that something was wrong. Ever since, of course, the parents have put an enormous amount of time and energy into bringing up a child who has needed special educational attention. It's been an education for *them,* too. They've taken her to various experts, and learning to reach her, and helping her to learn to talk, has been a great challenge for them. They took her difficulty very seriously; I mean, they have put the girl's needs first. At one point Walker was ready to move anywhere in the world, if Ann could be helped to live a more normal life — learn how to speak normally and understand what others are saying. But he didn't have to move. They were able to stay right there in Covington, and Walker got more and more interested in linguistics as he was going through the experience of Ann's deafness — one more branch of philosophy for him to explore. And what happened? Ann became a lively, intelligent woman, who has lived a full, active life. She went to L.S.U. [Louisiana State University] and is now Mrs. John David Moores.''

Covington had become the Percy home about 1950. New Orleans, twenty-five miles away, was a little too much for them — too charming, attractive, tempting. They wanted quiet rather than diversion — and maybe, to draw on Kierkegaard's way of putting things, they wanted a certain freedom from the "aesthetic stage" in order to pursue life "on the plane of the ethical": the responsibilities of parenthood, the steady acquisition of knowledge, which then must be sifted and evaluated rather than used (as are children, all too often) to preen oneself and show off. Even in Covington they sought seclusion, though by no means were they hermits. They went to church regularly, sometimes on weekdays as well as Sunday. They had their friends — and not far away, on both sides, there were relatives to see. And always, there were the movies: "In the nineteen forties and the nineteen fifties, much more than today, I'd keep on going to the movies. Of course, now you can see movies on television. But it's different, going out, and sitting there in a theatre with others. It's more active: you've all left home to go *see,* to *find* something — an hour or two of rest from the world, or a little uplift, or some amusement amid all the craziness and seriousness of life, or a clue to something important. Don't ask me for my reason; don't ask me why I go to the movies. I just like them. Of course they do get my mind going."

His mind was indeed "going," and finally, in 1954, well over a decade since he'd recovered from tuberculosis and decided that he would never return to medicine, and some twenty years after he'd last written an article (as an undergraduate), he sent off an essay called "Symbol as Need" to *Thought*, a "national review of Catholic and contemporary culture," edited by professors of the Fordham graduate school. In the autumn of that year the essay was published and Dr. Percy's family could begin to think of him as a writer.

"Symbol as Need" is not long, but it is scholarly, and sometimes dense. Much of the argument is a response of sorts to Susanne Langer's *Feeling and Form* (1953), which clearly impressed the author. He refers to the book's "power" and the "contagious excitement" it generates: "a first-class mind exercising a valuable new insight." Mrs. Langer, who had for a while been quite taken with logical positivism, slowly began to see that human beings, on their own and especially with the help of artists, respond to "symbolic transformation"; thereby they learn something which has its own integrity, is not reducible to something else, does not stand for something else. The symbol conveys the "felt life" of the artist, the writer, the man or woman who lives in and observes the world, but who, prompted by what Maritain would call "creative intuition," is inspired to go a step further: make another world, the form or structure of which is the symbol.

Art in Mrs. Langer's view is not a series of discursive expeditions, with words harnessed to the elucidation of concepts. Art develops "forms symbolic of human feelings." One meets up with a revelation. One feels "deep intellectual satisfaction." One is not, however, made to have a "consciousness of intellectual work (reasoning)." The artist sees, apprehends, uses his energy in a struggle for symbols, which when given shape become the poem, the painting — in Maritain's words a labor "made object," and as far as an audience goes, a sign: "both a *direct* sign of secrets perceived in things, of some irrecusable truth of nature, or adventure caught in the great universe, and a *reversed sign* of the subjective universe of the poet, of his substantial *Self* obscurely revealed."

In his article Dr. Percy quotes at considerable length from

Mrs. Langer, Maritain, St. Thomas's *Summa Theologica,* and Ernst Cassirer because he needs help in establishing the difference between man and animals — which he wants to do not to indulge our vanity, but to bring some of today's scientists back to those elementary distinctions which, ironically, get blurred from time to time by those who possess a great deal of, rather than little, knowledge. He insists upon the difference between a sign and a symbol, between events that trigger reflexes and a mode of expression by which human beings make known the nature of various things. The signs behaviorists see everywhere herald something: "Thunder announces rain. The bell announces food to Pavlov's dog. When I say James to a dog, he looks for James; when I say James to you, you say, what about him? — you *think* about James. A symbol is the vehicle for the conception of an object and as such is a distinctively human product." Percy will have no part of the symbol as a "variation of the sign function." Nor does he see any evidence that in more "primitive" forms of life the beginning of symbolization can be found. Like Mrs. Langer, not to mention the philosopher Maritain, he sees symbolization as possessing "a transformational character"; it is not an elaboration of something else, but a *beginning:* it is that point, really, where man begins to be his distinctive self. Needless to say, biologists, physical anthropologists, experimental or behavioral psychologists have no trouble being quite categorical about animals, including those thought to be our predecessors, and quite willing to accept their behavior at face value. A rat or pigeon or monkey is proclaimed to execute one or another maneuver, is said to function at a certain "level." But man must always be reduced: anything we do is but a version of what other creatures do more directly or simply. Their actions are accepted outright; ours are regarded as deceptive. Percy quotes disapprovingly what he calls "the old biogenetic motto": "Nihil est in homine quod non prius in amoeba erat."

For him the inclination toward symbolization is not only a uniquely human one, but one in no way explained by reference to either evolution or biology. With respect to the former, Mrs. Langer would agree with him, but not, apparently, the latter:

she refers to a "basic need" we have to use symbols. At one point she says: "This basic need, which is certainly obvious only in man, is the need of symbolization." Many would agree with her, place that "need" somewhere in the highly developed cerebral cortex, man's pride if not always the source of his joy. For Percy this way of thinking serves little purpose, though the reason we in the twentieth century feel so comfortable calling the resort to symbolization a biological "need" is eminently interesting to him. Anything explained in biological terms appeals to us — not only "ordinary" human beings but the most educated of the educated — as more "scientific," as nearer to what we think of as "the truth." Percy can perceive no "need" on our part to symbolize that compares with our "need" for food; and to say there is such a need is like "saying that bees store honey because there is in bees a need of storing honey."

He is quite willing to say good-bye, for a moment at least, to his considerable scientific education, because he believes that even in the twentieth century, so immersed not only in scientific enterprise but scientific imagery, there is room for, indeed warrant for, other ways of thinking — if you will, other symbols. "Symbolic transformation" for him is not a "need," but rather "a means of *knowing*." He wants not to put labels on people, but understand what they are doing. He believes that symbols enable us to acquire not "facts," but rather knowledge "in the Thomist and existential sense of identification of the knower with the object known." Through words and the symbols they evoke we come to terms with objects, things, the world; we grab them, it can be said, from what St. Thomas or a modern existentialist philosopher would both call "the flux of Becoming."

In the past, Thomists have spoken of "the interior word," of "knowing something and becoming something." All rather mysterious, rather difficult to visualize or even comprehend; but for Percy this refers to something we, in fact, do all the time when in a flash we find a word or a series of words that bring us nearer together: where we share understanding with another. For instance, it is possible for one person to seize upon two words, *the Cross*, speak them, and thereby evoke a whole world of meaning about Christianity to another person. Similarly, when I refer to the abstraction *courage* by evoking "the lion" (as in the expression "the courage of a lion"), I am getting a hold on the meaning of courage for myself and my reader or listener. Together we have shared something; one might even argue, as St. Thomas did, that insofar as we have both appreciated what it is about a lion that prompts us to think of "courage," we have at the same time experienced a measure of what courage is all about.

The same holds for the simple act of designation. Percy is especially indebted to Gabriel Marcel for the approach he takes to words and their meaning. Marcel points out *(The Mystery of Being,* 1951) that we don't want definitions when we ask, "What is that flower?" but rather a designation — such as the one he provides: "That flower is a lupine." Indeed what Marcel calls "the interpretation by reduction" only frustrates us — unless we are philosophers sitting alone in our studies and asking the broadest of questions, such as "What is life?" or "What is that flower?" No, we want to be given a name. Is that because we are "infantile," because we still resort to "pre-logical" or superstitious thinking, hence prone to identifying words with things? Or is it that, as Percy puts it, "our common existence is validated" when one person learns from another that not only does a particular flower exist, and not only does it have a name, but it exists for each of them, and that state of existence can be jointly affirmed by two human beings through the use of words.

In Marcel's way of expressing it, one has moved from the metaphysics of *I think* (or *name,* or *categorize,* or *come up with a formulation*) to the metaphysics of *we are.* To go back to the title of Dr. Percy's first philosophical article, the symbol is not something we use because of a biological "drive," a "need," but rather is an activity we have discovered in human society; a manner of looking at the world, then reaching out for company, so that where first there was one person, now there are two or more, and two or more who have, by virtue of their activity — that is, the use of words in a certain way — moved a substantial distance closer. The symbol carries people along. The company they become for one another as they move is for them an "existential" occasion — because they have been brought just a little bit closer to appreciating what it is like to be a human being: a human being not only can behave as a certain King Richard of England did, but also think of a lion, then use the word as a symbol, so that others will join in a shared under-standing — at least to a degree — of exactly who that "lion-hearted" king was.

In June of 1956 Dr. Percy continued his exploration of what a "symbol" means and can help us do for each other. This time he published an even more scholarly article in an even more scholarly journal: "Symbol as Hermeneutic in Existentialism: A Possible Bridge from Empiricism," which appeared in vol-ume XVI of the quarterly *Philosophy and Phenomenological Research*. It is not a very long article, but it is difficult. It is, really, a statement to professional philosophers, mostly written in the technical language they find congenial. It is a development of ideas pursued earlier — not only in the article already discussed, but over the past decade of the author's life. All along, as Percy has moved from a strictly scientific career (in the conventional definition) to a life dedicated to a diversity of speculative inquiries, he has tried hard not to give up what he had once so exclusively believed in, the value of the scientific method, but instead to add new ideas or values of his to old ones, and when necessary try to reconcile apparent incom-patibilities. As a young doctor and pathologist he had quite naturally been an empiricist; almost without thinking one sub-scribes to what he calls in this second article "the canons of induction-deduction." They have to do with "data." One makes hypotheses, comes up with inductions or deductions. One does tests in order to verify. One shows oneself able to predict. All very well, when it is the physical world or the life cycle of plants and animals that is under scrutiny. Let man himself be the subject of "research" and we have what are sometimes called the "human sciences," and (in Percy's words) "certain notorious difficulties."

He examines them, and for a while anticipates himself as the novelist who can in a paragraph or two make his readers smile at the pretensions of various social scientists. There is what he calls the matter of "imperialism." Some self-declared empiricists cling tenaciously to their words (often enough confused with actual "data") and scoff at the words or concepts others use: man is a "cultural unit"; he is "libido" exerting itself and being warded off or channeled or whatever; he is the sum of his "genetic traits" or the product of his "environment" as it works its power over him; he is a "social monad" — and, clearly, the list is a long one. Nevertheless, for all the assurance, if not arrogance, of the various definitions, man remains elusive: "sociological material resists fixed inductions." Even more complicated, the best description of a really sensitive sociologist or psychologist results in what Percy calls a moment of "transcendence"; the words have more than likely become wonderfully suggestive: for example, David Riesman's "lonely crowd." But such moments are at odds with scientific tradition. David Hume would obviously have had trouble with such a way of using words (at least on the part of a man who gets called a "scientist"). Percy believes that Hume would be bothered by Riesman's expression because the former's empirical "method," his philosophical tenets, are quite inadequate when applied to man's life as it is lived by each one of us human beings — something Riesman surely felt when he struggled to go beyond the particular observations he had made of Americans alive in the 1950s, and did so not by coming up with something that is testable, but something nearer to the symbolic.

Of course, those determined to regard themselves as scientists at all costs can go through the motions of scientific elaboration, even when they learn not a thing by doing so, and maybe confuse a few issues. Percy refers to smuggling: "The practice of smuggling in existential activities in a deterministic discipline." For example, psychoanalytic determinism, surely one of the most influential kinds in this century, constantly explains contemporary behavior as derivative — the result of antecedent experiences. In our everyday lives what we say or do is attributed to the outcome of a struggle within the mind: the Id urges one thing; the Superego has its say in the matter;

and the Ego is constantly and energetically working off impulses or mediating between internal demands and external realities, or not least, coming up with ingenious "mechanisms of defense," which for a while, at least, cause things to simmer down. Such a state of tension (the basis for the "psychopathology of everyday life") is no surprise to the thousands who have regarded themselves as "neurotic" or "sick" and taken themselves to a psychoanalyst; but for Percy it is indeed surprising, given the determinism of psychoanalytic theory, that a decision to seek "help" is ever made. How to account for the *decision*, the *choice*, the act of *will?*

Needless to say, those who want to regard themselves as scientists and nothing else don't take to words like those three: how does one quantify them, or for that matter fit them into an abstract, mechanistic scheme of forces and counterforces, drives and "defense mechanisms" designed to "push back" drives? Years after Percy's article, certain psychoanalysts began to ask precisely the questions he did, notably Avery Weisman in his *Existential Basis of Psychoanalysis;* but in the early 1950s and, to an extent, even now, the "smuggling" has to go on. The patient does get to the office, or the patient does decide to do something unexpected but enormously significant, or the patient does quite suddenly become "different" — and rather than openly resort to words like *choice* or *will*, or even more suspect, *fate* or *destiny*, psychiatrists often enough shrug their shoulders, are grateful when it all goes for the better (the patient's decisions, the patient's manner) or, when it doesn't, speak of the "difficulties," often called the "unknowns," which still confront any science. To existentialists the word is *mysteries*, and they are irreducible; that is, not ultimately objects of classification and reduction — to atoms or molecules, to "libido quanta," to a "mechanism of defense" or a unit or integer of some kind. Percy is quite comfortable with those mysteries; they lead, he knows, to other mysteries; and however unacknowledged, they persist in their obviousness and importance.

Especially important for Percy is what he and others drawn to existentialism have called intersubjectivity. It is a word hard to pin down, as are many words favored by existentialists (hence the annoyance of empirical-minded scientists). The sphere of intersubjectivity is shared reflection: Marcel's *we are*. *Knowledge* and *meaning* are the mere beginnings of intersubjectivity — because both have to do with individuals directly or indirectly calling upon one another for assistance, and not least, rejoicing together when the mutual appeal is successful. Percy insists that it is the "intersubjective" aspect of social science which many of its practitioners shun; they are determined to emulate natural scientists at all costs, and the price eventually gets not high, but absurd: cultural traits are isolated, social forces quantified, and one reads the result as if the objects under analysis are rocks or trees, chemicals or particles caught by an electron microscope. He acknowledges, however, that for many scientifically minded intellectuals, never mind scientists themselves, be they self-assured physicists or insecure psychologists or sociologists, "existential insights appear to be 'up in the air.' " They are regarded as murky, not subject to measurement.

As he goes about criticizing social scientists or acknowledging the vagueness of existential terminology, Percy generally speaks the difficult language of the philosophers he is addressing: "The task is to take account of Kierkegaard without surrendering to Kant. This is to be achieved, as far as the sciences of man are concerned, not by a precipitous search for a regional ontology, such as the ontologizing of the *existentialia* of the *Dasein*, but by an 'open' experiential empiricism which tacitly posits the world." Social scientists are thereby asked to be specific and concrete in their inquiries, though reasonable generalizations are not out of the question.

Yet it is, ironically, the subject of language itself which prompts the author to write quite otherwise, regardless of his audience — write in a nontechnical, lively, narrative vein. He is about to make the important point in his article. He is about to indicate the possible "bridge" he mentioned in the title. He is about to show that at a certain point traditional, empirical methods simply won't work, and the viewpoint of "existentialists," properly stated, becomes not only helpful, but even subject to a kind of verification: experience as one takes notice of it in oneself and in others. He is about to show, as he did in his first article, that a symbol is no elaborate reflex, but a means by which people learn about something, calling upon other people in the process. He is about to show that a kind of "deliverance" takes place when symbols are used — but one that can be witnessed, recorded almost, hence not something "mystical" or elusive. Rather than explain himself at great theoretical length, he summons an example, perhaps out of his own experience as a father of a deaf child: "It is the very indispensability of the role which symbolization plays in cognition which prevents our seeing its unprecedented character. The most graphic warrant for its uniqueness and for the qualitative difference between the signal world and the symbol world is the unwitting testimony of blind deaf-mutes like Helen Keller and Laura Bridgman. Helen Keller's experience is extremely illuminating. She had used words before — but as signals. When her teacher, Miss Sullivan, spelled out *water, mug, drink* in her hand, she 'understood': she responded by drinking water, going to water, fetching the mug, etc. — that is to say, she interpreted the word in a signal context and *did* something. What Miss Sullivan could not make her understand was that the word water was not a command to *do* something with water, but *meant*, denoted water. Then at last and in a sudden flash of insight, Helen understood that the gesture in her hand *meant* the water. It was an experience of tremendous excitement. Having learned that this 'is' water, what she had to know immediately was *what everything else was!*"

So it is that the mind is awakened. We begin looking, if not searching. And it *is* "we": "There is the 'I,' the consciousness which is confronted by the thing and which generates the symbol by which the conception is articulated. But there is also the 'you.' *Symbolization is of its very essence an intersubjectivity.*" In other words, we don't only come to terms with the world by adapting to signals of various kinds (the province of behavioral psychologists to study); we also gain what Percy calls "possession" of the world by using symbols, and that second kind of knowledge is existential because what is comprehended has become part of ourselves, *is* in us — does not require signals, however indirect or unobvious, but has been "made" by us, exactly as a poet comes up with his symbols, uses his words suggestively, so as to convey meaning. Percy believes such mental activity cannot be further reduced; it is what uniquely characterizes human beings — and it is what he calls a hermeneutic, a way of looking at and comprehending something, in this case the existential "facts" of our daily lives.

Drawing upon Kierkegaard and Marcel, Percy criticizes those who belong to three schools of philosophy — empiricists, idealists, and even some existentialists — for the way they look at "consciousness." The point is not that "I am conscious of this chair," or that "there is a consciousness of this chair," but that "this is a chair for you and me." For him such a "joint act of designation and affirmation by symbol *is itself* the constituent act of consciousness." (Clearly, there are dangers to that kind of "act." One part of it may come to overweigh the other: the object is "designated," but not really "affirmed"; it becomes "a picture-book entity." We can name things to pigeonhole them, rather than to acknowledge them to ourselves and to others.)

There is, Percy goes on to point out, a great exception to human powers of symbolization: "The one thing in the world which by its very nature is not susceptible of a stable symbolic transformation is *myself!* I, who symbolize the world in order to know it, am destined to remain forever unknown to myself."

Percy was writing as one who had steeped himself in the existentialist literature. He knew that for Sartre, when the self tries to treat itself as an object, something to be grasped, the result is a sense of "nothingness." For Marcel, there is the "aching wound of self." Or there are those sad and desperate "impersonations" — a fall into "inauthenticity." He summarizes the existentialist's predicament: "This is a chair for you and me. That is a tree, everything is something, you are what you are, but *what am I?*" If the answer is elusive, or never really to be obtained, this side of heaven, the effort to find the answer goes on and on. Not only philosophers make such an attempt; we all do — and as he indicates how, Percy gets vivid.

He speaks of "zones," a way, really, of getting specific about what gets called in the article "the-situation-in- which-we-find-ourselves." (Like many existentialists, he often feels driven to link up a number of words, through use of the hyphen, into one long noun.)

There is, for example, the "zone of the nought": new things are grabbed and devoured; goods are endlessly consumed. We crave a piece of furniture or a painting not because we really need it, not even because we are interested in it, or curious about how it will "work" in our house, but in order to have, and ultimately, in order to prove that we *are:* If I can lay my hands on that painting, then things will change — in Percy's words, "my life will be different, for my nothingness will be informed by the having of it." I feel empty deep down; I remember only too well the saying "ashes to ashes"; but for a second or two I can stand up, make my bid, be known as the buyer of that object, be known, *be.* But alas, once possessed, once in "the zone of my nought," the object loses its allure, its promise, and becomes of no consequence whatever; it "only participates in my nothingness." So it is that a week later, days go by and I ignore what once I lusted after, couldn't take my eyes off. Likewise with "impersonations": we try to be this kind of person, that kind of person; we imitate so-and-so, pursue one after another "ideal," and mold our behavior or appearance accordingly. Once we succeed there is, again, restlessness, unease, dissatisfaction, boredom, the "anxiety" Kierkegaard spoke of long ago, and knew enough not to try to treat. (He would not, of course, deny that other kinds of anxiety exist and can indeed be fathomed empirically, hence by exposure robbed of the power which inscrutability provides.)

There is also the "zone of the other"; and it is interesting to contrast Sartre's way of looking at the other with Percy's. Sartre exerted a strong influence on Percy — his plays and novels especially did. But Sartre's existentialism is emphatically not Percy's. Sartre emphasizes the critical, sardonic, aggressive side of the "other," and he emphasizes the power that other person possesses: he or she is not bound by my self-infatuation, the illusions I summon for myself, the tricks I pull on myself. Others regard us with honesty, and show us — through the glare in their eyes (Sartre's much discussed "stare") — what we have been up to. For Percy, however, the "other" is the knower all right, but not always in the sense of one who criticizes, exposes, reveals dozens of blind spots, weak spots, and just plain spots: stains of disgrace a given self has accumulated over the years. Percy sees the "other" as one who shares and affirms as well as takes note of various failures. He refers to "the communion of selves," a term Marcel — or the novelist Georges Bernanos — would find agreeable. And in a devastating section Percy takes strong issue with Sartre's "nothingness as the prime reality."

Sartre's fictional characters again and again discover how empty they are, how "zero at the bone" (Emily Dickinson's phrase) life is for them. In *Le Sursis* Matthieu is walking on the Pont-Neuf and suddenly stops; he has had a moment of revelation: "Within me there is nothing, not even a wisp of smoke; there is no within. There is nothing. I am free." But Percy notes the man's pleasure, his self-delight, his virtual elation. At last he does indeed have some sense of what kind of person he is: "He is something after all — Nothing!" Thereby Sartre (as Percy sees it) commits the same error he so severely condemns when made by others: this "nothing" which Matthieu finds in himself and proclaims is yet another of those many "impersonations" Sartre has portrayed. Nevertheless, at least Sartre is struggling to find, then use words to describe, what Percy calls "the uniqueness of human being." Empiricists, he charges, are on the contrary all too commonly engaged in an "obsessive quest for reducibility and quantification."

With that second article Dr. Percy had begun a philosophical career; other more or less technical articles would later be written to philosophers in various journals. But his next article, also published in 1956, though a few months later, appeared in *Partisan Review* under the title "The Man on the Train: Three Existential Modes," and was clearly written as an essay for the educated general public. This particular piece was a critical one in Dr. Percy's career; his writing becomes entertaining as well as thoughtful: "It is related," Percy observes in the first paragraph, "that when Kafka read his work aloud to his friends, they would all roar with laughter until tears came to their eyes," and perhaps some of his own readers, quoting parts of this article aloud, have experienced a similar reaction. Many of the images summoned and themes discussed in the fairly long (sixteen-page) and wide-ranging statement foreshadow his later interests as a novelist, though at the time he wrote the piece he was emphatically not plotting out *The Moviegoer, The Last Gentleman,* or *Love in the Ruins.* Yet in the first of those three novels there is a critical scene on a train; the second novel can be regarded as a major effort to deal fictionally with the "three modes" discussed in the article; and as for the third, its "ruins" — at one point the author quotes "love among the ruins" — were almost certainly first given description in one of the last phrases of the essay: "When the vines sprout in Madison Avenue and Radio City lies greening like an Inca temple in the jungle . . ."

"Alienation" was all the rage in the 1950s; an existentialist term had been imported from Europe and soon enough was tried on for size by just about everyone: the most fashionable thing around. Percy, despite his interest in European existentialists, was clearly amused by the way a word like *alienation* had become absorbed into America's culture. He wrote the article for *Partisan Review* in order to redeem, as best he could, an interesting and valuable notion from its ironic fate: alienation as the norm. Taking on countless critics in his first sentence, he insists that "there is no such thing, strictly speaking, as a literature of alienation." When one is riding a train, he points out, and reading a book about a person who is alienated and riding a train, then one is not by any means the "alienated commuter," sitting on the train quietly and smugly, and quite untroubled by something called alienation. The word, the symbol, a whole so-called literature, have conspired to make a difference — not that the awareness enabled by a reading of a book or two necessarily is redemptive. A man or woman can be all too miserably aware, all too conscious, of a given kind of life's confinements. But he or she is not alienated. Here is Percy's definition, along with a glimmer of his serious but never self-important manner of approaching issues: "I hasten to define what I mean by alienation, which has become almost as loose an epithet as existentialism (if you do not agree with me, it is probably because you are alienated). I mean that whereas one commuter may sit on the train and feel himself quite at home, seeing the passing scene as a series of meaningful projects full of signs which he reads without difficulty, another commuter, although he has no empirical reason for being so, although he has satisfied the same empirical needs as commuter A, is alienated. To say the least, he is bored; to say the most, he is in pure anxiety; he is horrified at his surroundings — he might as well be passing through a lunar landscape and the signs he sees are as absurd or at least ambiguous."

The alienated man in Percy's mind is not the stylish reader who pats himself on the back and says, "I am alienated," one more distinction that makes me no member of the mob. Percy's alienated man is the one who has made every possible effort to leave the mob, become his own person, go along with the "enlightenment" of his age. We are given a sample of the kinds of "needs" such a man may have conscientiously tried to fill: "sexual needs, nutritional, emotional, in-group needs — needs for a productive orientation, creativity, community service." Why is he alienated, then? Percy has no all-inclusive answer, but he indicates that the most likely candidate for alienation is the one who has for a long time gone along with the prevailing mood and sensibility of twentieth-century civilization. He uses the term *objective-empirical* as a noun to summarize that civilization's dominant ideology: scientific, rational thinking, along with, of course, its various "applications," which result in concepts like "the mature personality" or "milieu therapy" or sociocultural norms."

For reasons psychiatrists would call "emotional" but a man like Percy would consider philosophical or religious, a person wedded to that ideology can go through a shift of attitude, a reversal really: what has caused anxiety now becomes a refuge from it. That is, assumptions are turned around, so that the alienated person seems almost to welcome disasters, unsettling surprises, even the possibility of an apocalyptic moment. Life as it is lived from day to day seems futile, purposeless, a tiring bore. No longer does it seem worthwhile to dig in, call upon the familiar explanations. Habits once cheerfully followed now seem pointless or absurd. Beliefs once almost automatically held now seem laughable or wrongheaded. And worst of all are those efforts on the part of the unalienated to "interpret" alienation, refer to it as the outcome of one or another "process." Percy here distinguishes between the writer, who presents or portrays alienation, and the social scientist who, of all ironies, tries to banish it, as a "disease," with the very instrument which, the victim is convinced, has helped make things so painful in the first place: "It is just when the alienated commuter reads books on mental hygiene which abstract immanent goals from existence that he comes closest to despair." That commuter, and maybe the author with him, "shook like a leaf" when he read this: "The most profound of all human needs, the prime requisite for successful living, is to be emotionally inclusive. Socrates, Jesus, Buddha, St. Francis were emotionally inclusive."

As he had before, Dr. Percy denies a wish to attack "the objective-empirical method": science with all its "truth and beauty and fruitfulness." He is quick to point out that "the European existentialists," alas, do just that all too often — "while at the same time living very well" off all that physicists and chemists, among others, have enabled. It is, to say the least, inconsistent (and maybe irresponsible) when one denounces Reason or Science in ever so sweeping terms, then gladly receives a shot of penicillin, picks up the telephone to reach a friend, or opens up a refrigerater in order to get something which has been kept quite fresh. For Percy the point is simply this: alienation is a "mode," a way of coming to terms with the world; it takes place when a commonly accepted world view, such as the "objective-empirical" one, no longer feels persuasive. Then the individual turns away from principles which have been previously held "true" if not sacred; indeed, discovers in them not a source of affirmation but the "root-source" of discontent.

The self Percy is interested in exploring can find another way of registering its unease, if not outright despair. Drawing on Kierkegaard, especially, the author tries to indicate what "rotation" is like. Kierkegaard wrote in *Either/Or* of "the rotation method." From childhood on we sense what he called "the ruinous character of boredom." He was a tireless observer of his fellow Danes, of all Europeans; the spectacle of their plight never bored him. He observed people going through one rotation after another: "change in its boundless infinity." Illusion is the essence of rotation, which he described rather vividly: "One tires of living in the country, and moves to the city; one tires of one's native land, and travels abroad; one is *Europamüde* ["Europe-weary," a literary expression of the 1840s] and goes to America, and so on; finally one indulges in a sentimental hope of endless journeyings from star to star. Or the movement is different but still extensive. One tires of porcelain dishes and eats on silver; one tires of silver and turns to gold. . . ."

More "intensively," as Kierkegaard phrases it, there is the "prisoner in solitary confinement for life," who finds that "a spider may furnish him with much entertainment." Whoever one is, the challenge is clear: be ingenious, lest the rotations go on and on, to no real effect. He speaks of "arbitrariness" as important — a capacity for sudden shifts, a willingness to be shrewdly, imaginatively unconventional: "You go to see the middle of a play, you read the third part of a book. By this means you insure yourself a very different kind of enjoyment from that which the author has been so kind as to plan for you." The world is full of the accidental; one is more alive in that world when one seeks and welcomes abrupt surprises. By being "arbitrary," one allows the unexpected to happen, and is, that way, in closer touch with things, rather than inertly under the spell of "everydayness."

That word comes up repeatedly in Percy's article and Kierkegaard knew how to describe the phenomenon of "everydayness" especially well. So did Heidegger: his *Alltäglichkeit* — an absorption into life's duties or routines which saps the person of an ability to look around, take notice of life's texture, gain a measure of philosophical distance, and in general be responsive to the many subtleties that are there, waiting for the eye to notice, the ear to heed, the mind to find worthy of attention. The hero of *The Moviegoer* would tell us: "Everydayness is the enemy." Five years earlier Percy was trying to take the measure of that "everydayness": what does it prompt in people who, one way or another, sense something is wrong? And something is wrong because one is confined — not only from the world's possibilities, but from oneself, as Roquentin was in Sartre's *Nausea*.

Sartre has his character finally see his hand, recognize it as part of the world around him — as if to indicate how cut off one can be: for years even a hand goes unnoticed. Usually it is otherwise, and with respect to more than our hands, as Percy suggests in this passage about the alienated commuter on the train: "Beyond all doubt he is in Metuchen, New Jersey during the few seconds the train stops there, yet in what a strange sense is he there — he passes without so much as leaving his breath behind. Even if this is the one-thousandth time he has stopped there, even if he knows a certain concrete pillar better than anything else in the world, yet he remains as total a stranger to Metuchen as if he had never been there."

Now one does not have to be an existentialist vagabond to experience the lurch of a rotation. Those with money, time, and sophistication can, of course, buy an endless succession of apparently transcendent moments: I am here in this strange country and I have thought about the world in a new way, and found myself conscious of the world around me as never before; or, I have just made this wonderful purchase, and it has virtually taken over my life, so wonderful it is — so that I feel different, almost euphoric because of my delight, and so much more responsive to people and my surroundings. But tragedies or calamities befall all of us, rich or poor, and with them come unexpected benefits — a rotation that changes for a while the way one person gets along with others, with himself or herself, and with "the things of this world." Here is Dr. Percy's man on the train, again: "It is only in the event of a disaster, the wreck of the eight-fifteen, that one is *enabled* to discover his fellow-commuter as a comrade; thus, the favorite scene of novels of good will in the city: the folks who discover each other and help each other when disaster strikes. (Do we have here a clue to the secret longing for the Bomb and the Last Days? Does the eschatological thrill conceal the inner prescience that it will take a major catastrophe to break the partition?)"

As the author tries to do justice to a whole philosophical literature, he feels compelled to become graphic, concrete; and increasingly, he does so by providing illustrative examples which, in essence, are brief but suggestive incidents, if not ideas for a short story: "Suppose the eight-fifteen breaks down between Mount Vernon and New Rochelle, breaks down beside a yellow cottage with a certain lobular stain on the wall which the commuter knows as well as he knows the face of his wife. Suppose he takes a stroll along the right-of-way while the crew is at work. To his astonishment he hears someone speak to him; it is a man standing on the porch of the yellow house. They talk and the man offers to take him the rest of the way in his car. The commuter steps into the man's back yard and enters the house. This trivial event, which is of no significance objectively-empirically, is of considerable significance aesthetically-existentially. A zone-crossing has taken place. It is of extraordinary interest to the commuter that he may step *out* of the New York Central right-of-way and into the yellow house. It is of extraordinary interest to stand in the kitchen and hear from the owner of the house who he is, how he came to build the house, etc."

These "zone-crossings," Percy knows, are the very stuff of novels and plays, radio or television soap operas, and, not least, the movies he has for so long found intriguing. We are told that *It Happened One Night* provides "a triumph of rotation." Why? Because in the film one sees "Clark and Claudette crossing zones without a trace of involvement, from bus to hitch-hiking to meadow to motel." They wander into a barnyard, get to meet and know people, as strangers become almost exquisitely aware of what is happening around them, then leave before they succumb to "everydayness": turn into "members of the community," neighbors who do their work, live their lives — and every once in a while dream of leaving, finding a new place to live, meeting new people, "seeing the world." Percy does not use that last phrase, but Heidegger does, and with full consciousness of its irony: we could, if we were more nearly free, see the world all the time, with no need of travel to do so. We would be responding to all sorts of sights and sounds, to subtleties of mood, nuances of feeling, which in their sum we quite regularly and completely manage to miss observing.

Why are we blind to so much? It is in our nature to be so. Kierkegaard traces the phenomenon back to Adam and Eve: Adam became bored, indifferent to the world, confined to himself; with Eve he was for a while newly alive — liberated and energetic enough to want to explore; together they were alive and in touch not only with one another, but their Garden, the so-called environment; but soon enough they, too, became bored — hence the arrival of Abel and Cain; and on and on it has gone. Kierkegaard is, of course, being sly; he does not intend the boredom he mentions to explain all aspects of the doctrine of original sin. He was simply exercising the right of a poet, trying with a word, an image, to condense many ideas, trying also to be suggestive: "The gods were bored, and so they created man. Adam was bored because he was alone, and so Eve was created. Thus boredom entered the world, and increased in proportion to the increase of population. Adam was bored alone; then Adam and Eve were bored together; then Adam and Eve and Cain and Abel were bored *en famille;* then the population of the world increased, and the people were bored *en masse.*"

A factory worker I came to know once said, "Once a year, I'd say, I stop in the middle of something and pinch myself and say, who in hell are you and what are you doing here and how did you get here and where are you going and what's it all about? And I'll tell you, I don't have the answers. Anyway, before I have a chance, there's a whistle blowing, or a lever to turn, or a guy shouting at me: What's the matter, you turning deaf? He's been calling me, and I've been off somewhere, so I get back to business, and that's all the time I have for those deep questions."

If everyone is more or less blind, more or less out of touch with so very much that really matters (all those questions of the factory worker, waiting to be asked and at least thought about, though pushed aside or "dominated through and through," and "for life," by machines and people and customs and demands and the voice of conscience and the requirements of conformity — the list is endless), then surely novelists or essayists or philosophers will be similarly "dominated." Personally, like everyone else, they only at certain moments "break through," free themselves of the routines, come into some contact with themselves, regard the world with awe or wonder or real interest, rather than take it for granted, while the foot presses on the accelerator, the radio blares forth, and maybe the mind has rapid-fire fantasies, none of which it will remember five minutes later, when the car stops, and there is an "errand" or "business" to do. As a result, when they use words they are often enough behaving like the factory worker; they do their job, go along with, rather than try hard to survey and challenge through questions and close attention things-as-they-are; and so the reader gets from the writer the stuff of yet another unsurprising fantasy, gets something quickly and easily absorbed into a complacent or hurried or all too exhausting life. ("Oh, yes, that's interesting; now let me see, what do I have on my agenda for today?")

The man Percy puts on a commuter train is the man he has been reading about in *Either/Or* or *Being and Time*. The article was meant to show how writers of movie scripts or novels at least struggle to obtain brief moments of partial liberation for their characters, and by extension, for those moviegoers or readers who for a while, anyway, are brought up short, jolted, made to think about themselves and their lives — perhaps in a way the factory worker sometimes finds himself thinking: "I'll be going along, and I never think about anything. Then I'll go fishing with my son, and we get lost for a few minutes — we don't know exactly where we are — and I'll look up at the sky and the trees, and instead of being scared, I'll say to him: wouldn't it be something if we could live here, and when we got up in the morning we could look at the sun coming up, and at night there'd be the stars, and we could be free of the rat race.

Once my boy and I spent an hour looking at different trees and their bark. Now, I ask you, who has time for that most days? I don't even remember driving to work a lot of the time; I'll be here, pulling my levers, and I'll suddenly stop and say: Mister, how did you get here — I mean, what happened to that auto ride; it's gone from your memory. I'm only thirty-four, and at times I think I'm going senile. I'm so caught up trying to beat the clock that I've become a clock myself: I just go around and around, and don't ask me what I'm doing or what I remember or what I noticed, because there's no time for that."

When a man says he has become a clock, he is remarking on the nature of his "being": he *has* no time, simply *puts in* time, rushes to make time, so to speak. Of course, there are those precious moments when he goes fishing, and, having become lost, finds himself, if ever so briefly. Percy mentions Hemingway's story, a fictional presentation the factory worker would find familiar: a fisherman leaves a train in the middle of the Minnesota woods and charts his course. "To leave the fixed right-of-way at a random point and enter the trackless woods is a superb rotation," we are told. But one has to be careful. Were the factory worker to go fishing in unexplored territory only because he'd read the Hemingway story, and, further, if he were to go because he worried that people would find him odd indeed if he didn't go ("What *does* he do on his week-ends or vacations?"), one wonders how much of the sun and sky and stars he would catch sight of. The next week, back home and on his way to work, dozens of cars before him and dozens behind him, the radio going but not being heard, he might wonder what happened to his vacation. What *did* he do with it? Not only alcoholics "lose" weekends.

Percy keeps trying to illustrate alienation and rotation — as if he hopes that the reader will experience a rotation of sorts as he reads "The Man on the Train." The article is a blend of literary criticism, social commentary, and philosophical speculation: "Travelers in Sweden report two national traits: boredom and love of the North country — alienation and rotation." On the other hand, it didn't work when Swedish planners, of which there are, no doubt, many, began to worry about such a "recreational need," and so provided wooded areas near residential neighborhoods of Stockholm, and set aside stretches of the north country for hiking: "There occurred a sudden increase of Swedish tourists in quaint out-of-the-way *English* villages." And back to literature: "The road is better than the inn, said Cervantes and by this he meant that rotation is better than the alienation of everydayness."

Percy is especially drawn to Huck Finn's adventures. He loves Huck on the Mississippi River. The boy is on water, "the mobile element." He is adrift, "the random on the mobile." And finally, he is on a river that provides a very special bonus to those who care to stop and think about their situation: one is between states. Huck was not in Illinois and not in Missouri, "but in a privileged zone between the two." It is a telling rotation: not extreme — a raft on the ocean would be too exotic, too removed from everyone's experience — and yet not too familiar, such as a raft on a local pond or river. Percy delights in the "businessman who sits reading his paper, immured in everydayness, while not two hundred yards away Huck slips by in the darkness." What has happened, existentially, is that "Huck has his cake and eats it: he wins pure possibility without losing access to actualization." On the other hand, if the factory worker were plucked out of whatever neighborhood he calls "home" and put in Bulgaria or Paraguay or Kuwait, and told he was going to stay there indefinitely, he wouldn't be looking at the sky and asking himself all sorts of trenchant questions, thereby in his new life becoming a contrast to his former self, or to others who lived where he once did and each day read the newspaper or brushed their teeth or watched television while half-dozing or daydreaming or keeping an eye out for the candy dish or the cookie jar. In Sofia or Asunción or in Kuwait's Al Kuwait the factory worker would be burrowing in, trying to find a house, work, a "routine."

As for science fiction, or comic-book serials, they are "way out," hence they may distract, but they never do so in such a way that one's everyday life is in the slightest degree brought into focus. Most writers do, however, try to give us a break, so to speak, and Percy gives us an amusing summary of some of

95

the directions they pursue: "Rotation may occur by a trafficking in zones, the privileged zone of possibility which is the River in Huck Finn; the vagrancy zones of Steinbeck: ditches, vacant lots, whorehouses, weed-grown boilers, packing cases; the parabourgeois zone of *You Can't Take It With You* with Jean Arthur and her jolly eccentric family (an exceedingly short-lived rotation: what could be drearier than the madcap adventures of these jolly folks experienced a second time?)."

The Western as a literary genre, referred to in the writing of the undergraduate Walker Percy, gets further study in "The Man on the Train." The Western is "an exercise in rotation stripped of every irrelevant trait." The cowboy who comes from nowhere, dropped off as the train or stagecoach keeps moving, is the outsider, the stranger, the man of mystery. In Percy's wonderfully rhetorical question: "Who is he, this Gary Cooper person who manages so well to betray nothing of himself whatsoever, who is he but I myself, the locus of pure possibility?" Others in the Western are all too familiar: "the loyal but inept friend, the town comic, the greedy rancher, the craven barber." But the main character, Gary Cooper or John Wayne, is either no one or what Percy calls "perfectly actualized actuality," a god of sorts, who "acts with a ritual and gestural perfection."

"But what of the moviegoer?" Percy asks. We watch those Westerns, are held to our seats by what Cooper or Wayne does. What happens, however, when for a second or two we imagine ourselves in their shoes, or try to imitate their marvelously perfect gestures? In no time we have realized that art (or amusement or diversion) is not life, and that their apparent lack of anxiety or fear is both misleading and revealing: no human being lives as they do, psychologically. Still, for all their apparent lack of the human limitations the rest of us have, they possess an ability to get to the heart of things, a canniness and a daring of mind and spirit (Kierkegaard's "shrewdness") that are really not beyond our reach, simply more or less pushed aside by the routines of life. Indeed, at any moment, and with far less exertion or melodrama, we can approach Gary Cooper's wise and apparently singular openness.

"The other day," the factory worker recalls, "I looked out the window as I drove away to work, and I thought of my neighbors and myself, and I said to myself that we're all locked in to our schedules and our routines, but in each of us there's the wish that we could escape. Don't ask me what we'd do, once we *did*, though. But I wondered if I couldn't just go and open everyone's door, and say, come on, run and keep running, and I'll help you, and we'll overcome the prison guards — the bank people and the mortgages they've got on our houses, and the foreman at the factory, and, worst of all, I guess, ourselves: because we're the ones who go along." That is the point, of course, when every Western ends. The hero has freed the various victims — the insulted, the intimidated, the injured, the innocent, the merely acquiescent — and they are standing there in the town square, for a moment given something (a gift of sorts). Meanwhile he rides off; or he stands there, all lights on his face — the benefactor. What happens the next day, though? The Lone Ranger is now off tending to another town; "everydayness" slips back upon those he helped so much.

Sometimes it turns out that with no help from anyone like the Lone Ranger and with no accident or incident that provides a rotation (amnesia, a war, a vacation trip) we manage to find relief from "everydayness," and even confront it more decisively than ever before. Percy calls the mode "repetition," and gives examples: "Tom Wolfe, lying in his berth while the train passes by night through lonely little mid-Western towns, is alienation re-presented and so reversed. He may be lost and by the wind grieved but he is withal triumphant." The rider is not finding a rotation in his train ride; he could, if he wished, get off, enter one of those Midwestern cities, and manage quite well a distracting scene for himself. Instead there is "a deliberate quest for the very thing rotation set out at any cost to avoid." The rider looks inward, seeks out his past, questions and examines himself: what was "it" like, what was *I* like, back then — and how did I come to live the kind of life I now live, and how did I become this person who I now am?

Percy cautions that such a "return" can be "aesthetic," one of those "interesting experiences" people mention, or alternatively it can become a "passionate quest": at all costs the person wants to explore his being — the roots of his character. *Remembrance of Things Past* and *Brideshead Revisited* are examples Percy offers — though he does not in either instance judge the quality of repetition rendered by the novelist: whether it is a matter of mere curiosity or something more solemn and important. He also mentions *East of Eden* and J. P. Marquand's *Point of No Return*, which portrays "exurbanite alienation." The hero does not find a new life — free of all the dreary, little moments he (along with everyone else) has to face day after day. He becomes resigned to his life, which to all appearances is no different. The point is that he has reviewed his past with seriousness and care.

Not that any such sustained review is always conscientious and "authentic." A patient in psychoanalysis can give over an hour a day (at enormous cost, financially) to a backward look which never really engages his soul. It is all very "interesting" — sometimes it gets called "fascinating" — but the dedication and commitment, the high seriousness of Percy's existential kind of repetition, are sorely lacking. And maybe the doctor sets the tone: the patient is a series of equally "interesting" or sometimes "fascinating" problems, and those problems are dissected intellectually, coldly — as if they have a life of their own, apart from the feelings of the person who possesses them: a series of complexes, difficulties, syndromes. Percy's repetition, akin to Marcel's "recollection" and a modification of Kierkegaard's version of repetition, has the contemporary "I" meeting up with an earlier version of itself: one's former self thereby becomes a "Thou." Unfortunately, both one's former self and one's present self can become an "It" to patient and doctor alike: once I was a "phobic"; now I'm less than that — a "mature personality" most of the time.

"Repetition," like "rotation," is the property of no particular class or cadre, a point that has to be emphasized. (Camus worked hard to make his "stranger" neither rich nor poor, neither intellectual nor political ideologue nor fashionable aesthete.) All too often "introspection" — and, certainly, psychoanalysis — has been associated with the well-to-do and the well educated; as if working people don't stop and think about the issues a man like Kierkegaard posed for himself, and as if analysts like August Aichhorn and Helene Deutsch and Anna Freud didn't, from the very beginning of psychoanalysis, try successfully to work with working-class people, and indeed, the poor and needy of Vienna. Here is the factory worker once again, now trying to convey what some would call a "repetition"; for him it was simply a "funny day": "I have a funny day every once in a while. I take my boy and we go ride on our bikes. Bless my wife for pushing that bike on me: a Christmas present. I thought she was nuts at first. But I stand all day, never move much. This way I get going and I discover that I have muscles in my legs. I go with my son to the quarry over in Quincy. The Quincy quarry: it wouldn't mean much of anything to anyone else. But to me, I'll tell you, it's like suddenly seeing a lot of my life stretch before me. I'll picture myself on my old bike, my Columbia: red and white, the bell and the light my father made — by taking a flashlight and clamping it on to the handlebar. I'd go there when I had fights with my parents. I'd go there with my friends. I went there with each girl I got serious over. Before I got married I took my wife there. She thought I was getting strange: what's in a quarry? But I'll be back there and all of a sudden I picture my old friends, I picture *myself* when I was nine or ten. Then I start wondering how I got to be the kind of guy I am.

"Don't ask me any more. I don't know how to explain how I feel over there. My brother, he's not me, and to him the quarry is nothing. My friends I used to come to the quarry with and play with, they're not me. They probably never think of that quarry, either. It's hard to figure out, why you have your own personality, and not someone else's, and your memories, and not someone else's who grew up with you. But I know that I put in a lot of time riding around that quarry, and singing to myself and talking to myself; and whenever I was upset, you might say, I'd go there to think. I wasn't one for sitting in church, like my mother would tell us to do. Maybe because the quarry is outside; maybe it's because I've known it since I was a little boy, and my father would take us there — he'd push me in a baby carriage, he once told me. So, you know, it's not every-place that you feel familiar with: the roads and the scenery, and you've got all the memories hitting you. You say to your-self: I'm the one who has these memories; no one else in the whole world (even if there are two billion people now) has them — just me. It's foolish, I guess; but I don't think I'll ever stop going to the quarry, not as long as we live here, nearby. I talk to my boy better when I'm there. He gets to meet his *real* father. I'll tell you: half the time I'm my Social Security number, and half the time I'm the number on our house! Once a priest asked me if I felt I was only those two numbers, and I said: Father, you are *so* right. He's pretty lucky. He hasn't got either; he lives in the parish house and I guess he took a vow of poverty — he's a Jesuit. But I don't regret my life, even with its hassles. The other day, near the quarry, I told my boy: 'I could have done worse. You have to be true to yourself.' I think I've been that."

The man doesn't read articles or books on "existentialism," but philosophers like Marcel and Heidegger and, before them, Kierkegaard, have recognized that such an open, frank state-ment, offered in uncluttered language and without the media-tion of elaborate theory, conveys what they, intellectuals, may have trouble fitting into the discourse of philosophy or psychology. Once, holding up an example to himself, Kier-kegaard said: "When the Eleatic School denied the possibility of motion, Diogenes, as everybody knows, stepped forth as an opponent. He *stepped* forth literally, for he said not a word, but merely walked several times back and forth, thinking that thereby he had sufficiently refuted those philosophers."

Marcel and Heidegger (not unlike, from another direction, Wittgenstein) ultimately had strong doubts about their own extraordinary efforts. Heidegger's language is not so much dense as circuitous, as if he knows that he must only approach human experience, not *define* it. Marcel is explicitly contemp-tuous of any effort to convey through conceptual thought a kind of reality which he believes is lived out in concrete situa-tions by particular individuals: the difference between think-ing about the world and living in it. In a sense, Marcel argues for a kind of repentance: it is pride which makes for so much philosophical speculation, his own included. Ultimately Marcel turned to novelists such as E. M. Forster at critical moments in his essays; and, too, he wrote many plays. That way individuals could speak, and speak for themselves, not as spokesmen of various ideas; and they come up with suggestions and approximations, rather than conclusions handed down as the law itself. As for Kierkegaard, he created those marvelously named pseudonyms, and had them come up with lyrical aphorisms and stories: Victor Eremita, Constantin Constantius, Johannes de Silentio, Johannes Climacus, Vigilius Haufniensis, Nicolaus Notabene, Hilarius Bogbinder — with their "Fragment of a Life," or "Dialectical Lyric," or "Mimicpathetic Dialectic Medley."

The author of "The Man on the Train" was experiencing some of the frustration (and inspiration) that drove Marcel to the theatre, Kierkegaard to his various poetic tirades, Camus and Sartre to novels. The "material," as it is put in the academy, resists or eludes the rational mind that writes scholarly articles. Though Percy once contemplated a book based on the subject matter of his various articles, already written or planned, he also began in the late 1950s to send editors more and more essays on general subjects (the South, the profession of psychiatry, social and ethical issues facing the nation). He even began to write his own kind of literary criticism, and to attempt fiction. He was addressing widely different audiences — doing so both fluently and in a rather broad range of styles.

But before he could break out, turn to storytelling a free man, he had a few hurdles to accomplish. In a rather abstract paper ("Semiotic and a Theory of Knowledge," published in May of 1957 in *The Modern Schoolman*), he tried to win linguistically minded scientists and philosophers over to the kind of "intersubjectivity" Marcel has written about. He was speaking to those who apply logical analysis to "the science of signs": semiotic. Scholars who work in the field have developed a highly complicated system of symbolic logic; they have also become rather well versed in the principles of behavioral

psychology. Such scholars might not be considered likely candidates for Percy's existentialist persuasion, and he has
achieved no great renown as a semanticist or linguist, though
his articles, the ones already discussed and this one, which
offers a more technical version of their argument, clearly anticipated the assault Noam Chomsky would later launch on
B. F. Skinner's behaviorism.

"To render human cognition physico-causally," Percy tells
his readers, "can only end in the hopeless ambiguity of current
semioticists." He spells out their dilemma, and suggests an
answer to it which conveys his faith that the wrong questions
are asked by Skinner and his associates in the first place — the
issue being not only the definitions and interpretations an
analytic, deductive mind always craves, but the human inclination to avow and profess. First he asks a tactful question: "Is
it not possible that what I primarily want in asking *what* something is, is not an explanation but a validation and affirmation
of the thing itself as it is — a validation which can only be
accomplished by laying something else alongside: the symbol?" Then he throws caution to the wind and states, tersely
and defiantly: "Knowing is not a causal sequence but an im-
material union." At some point we speak to one another, help
one another know the world, and thereby move toward that
world — all of which is not a matter of external buzzers and
bells and verbal "associations" prompting sounds from our
mouths as "responses."

In 1957 Dr. Percy also took on those in the profession of
psychiatry (be they psychoanalysts, "organically oriented," or
interested in "cultural factors") who see men as a *driven* or
socialized animal, or who shun ethical judgments, claiming to
be scientists whose work demands that they be "value-free."
"The very men," he insists, "whose business is mental health
socialized animal, or who shun ethical judgments, claiming to
tional impoverishment, his sense of homelessness in the midst
of the very world which he, more than the men of any other
time, has made over for his own happiness." He was writing in
America, published by the Jesuits. It was a two-part piece titled
"The Coming Crisis in Psychiatry." Now over twenty years old,

the message has by no means become dated. "Who is mentally healthy?" the author asked; and from one who wrote "The Man on the Train" the answer is no surprise: not those who "adjust," who live up to every "norm," every passing fancy a given community takes to its heart; and not those who try to impose those standards on everyone — in the name of "loyalty," "patriotism," "the common good," or "mental hygiene."

Why, anyway, ought we raise our brows in the presence of anxiety, guilt, and fear — when, the author points out, there is every reason to have such emotions? Nor are they necessarily "residues" of earlier "neurotic conflict." A man who feels himself wasting a life, living it to no good purpose, will (or *ought* to) feel anxious, guilty, and fearful. A man who feels himself caving in to "powers and principalities" he knows to be morally indifferent, or corrupt, or even thoroughly wicked, has good reason to be alarmed about the direction of his life, if not in a state of complete panic. If such a man feels quite satisfied with what he has come to, then he has become lost to himself — and so is the psychiatrist who has been patting him and others like him on the back, telling them that they are O.K., everyone is O.K., or telling them that true, they have "problems," but that is inevitable, and therefore one can only make a series of accommodations.

Percy even goes after the newer "schools" of psychiatry and psychoanalysis. He nods approvingly at what they mean to do, tone down some of the crudities, if not downright absurdities, of the mechanistic viewpoint. But he takes issue with Erich Fromm, whose ideas (in *The Sane Society,* 1955) had initially impressed him a great deal. He does so because he can't accept man's ultimate difficulties as the result of any particular economic system's injustice or irrationality, though he doesn't at all discount the devastating effect of poverty or exploitation upon the spirit of the worker.

He notes that Erich Fromm corrects his categorical-minded colleagues, who tend to ignore social and economic realities, which exert a decisive psychological influence on children, as well as on grownup analysands. They tend to go along with the status quo, become the same greedy consumers their patients are: "market-oriented," in Fromm's scheme of things. But Fromm's prescriptions are themselves rather facile. He wants both his colleagues and their patients to achieve a "productive orientation." Then they would be "creative" and "productive"; then they could "love." It is no great leap from Fromm with his "live productively!" to the Overstreets with their "goal" of "emotional maturity." Percy mentions a "weird, abstractive" quality in *The Sane Society* — not by any means something that distinguishes the author of that book from others who call themselves "social scientists." A "reformer's zeal" has somewhat taken over where a secular critic's disenchantment with the capitalist world has spent itself. For Percy the result is a disappointing return to yet another kind of mechanistic straitjacket: Fromm's categories are no less suspect than any other social scientist's. We are back to that "man on the train," that compliant commuter, that willing consumer: "But what of the alienated man of the 20th century who reads this vast library of popular mental hygiene and dutifully sets out in quest of 'emotional maturity,' 'productive orientation,' 'cultural integration' and suchlike? To the degree that a man stakes everything on a goal isolated by the scientific method, to this same degree is he destined to despair. Somewhere there has occurred a fatal misplacement of the real. To hold out to a man lost in the abyss of anxiety and anonymity the solution of a 'productive orientation' is like telling a man who has fallen into a pit that the answer to his trouble is a pitless orientation."

The Louisiana doctor, who asked that the editors of *America* specify him as "not a psychiatrist," comes up with no alternative "answer." Transcendence, he knows, is what Fromm and many other social scientists fail to see as the most important if most elusive "trait of human existence." It is a trait no one can elicit with a buzzer; nor is it one that can be found on a Rorschach card, or on the Minnesota Multiphasic psychological test. For a religious existentialist like Marcel, transcendence has to do with man's capacity to see and be part of the world around him in a unique way, and ultimately, in a way that moves the person closer to God: each of us is not the sum of what the body urges, the environment demands; each of us is, or at least can be, *homo viator,* man en route, possessed of an active, responsive nature which fathoms, reaches out, defies those who would come near with the chains of the abstract, the categorical, the empirically measurable.

Another existentialist, Heidegger, also describes man as uniquely free to transcend himself — regard himself, hence obtain a distance from his constituent parts: his reflexes and needs, even his thoughts or ideas. The freedom existentialists mention is part of man's essence — not reducible phenomenologically: not, that is, an "illusion," or a result of rationalizations or denials. For Marcel (and Buber) man is free to realize his solidarity with significant "others"; he actualizes his freedom in love, and with another becomes transcendent. Two people thus bound are more than each of them was or is. That "other" can be God, as well. All existentialists, religiously inclined or not, stress that man is not a mere sum of what any particular observer sees. Even Sartre, a convinced atheist and a kind of Marxist, insists that man is capable of transcendence; he has the "useless passion" — the desire and ability to see more than he "needs" to. In Nietzsche's words: "Man is he who must surpass himself." And in doing so, he wriggles out of descriptions, slips through the fingers of those, however well intentioned, who want to submit his "life," his "nature," his character and his destiny to a series of specifications.

Man's capacity for transcendence is not the only psychological reality worth consideration. Percy is grateful to Fromm for his social criticism and psychological canniness. He simply doesn't believe that "an objective-explanatory-causal science can discover and set forth all the knowledge of which man is capable." He said that in an article written for the University of Houston *Forum* in the summer of 1957 ("The Act of Naming") and went on to point out, so simply yet suggestively, that "science is one of the things that man does, a mode of existence. Another mode is speech." That article, like those that preceded it and those that would follow, is devoted to an exploration of Being in the tradition of philosophers like Heidegger, Karl Jaspers, and Marcel. Animals respond to the world around them and to their own "needs" or "drives." So does man. But man also stands apart, names, and signifies. Percy draws on Heidegger and characterizes man as "that being in the world whose calling it is to find a name for Being, to give testimony to it, and to provide for it a clearing." And he makes quite clear the "consequences" Heidegger's viewpoint has for him; there are implications to be developed — which he lists as "epistemological, existential, religious, psychiatric." In a series of articles to follow he would pursue those implications.

Between 1958 and 1961 the articles came forth, one after the other. In three years Percy published seven major philosophical articles, along with a number of book reviews and essays for *Commonweal* and *America*. For *The Sewanee Review* he wrote "Metaphor as Mistake," an effort to show in great detail how so-called misunderstandings, misreadings of poems, slogans and mottos, or colloquial errors are, even so, instances of symbolization, means by which people attempt to educate themselves and one another: in their literal failure they achieve the success that goes with heightened comprehension — what Gerard Manley Hopkins called an "inscape," with its "unspeakable stress of pitch, distinctiveness, selving." When the Mississippi black makes such a "mistake," refers to a coin record player made by the Seeburg Company as a "seabird," it is not enough to say that he is being wrongheaded, showing evidence of illiteracy, or being quaint and in a naïve way "poetic." Nor will the author accept a psychological interpretation: "It is less than useless to say that in calling a machine a bird [he is] regressing into totemism, etc." The point is that for a particular person, and for those who hear him and understand him, the machine is appreciated, seen, felt, *known* by virtue of the use of a particular symbol: seabird. It matters not whether the black people who use the expression are right or wrong, are sensitive and poetic or given to slips of the tongue or sly exercises in "hostility": disfigurement of the white man's language, not to mention a given company's name and property. One is obliged to understand an effort by others to understand: "We may make a long cast and guess that in conceiving it as a *seabird*, the namer conceives it with richer overtones of meaning, and in some sense neither literal nor figurative, even as being more truly what it is than under its barbarous title, Seeburg automatic coin record player."

Another "mistake" is autobiographical: "I remember hunting as a boy in South Alabama with my father and brother and a Negro guide. At the edge of some woods we saw a wonderful bird. He flew as swift and straight as an arrow, then all of a sudden folded his wings and dropped like a stone into the woods. I asked what the bird was. The guide said it was a Blue Dollar Hawk. Later my father told me the Negro had got it wrong: it was really a Blue Darter Hawk. I can still remember my disappointment at the correction. What was so impressive about the bird was its dazzling speed and the effect of alternation of its wings, as if it were flying by a kind of oaring motion."

How does one distinguish between all the "variables" at work — the black man's reasons for using his expression, the boy's preference for it, the aesthetic and cognitive issue: what does "blue dollar" mean to the boy — as opposed to "blue darter"? The boy's reply would be brief and simple: a person, a guide, a namer, had spoken, and he the listener had heard and been told. In Percy's words: the child's "mind, which had really suffered a sort of hunger (ontological hunger?) now had something to feast on." Had just anyone come upon the scene and pulled the name "blue dollar" out of a hat, the boy would not have had his feast. And when the father came up with appropriate logical and definitive correction, the boy felt disappointed or cheated. Was the child a victim of the use of "prelogical" language? Was he having his "problems" with his father, hence unable to accept the correction? The man and writer who was once that child says no. "Blue dollar" clearly was a guide's "mistake." The correct name, "blue darter," does indeed serve its purpose; we learn what *color* the bird is and what it *does* so swiftly and unforgettably. But "blue dollar," in Percy's words, tells "what the bird *is*." It does so even though it has an origin, no doubt, in some other experience of that guide — though an experience which possesses "the same ontological status as the bird."

Perhaps the guide never could give the boy (or some curious linguist or social observer or literary critic) a brilliant and convincing explanation. Percy makes clear that he has no answer for us from that guide; but one can imagine him coming up with something rambling though not completely farfetched, like this: "I don't know why I use the words 'blue dollar.' I just do. But I'll tell you something. Yes, sir, I will. I know of the Green Dollar Express; and it picks you up not far from Midnight, Mississippi, and before you know it, faster than God Himself running, you're up there in Chicago, and there's money there, they say." Such a man, a backwoods tenant farmer, reciting this tale, has indicated a notion of speed, astonishing speed — of a kind that captures the imagination. Were the guide and others to hear a white man talk about the blue darter hawks, then change the description to blue dollar hawks, with that speedy Green Dollar Express in mind — then they would, as we have seen, been as "wrong" as can be, yet "right." Right about what? Their "ontological pairing," as Percy says, "or if you prefer, [their] 'error' of identification of word and thing, is the only possible way in which the apprehended nature of the bird, its inscape, can be validated as being what it is." Needless to say: we are talking about that boy and that guide, and a concrete (but not unique) situation in Alabama. A Harvard graduate student of zoology who grew up in Brooklyn or near downtown Cleveland and went South on a hunting vacation might scratch his head and wonder what in the world is wrong with both Dr. Percy and that guide he writes about.

There are no such "regional references" in the article "Symbol, Consciousness, and Intersubjectivity," published in the July, 1958, issue of the *Journal of Philosophy*. Dr. Percy is again writing to his fellow philosophers. He is more scholarly, less literary, as might be expected. He wants to reconcile two points of view often opposed to one another — the philosopher George H. Mead's approach, with its emphasis on consciousness as the result of social experience, mediated through language, and the philosopher Edmund Husserl's so-called transcendental phenomenology, with its interest in the most rigorous and exclusive analysis of pure subjectivity. Mead was constantly showing our life to be a series of responses to the world's demands. Husserl spoke of *epoché*, a different way of apprehending experience; common sense must be suspended, the reality of the outside world ought to be ignored and our natural beliefs and judgments held suspect — so that one might go deeper and deeper inward, and come to understand the structure of the self, its *internal* operations, which Husserl granted a life of their own, and one not ultimately subject to the authority of society.

Mead was a "social behaviorist." His emphasis was on a subtle kind of social conditioning: signals of various sorts impinge upon us, and we respond; and, having responded, yet additional "connections" are touched upon, until an "attitude" develops. Yet, for Percy, there is, at the very least, a touch of paradox to all behaviorism, even the broadest and most sophisticated kind. When George Mead wrote his essays and books he hoped for more than a series of reflexes from his readers. He wanted understanding. He wanted to convey meaning, so that one person, and another, and on and on, would come to look at things more or less as he did. Is that kind of awareness, is the awareness B. F. Skinner wants to offer his readers, a matter of an intricate series of "reflexic responses" to a range of symbols? Or is the issue one of the mind's ability to synthesize, pull together out of a range of facts and figures, signals and signs and sights, something coherent — and do so *for* someone; for another person (the reader, a teacher); for oneself, too?

On the other hand, Percy does worry about the existentialism of Husserl and his followers. It is all very well to probe phenomenologically the "self"; but the "self" can thereby become an object of exclusive passion. The "essences" Husserl sought belonged to that "self"; there is for him no outside world, only pure subjectivity: *solus ipse*. Husserl acknowledged the world of everyday experience, a world of you and me and your friends and mine (his *Lebenswelt*); but he cared little about exploring it. Max Scheler, a contemporary of his and much influenced by him, urged the "intersubjective" upon him, but to no real effect. Percy, rather like Scheler and the French philosopher Maurice Merleau-Ponty, wants the existentialist emphasis on the "self" maintained — the "self" as transcendent, as more than impulses exerting themselves, reflexes being prompted, defenses going into action; at the same time he holds out for the wonderful attentiveness of the experimental, scientific tradition. I suppose it can be said that he wants an existentialism that keeps in touch empirically with people and the kinds of communion they seek and find with one another. He wants, that is, each person to be exalted — not necessarily (though it is his own bias) as a unique gift of God, but as a man or woman whose nature and spirit, whose particular "self," amount to more than the constituent items any one scientific "methodology" would propose.

One doesn't deny the validity or importance of reflexes, libido, drives, instincts, or socialization, with the needs it generates; one simply refuses to let any line of formulation assume ideological control over the way Being itself, as men and women experience it, gradually unfolds. And very important, consciousness is something shared: not only obtained from others (the social behaviorists would certainly agree) but something constantly affirmed by others, even when they are not to be seen — for instance when a person all by himself figures out a mathematical equation or works his way through a chemical experiment. Though he is alone, "voices" from his academic past have made themselves heard. Another way of stating the point Dr. Percy wants to make might be: social behaviorists are good at seeing how we take in the world; but they don't accord our efforts to reciprocate a similar degree of complexity. What we hear and see and respond to becomes part of our "consciousness"; but we initiate sounds, become objects of scrutiny, cause others to pay heed. The mind is active and searching as well as passive and reflexic.

Over and over again in that technical paper Percy aligned himself against the nominalists, who in the 1950s were riding high in the social sciences. (And it is the pronouncements of social scientists on man and society, rather than what philosophers, even existentialist ones, have to say, which are most heeded in this nation.) He would let no noun claim victory over the mystery of man's situation in this world — as the one who speaks and knows, who is driven to watch rats run through mazes, who is moved to declare people going through their paces as very much like rats; but who also strives to make sure that others get the point and say yes, indeed, hence the effort that produces a book like Skinner's *Freedom and Dignity*. By the same token, man does not begin to have dreams or daydreams or fantasies *only* because his drives (making up the Id) crave satisfaction, hence the mental "response" which is "the psychopathology of everyday life," and the stuff of so many thousands of analytic hours. Man has dreams and daydreams because he wants to make his ideas known to others. Our minds are forever carrying on conversations, even when we are alone — letting people know that we and they agree or disagree, but in any case, we are here together for a spell, called a lifetime. Those conversations, often silent rather than spoken, are a "need" we have; we are driven, if it must be phrased that way, to have them.

But the "everydayness" Percy mentioned in "The Man on the Train" throws a pall over those conversations. We become so tied to routines, so compliant in our membership in a neighborhood, an occupation, a fraternity or club, that we stop having any but the most predictable of words with ourselves or anyone else. We say the expected, the required — often automatically. We see what we feel is safe to see, what we have quickly *told* ourselves to see. In a sense, we come rather close (but never fully — because, one hopes, even the most "alienated" are free to see and hear things for themselves) to fulfilling the behavioristic or psychoanalytic formulations. The alarm rings, and off we go to the daily grind, the marathon from suburb to city and back; or alternatively, hunger strikes and we eat, sexual tension makes its presence felt and we find a "libido object," as a result of which we no longer experience said tension, or an "aggressive instinct" pushes its way upward, and soon enough, sometimes but not always after appropriate mediation by the Superego and Ego, there is a sour face, a nasty remark, or worse.

In a second article written for the University of Houston *Forum*, published in the fall of 1958, Dr. Percy tried to connect his more formal, philosophical articles — they are essays on phenomenology — with the kind of narrative social scrutiny, with an existential tone to it, that characterized "The Man on the Train." The article "The Loss of the Creature" is a delight to read — the best writing Percy had so far managed. "Every explorer names his island Formosa, beautiful," he begins. But next came the rest of us, visitors; the danger is that we won't on our own look at that island, and join with the man who discovered it in a conversation: I, too, looked, and I was also struck by beauty, and so I speak to you in affirmation. Rather, we read before we set out that the explorer said this and he said that; and when we arrive we don't ready ourselves for a possible alliance, but instead have in our minds what we are supposed to see. In a sense the "symbol" Percy had written about earlier becomes all too effective — stifling, indeed. The explorer wanted to tell us something: "I saw the island and it was so beautiful that I will even call it Formosa, beautiful." When we go there, he might hope, we would be enough kindled by the message he has given us to look intently and see for ourselves. But we don't; we see what we believe we ought to see — his version of the island — and as we travel across the island the word, *his* word, buzzes in our ears: beautiful, just beautiful.

Nearer to us there is the Grand Canyon, an island of the "beautiful" or the "panoramic," surrounded by stretches of desert. When the doctor who went to New Mexico from Louisiana wrote his article, he had not forgotten what he saw at the Grand Canyon National Park: tourists flocking to the place, all too sure of what they would see, based on the post-cards, the geography books, the travel folders, the documentaries they had already seen — and ready to go along instantly: it *is* a "grand" canyon. The next step, of course, is the camera: recording the scene, recording the presence of so-and-so at the scene. Before arrival there is a firm notion of what to expect, and now there will be permanent evidence. Lost in all this, Percy insists, is nothing less than the Grand Canyon. The tourist doesn't dare let himself study the canyon on his own, come to any number of ideas about nature, time, the elements, God's will, man's fate. He may not even permit himself a particular, idiosyncratic view — a function of where he stands, the weather that day, the season of the year, his eyesight, his mood, his age, and on and on. For him the chances are high that there is *a* view, and he has either seen it and exclaimed his satisfaction or failed to do so, in which case he is not challenged to find another view, but disappointed: the clouds or the rain "ruined" things. Likewise with the guides or forest rangers — they see the canyon every morning, every afternoon, yet for all the world they could be working amid the canyons of Manhattan. They have work to do, people to escort, paths to keep clear, controls to exert — and that is that.

For Percy the problem, again, is "everydayness." As he did in "The Man on the Train," he wants to suggest ways a person can actually come face to face with the canyon, "recover" it. Once more Kierkegaard's *Either/Or* is summoned; the "dialectical movement" Percy describes are the Danish theologian's. One approaches the canyon at an odd time, or in an odd way. One is aesthetically ingenious, Kierkegaard might say. Without visitors early in the morning, or at night under a full moon, the canyon may not quite be what it is for those brought to it *en masse* along the approved paths and at the regular hours. Of course an insistent refusal to go along with conformist postures, as a tourist or in other respects, can itself become a predictable routine that forecloses independent observation or judgment; so no one is safe from "everydayness," and everyone must be ingenious: "After a lifetime of avoiding the beaten track and guided tours, a man may deliberately seek out the most beaten track of all, the most commonplace tour imaginable: he may visit the Canyon by a Greyhound tour in the company of a party from Terre Haute — just as a man who has lived in New York all his life may visit the Statue of Liberty. (Such dialectical savorings of the familiar are, of course, a favorite stratagem of *The New Yorker* magazine.) The thing is recovered from familiarity by means of an exercise in familiarity."

If only one might recover one's "sovereignty"; that is what Percy sees at stake — the freedom Martin Heidegger declares ours by virtue of our being human beings. Men or women who see only what postcards or fads or social pressures dictate are slaves. An accident, a tragedy, a surprise of some kind can bequeath at least a moment of freedom — the fresh breath of air, the sense of discovery, the feeling that the world is not quite as set and predictable as it sometimes seems. Often, however, even the most sophisticated, alert, and assertively independent people become victims; in Percy's words, they suffer "a radical loss of sovereignty." He is a gentle but determined satirist as he portrays those latter people: on a safari, on a trip deep into Mexico. Far be it from them to stumble into the mob of tourists who visit the canyon, Carlsbad Caverns, the Empire State Building, or Niagara Falls. They are adventurers, and they seek out the exotic. They thrill to the sight of a village not even marked on the map. They risk death itself going up unmarked mountain roads. A religious festival in a strange setting has them spellbound; afterward they discuss the "implications" of what they "experienced."

Perhaps they've read Kierkegaard and put in their difficult moments with Heidegger. They are not remiss in making an "application" of psychoanalytic theory to the "native ritual" they may have encountered in South America or Africa. Their questions are Sartre's or Camus's; indeed, they know the latter's writing far better than the Bible or the Book of Common Prayer. If there is injustice, they are quick to spot it. If there is ignorance or the presence of one or two superstitions, they note them. If a new and somewhat impenetrable "world view" is there, they stop and reflect and even take careful notes: not because they want to keep a diary, but because they know an ethnologist back in the U.S.A.; he lives in Cambridge or in New Haven or Palo Alto, and he would be absolutely "fascinated" by what goes on "out there."

Percy is not only being a good storyteller and social observer when he describes such a couple, provides dialogue for them: "This is *it*"; or "This is too good to be true." He senses a kind of desperation which he wants to understand; there is "spuriousness" in all this earnest originality, this brave and thoughtful desire to push aside the restraints which press upon others and find something *different*, something *exciting*. "Now we are really living," they say — and why isn't Percy glad, even as, presumably, any number of twentieth-century phenomenologists would be?

Unfortunately, the very "higher consciousness" which the couple has cultivated works to undercut the "experience" they claim to seek. They can't make a move without having in mind an "expert," the ethnologist or cultural anthropologist or whoever; they look to their "expert" as thousands of visitors at the Grand Canyon look to postcards before and after they glimpse the "view." From the expert will flow sanction: you are right, this is an extraordinary discovery you have made, and I will tell you why. So it is that "theorists and planners," as Percy refers to them, gain so much authority; the rest of us are almost desperate to surrender our right to structure the world, our right to make plans: "A poor man may envy the rich man, but the sightseer does not envy the expert. When a caste system becomes absolute, envy disappears." And, of course, the most cultivated become their own kind of consumers, in an instant ready to obey "a class of privileged knowers," who in turn have *their* experts to worry about. The result, for a religious person like the author: secular piety everywhere.

Percy doesn't stop there. He wants to analyze more than the "dynamics" and varieties of tourism. The second part of the article, perhaps its more valuable part, ventures into what might be called "educational criticism." Well before the 1960s, when our schools and colleges were thoroughly examined and so often found wanting in one or another respect, Percy was making this comment: "A young Falkland Islander walking along a beach and spying a dead dogfish and going to work on it with his jack-knife has, in a fashion wholly unprovided in modern educational theory, a great advantage over the Scarsdale high school pupil who finds the dogfish on his laboratory desk. Similarly the citizen of Huxley's *Brave New World* who stumbles across a volume of Shakespeare in some vine-grown ruins and squats on a potsherd to read it is in a fairer way of getting at a sonnet than the Harvard sophomore taking English Poetry II."

Why so? As students come to terms with something called a

"curriculum," they become consumers, tourists of sorts: they go from one scene (called a "course") to another, and they are constantly told what to think, what to say, what is the "right" answer to the "right" question. Books or "audiovisual equipment," which are meant to transmit a play or a sonnet of Shakespeare's, become much more: there are introductions and explanations, and teachers who use them, and give tests to find out whether readers have got the "point" or "theme," and on it goes. As for that dogfish in Scarsdale High School or Sarah Lawrence College, by the time the student has been given a "specimen" of dogfish, then told what to look for, and how to find it, and what the "experiment" (if it can be called that) means, a "spoliation of the dogfish by the theoretical method" has been done. The poor "specimen" has been comprehended as a rather pedantic version of the reality: species *Squalus acanthias*, the dogfish. Percy sees the student as encouraged to shift "from the concrete thing to theory"; the result, in Alfred North Whitehead's term, is "the fallacy of misplaced concreteness." An abstraction becomes mistaken for the real. The dogfish is seen categorically or hierarchically, A species on B phylogenetic chart. "Through no fault of the zoology instructors," the author adds, "it is nevertheless a fact that the zoology laboratory at Sarah Lawrence College is one of the few places in the world where it is all but impossible to see a dogfish."

The answer, he makes clear, is not a "revised" curriculum, or a different mixture of age groups or instructional "methods." Nor will Shakespeare's sonnets be met, appreciated directly and in each person's particular way, by yet another "with-it" exegesis. Here is an essayist, a philosophical "thinker," become practical: "I wish to propose the following educational technique, which should prove equally effective for Harvard and Shreveport High School. I propose that English poetry and biology should be taught as usual, but that at irregular intervals, poetry students should find dogfishes on their desks and biology students should find Shakespeare sonnets on their dissecting boards. I am serious in declaring that a Sarah Lawrence English major who began poking about in a dogfish with a bobby pin would learn more in thirty minutes than a biology major in a whole semester; and that the latter upon reading on her dissecting board

> That time of year Thou may'st in me behold
> When yellow leaves, or none, or few, do hang
> Upon those boughs which shake against the cold —
> Bare ruin'd choirs where late the sweet birds sang.

might catch fire at the beauty of it."

As for those who are "creative," there might be a way of looking at them that does not stress their peculiar mental makeup or their "defensive operations" (the novels they write ward off severe anxiety or God knows what) but also does not completely rely upon "mystique" — the writer or artist as one smiled upon by the gods: "The biography of scientists and poets is usually the story of the discovery of the indirect approach, the circumvention of the educator's presentation — the young man who was sent to the Technikum and on his way fell into the habit of loitering in book stores and reading poetry; or the young man dutifully attending law school who on the way became curious about the comings and goings of ants. One remembers the scene in *The Heart Is a Lonely Hunter* where the girl hides in the bushes to hear the Capehart in the big house play Beethoven. Perhaps she was the lucky one after all. Think of the unhappy souls inside, who see the record, worry about scratches, and most of all worry about whether they are *getting* it, whether they are bona fide music lovers."

We are in constant jeopardy, existentialist philosophers say, of losing ourselves as sovereign observers and listeners. The lines go: "In the room the women come and go / Talking of Michelangelo." Percy has some painful words about museums and the people who glide through — and about movie houses, parks, theatres, or indeed any "place" where people assemble. The poor museum curator, for instance; he wants people to look carefully and thoughtfully at the work of Michelangelo he has acquired at such cost and worked so hard to display in the most arresting way. Nor is it simply the boredom or distraction of T. S. Eliot's "women" that interfere with the curator's wish. The most earnest and silent of viewers can also fall into the state of mind, the state of being, really, which both Eliot and Percy describe: disinheritance. One follows the curator's lead, and the writer's, who has prepared "notes" for the exhibition, and the art professor's (or friend's or relative's) who has recommended the "show" in the first place: "It's *marvelous,* and don't forget to notice how . . ." In the end, tongue only half in cheek, Percy suggests that curators keep hidden their paintings, archeologists their "finds," and show them only "now and then to strangers." He has nothing against museums, nor against curators or the planners and theorists he keeps mentioning — only a sense of regret that so often we all experience "loss." We forsake the freedom we have to make judgments of our own, he keeps insisting: to know the world with our eyes and ears, minds and hearts. Instead, we abandon ourselves to others, who in turn have done so — since behind every expert is another expert: often enough, the blind leading the blind.

About the same time "The Loss of the Creature" appeared, another of Dr. Percy's essays, "Culture: The Antinomy of the Scientific Method," was published in the periodical *New Scholasticism* (October, 1958). It is a long piece, and a learned one; again philosophers are addressed. The author's purpose is to show some of the ambiguities scientists, especially social scientists, have to face as they go about their work. They are interested in so-called facts, in accomplishing observations that make sense of the world. But they are human beings, too; they believe in certain things, have assumptions and values. When a chemist says that sodium (Na) combines with chloride (Cl) to make sodium chloride, he can be a conservative or a liberal, an agnostic or a devout believer in the letter and the spirit of a given religious creed, and it makes no difference, so far as his assertion about sodium chloride goes. It is quite otherwise with those who study "man" or "the mind" or "society," even with those, Percy indicates, who make the most of their adherence to "the scientific method," who insist loudly and often upon their "value-free" approach, who are interested only in the "functional": does a given way of behaving "work" for the person, or does a certain "myth" still have a purpose in this or that "culture"?

Antinomy refers to paradox, to intellectual contradictions. Percy believes they abound in the social sciences. Rather obviously the psychiatrist who is "neutral," who wants only to *analyze*, has dozens of preferences which all the time determine what he does with the "analysis" he undertakes. In an example — from my own clinical work: a man has been flying bombers over "enemy" territory and one day becomes "nervous"; he cannot sleep and his appetite is poor. He is afflicted by nightmares. Eventually his commanding officer sends him to a doctor, who in turn recommends a psychiatric "evaluation." The psychiatrist makes a careful, "objective" appraisal: the man is in difficulty, but some "sessions" might well help him out. They talk. After a month or so the psychiatrist is satisfied that his patient has done rather well. "You are ready to go back to duty," the patient is told, and he is delighted. He thanks the doctor for his help, and walks away from the clinic in the best mood possible. Later that day he tells his wife that she was wrong to think of psychiatry as mumbo jumbo. "It is a science," he tells her. "That doctor listened very carefully to me. He told me, on each visit, what was on my mind. *I* didn't know, because I couldn't be objective about myself. But he could be. Then he explained to me why one thing followed another — you know, cause and effect: I said *this* because I'd been thinking *that*."

The wife was pleased, too. She may have had her reservations about psychiatry, but she was glad to find them proven wrong. So, a month later, when a neighbor of hers talked about *her* husband, also a pilot actively engaged in bombing the enemy, the advice was easy to give: "Have him see a psychiatrist. They are well trained. They are scientists. You need an outsider's opinion — someone who isn't 'involved' and is a professional man, able to size up emotions." Meanwhile, the psychiatrist who saw the first pilot has indeed sized up "emotions" — as opposed to a person. He doesn't, anyway, like to write about the particular individuals he sees. He prefers to see their "complaints" in terms of the larger generalizations any good scientist is capable of making: patient is counterphobic; had decompensated, due to precipitating stress; with insight his defenses were reconstituted, and now he can be recommended for return to duty. Diagnosis: Anxiety Reaction, secondary to external stress, in an essentially stable personality structure. Follow-up shows patient is able to perform his duties.

A thousand miles away another psychiatrist has just seen a patient, whom he asks to remain in his office while he goes outside to consult with a colleague: "This patient came to see me because he had 'bad thoughts.' For almost an hour he wouldn't tell me what the 'thoughts' were. I told him that I was no judge, no priest, no moralist. I told him I only wanted to know *what* was on his mind, so that I could help him understand *why* he felt as he did. Finally he said he believed me. He told me. He wakes up picturing himself shooting people. He tries to get the thought out of his mind, but with no success. At work he has had to take more and more breaks. He goes for a walk and tries to clear his head, but no, the thoughts keep coming back. Last week he pictured himself on top of a building. Someone was telling him to jump; instead he pulled out a hand grenade, from a paper bag he was holding, and threw it down on the people below. He hasn't thought any more about hand grenades, though — only guns. Yesterday he went to a store and bought a long-range rifle. Today his wife called up and asked for an appointment; she said her husband had 'terrible insomnia,' and she didn't know how much longer he could 'hold out.' "

The colleague asks a few questions. The two doctors exchange "ideas." Soon they decide upon a diagnosis and a recommendation, which they jointly write: the patient is actively psychotic; he is most likely a chronically paranoid schizophrenic, now in a "state of exacerbation"; his homicidal obsessive thinking is obvious, and has been persistent for at least a week or two. His "affect" is neutral and inappropriate. He talks about using a rifle on people, but shows no evidence of alarm or concern or apprehension. He may well begin to "act out"; the purchase of the gun is ominous. Analysis of his remarks and the results of his responses to the Rorschach card indicate that he is quite possibly homicidal. He is also a potential suicide.

Therefore, he ought to be hospitalized forthwith. He will most likely refuse such a course of action; he has already told his wife what we would decide, and that he would not go along. He is committable, and should be so handled.

Rather obviously the several psychiatrists involved in these two "cases" have been sincere men, dedicated to a pursuit of the "truth." They have learned what they think of and what they call an "analytic method." If asked, they would without hesitation call themselves scientists — maybe not physicists but in the tradition of those who aim to be objective, discover certain "laws" about what happens around them, and formulate those laws as precisely as possible. Yet, one man who was all the time dropping bombs on people, killing them, was seen for a while, called "stable," and sent back to such a pursuit. Another man, tormented by thoughts of killing people, and likely in the clutch to turn on himself, rather than actually harm anyone, is deemed committable, and carted off. The issue for Percy, who does not use the instances I have just given, but others in a similar vein, has to do with the implied conflict or contradictions in a given creed, the scientist's — hence the "antinomy" of the article's title.

On the one hand the psychiatrists claim that they probe "emotions," the equivalent of atoms or molecules — or so their language tries to indicate: the aura of objectivity and impersonality, the offhand, unqualified assertiveness. On the other hand they make judgments of social significance: permit an Air Force officer to resume his "missions"; insist that a man go to the hospital. When questioned closely they might get as "defensive" as they sometimes describe their patients as being; that is, they might at great length try to show how their "decisions" are simply "applications" of their scientific knowledge. Yet killing is killing, and when one psychiatrist worries that a man who has *thought* about killing might well do so, and calls the man "sick" and in need of prolonged "treatment," whereas another psychiatrist regards a man who drops bombs all the time on people, thereby killing untold numbers of them, as "stable," and in no time at all ready for duty — after having proudly helped him a bit, by talking with him, and certainly never having considered hospitalization for him — then we are up against, at the very least, a somewhat puzzling state of affairs.

If only both psychiatrists would come forth with disclaimers: we are not scientists in the nineteenth-century tradition of natural science; we are members of a given society, whose standards we more or less adhere to, and those standards not only impinge upon us, as they should, in our lives as citizens, but in our so-called scientific lives as well. Some psychiatrists have recently said just that, but to do so they have had to rebel openly against the canons — occasionally they are rigidly defined strictures — of their profession: the psychiatrist's urgent and firmly believed credo, "I am no judge or priest."

In Percy's article the emphasis is on the dilemmas of the cultural anthropologist rather than the psychiatrist, but as he examines various professional commitments and ambiguities, he shows quite clearly how all social scientists cannot, at some point, avoid taking ethical and philosophical positions in the course of their work. For example, anthropologists and social psychologists have spent years examining the nature of the "myth." There are "spurious" myths and "genuine" myths — those that don't "function" and those that do. Not that the social scientists who study those myths necessarily believe them; at times, in fact, one wonders what myths various sociologists or anthropologists do believe. Suddenly fascism or communism arrives on the scene, and whole nations are aroused by those political philosophies — myths, of sorts, which by various "criteria" seem to be "functional," at least for a while. How does the usually "liberal" American social scientist deal with *those* myths? In the classroom he is "objective": what works is "genuine" (the anthropologist Edward Sapir's word) and what doesn't is "nonfunctional" or again, "spurious." At the same time the social scientist leaves his office and rails against totalitarian ideologies, upholds democratic "values," and maybe works hard indeed to find a way to fit fascism, say, under the "spurious" category. He may well fail, however; and if he is honest with himself he will see the anomaly: he has been content to distinguish the "functional" from the "nonfunctional" — and in doing so has experienced no moral or professional conflict, so long as he was dealing with natives in the South Seas or African tribes. When the issue comes close to his own life, the "functional" won't quite suffice: he has ethical assumptions, deeply felt convictions — a *faith* of sorts. He can't take up a neutral posture with respect to fascism — even as a "scientist" he can't. He is, therefore, lucky professionally as well as happy as a human being and citizen of the United States when Germany falls, and Italy. Spain is a bit of a problem, not to mention the Soviet Union or China. He has to juggle his loyalties, maybe his definitions. Perhaps it is best to stay with those distant tribes, which enable him to maintain, in several senses, distance.

Equally anomalous is the position of a certain kind of natural scientist, whose only reality is the scientific method. Percy draws on the "operationalism" of the theoretical physicist and philosopher Percy Bridgman, whom he quotes: "It is obvious that I can never get outside myself. There is no such thing as a public consciousness. In the last analysis science is only my conscience." Yet Bridgman wrote articles for journals and wrote books, and no doubt received from readers letters which he found satisfying. They certainly did understand what he had in mind. Then, there are the semanticists or behaviorists, who study the way "responding organisms" act, or classify the words people use for various purposes. The semanticist or behavorist considers a sentence: The flower is yellow. He describes the sentence as a response to stimulus, points out the interesting fact that despite the ambiguous syntax the flower is not to be confused with its color. But he won't grant the "reality," maybe it is the integrity, of the sentence as an *assertion*, an affirmation embraced by a speaker and a listener.

Meanwhile he himself goes on, quite justifiably, making one assertion after another, and is, presumably, understood, even though as a matter of principle he views all assertions as not "real" or "objective phenomena," but rather, reducible to something else. Needless to say, neither B. F. Skinner nor the semanticists spend their time explaining after each sentence what prompted it or apologizing for its very use — because they have resorted to what they refer to as a "semantic operation," rather than come up with something "real" or "scientific." They quite naturally want to convey what is on their minds, and receive from readers or listeners a reaction: Yes, we see. Why cannot that effort be regarded as fundamental, as a "unit" or an "element" of "reality" which warrants its own kind of study, not to mention respect? Addressing a whole generation of natural and social scientists, and especially anxious to be heard by behaviorists, Percy wryly and quietly makes this observation: "It seems reasonable to approach the organisms who are scientists with the same objectivity with which he approaches organisms who are searching for food or organisms who are making a myth."

It can be said that everything is grist for the scientist's mill except his own activity as someone who hands down one statement after another. For that latter activity he has either indifference, or outright contempt: mere subjectivity. The more perceptive and ironic scientists or philosophers of science smile and either wash their hands of the whole business of words, or note the "antinomy" Percy discusses in his article. Here is Einstein: "If you want to find out anything from the theoretical physicists about the methods they use, I advise you to stick closely to one principle: don't listen to their words, fix your attention on their deeds." Or, from another vantage point: "Whitehead once remarked that it was a matter for astonishment that while scientists have succeeded in learning a great deal about the world in the past two hundred years, philosophers of science seem equally determined to deny that such knowledge is possible."

Scientists, so sure about the world, or at least about larger and larger portions of it, stop short at acknowledging themselves as human beings who speak out constantly, win adherents if not converts, establish their own versions of myths, set off an assortment of reflexes, and influence what is or is not considered worth examining. For Percy the philosophical issue is precisely the one Kierkegaard grasped when he went after Hegel so critically, or Heidegger when he expressed his dissatisfaction with the social sciences — not so much because they are "wrong" but because of their willful inattention to matters that are terribly important. Hegel claimed to understand all history, the future as well as the past, yet could offer no ideas about how man is to live a life: man was the "leftover" in such a scheme of things. Many social scientists, Heidegger knew, distinguish all too arbitrarily (to their own gain, a sharp critic might insist) between themselves, whom they think of as objective observers and recorders of the "truth," and everyone else, whom they think of as belonging to a "culture," and having "needs" for myths or responding to "signals."

Scientists, like everyone else, live certain kinds of lives, and the judgment of *what* kind is something that also requires "study" or "analysis." The issue is not only "functional" (does the person fulfill various social or biological purposes?) or "aesthetic" (does he do so in a manner that is "integrated," fits into the prevailing customs of his society?) but also "normative." In Percy's words, a person "may be a good organism and an integrated culture-member and at the same time live a trivial and anonymous life." More than anything else he argues against the narrowness of behaviorism and the ultimate and stultifying impasse that cultural relativism forces upon those who follow it to the bitter end: "For if one takes seriously the position of the cultural relativist, that there is no reality but a cultural reality, that 'even the facts of the physical world are discerned through an encultural screen so that the perception of time, distance, weight, size, and other realities are mediated by the conventions of a given group' — if we take this seriously, we can only conclude that science itself, even ethnology, is nonsense, since it is at best only a reflection of the culture within which it is undertaken."

Scientists all the time assume that they, if no one else, go beyond the "enculturative screen." They are not "data," but men or women who see, find out, and tell the rest of us what they have discovered. There are "data" out there, and there is that part of my mind which recognizes and makes sense of those "data," and does so, it is assumed, independently; that is, apart from the contingencies of class and caste, race and religion. This split, of utter importance in their work, is the psychological "distance" Heidegger refers to, the "clearing in the woods" that man is capable of making for himself. The split implies a faith, an assumption of a "metascientific, metacultural reality" — an order of being that stands apart from the scientific concepts, data, or theories which are used and then written about: the Being existentialists refer to, the Being whose achievement it is to devise mazes, analyze speech patterns or cultural myths, come up with psychological formulations — or with the existentialist notion of Being. But when an observer studies not "data" out there — the way sodium (Na) and chloride (Cl) come together in a test tube, or the way rats run down mazes — but himself or his neighbors, in all their complex humanity, the "distance" between observer and observed may be an illusion, however wordily proclaimed as real and substantial. Anyone who has struggled with Heidegger's writing knows how complex and demanding the task is — to gain an order of knowledge about oneself and others that is at once unashamedly intimate and explicitly detached. The observer must look at himself or others without the protection of abstractions and then go on to describe what has been seen, in a way that encompasses the observations (hence the act of detachment) but does not trim them to fit the needs of a theory.

Percy knew that it is a "radical" step, the move Heidegger asked of social observers. Percy's "radical anthropology" is very much the "phenomenological anthropology" of the European existentialists. Above all, they ask: Who is this "one" who asks these scientific or philosophical questions, makes these inquiries? And how to convey the answers, the "results"? Words are treacherous; they have dozens of connotations. They have become the property of one or another person or "school" of thought. How to put all those words together? Ought one to write a paper or an "article," as Percy had been doing? Ought one to walk up and down the street and converse with friends, a twentieth-century follower of Socrates, or seek out an original, aphoristic style that to a degree subdues language but also explains and enlightens? The intellect, Percy knew, is both a friend and (potentially) a most dangerous enemy. The intellect sees, but it also wants to take matters into its own hands — and the making of abstractions can be an act of usurpation: part of the world is torn away, fitted all too snugly into a theoretical statement, then offered to others as a separate world of its own. The result is a world simplified and distorted — once by the observer's desire to adapt and accommodate events to suit a particular theory of his, and a second time by the various implications of the words used to make that theory known to others.

In the autumn of 1959 another article of Percy's appeared in *Thought*, but this one, "The Message in the Bottle," was a parable rather than an analytic essay. Heidegger had once used the word *Geworfenheit* to describe man's existence: the condition of being a castaway. Percy was anxious to escape what he knew to be the hazards of the theoretical article whose subject matter is man himself and his situation or "condition." He decided, as an alternative, to pick up Heidegger's image and use it to tell a story about a man who has lost his memory after a shipwreck, and is now on an island. For a long time he tries vainly to find out where he came from, who he is. Eventually he settles in. He is no Robinson Crusoe, however. The island is inhabited, has what we call a "well-integrated culture." There is a university. Industry flourishes. Artists, writers, and scholars are very much in evidence. The castaway is welcomed and rather quickly marries, fathers children, gets a job, started cultivating hobbies. He becomes, as Percy puts it, "a useful member of the community." As such the man was no longer regarded as an outsider or castaway. He was, as the phrase goes, "one of us."

But something in him prompts restlessness and curiosity, so he takes long walks, and always seem to end up on the beach. There he comes across bottles, many of them, washed up by the waves. The bottles are corked, and inside each is a piece of paper with a message written on it. The messages at first seem without rhyme or reason; they assert facts, tell about feelings, narrate bits of history. The man is puzzled, but he is also conscientious. He shows what he has found to others, and hopeful of finding clues, they set about sorting out the various messages. Perhaps in time, they tell one another, a discovery will

be made; in today's language, the discovery would be referred
to as the existence of a "meaningful, relevant pattern."
Through the man, his friends, and the messages they are examining, Percy has an interesting opportunity to deal with
broad subjects like "the nature of science," "the nature of religious faith," and "the use of language to convey knowledge."
He can make a list of statements, and have his castaway distinguish among them. He can tell a story which at the same time
helps clarify certain scientific, linguistic, and philosophical issues which had been preoccupying him for a long time. In an
amusing footnote he tells the reader that "some of the bottles
must have been launched by Rudolf Carnap since the sentences
are identical with those he uses in the article 'Formal and
Factual Science,' which appeared in the book *Readings in the
Philosophy of Science.*"

There are some twenty in all — sentences like "Lead melts at
330 degrees" or "2 + 2 = 4," or "Chicago, a city, is on Lake
Michigan," or "Chicago is on the Hudson River or Chicago is
not on the Hudson River," or "Jane will arrive tomorrow," or
"Truth is beauty," or "In 1943 the Russians murdered 10,000
Polish officers in the Katyn forest," or "Being comprises essence and existence," or "The Atman (Self) is the Brahman," or
"A war party is approaching from Bora Bora." The castaway,
nudged by the author, sets to work. Some sentences, he concludes, contain empirical facts which are discovered through
observation. ("Lead melts at 330 degrees.") Other sentences
refer to aspects of what is called "reality": "2 + 2 = 4"; or
"Chicago is on the Hudson River or Chicago is not on the Hudson River."

But there is yet another way of dividing up the sentences, a
way which the castaway feels makes more sense to him in his
situation — because, though he no longer is considered by
others a castaway, he has not forgotten that one day he found
himself on a strange island, and he has still not discovered
whence he came, or whither (if anyplace) he might someday be
going. In one group he places all "those sentences which are the
result of a very special kind of human activity, an activity
which the castaway, an ordinary fellow, attributes alike to sci-

entists, scholars, poets and philosophers." Those are the people who for varying lengths of time stop going about "living" in order to learn something and express it: "in order to discover underlying constancies amid the flux of phenomena, in order to exact measurements, in order to make precise inductions and deductions, in order to arrange words, or sounds, or colors to express universal human experience."

Such people pursue knowledge in its broadest sense: they want to know the world, understand what is happening about them, be they sculptors, nuclear physicists, or philosophers — the German word *Wissenschaft* provides an umbrella for their activity, and for a number of the messages the castaway has examined. In quite another category are the messages which quite directly pertain to a particular person's situation: "There is fresh water in the next cove," or "A war party is approaching from Bora Bora." They have to do with the life of the islander. Is he thirsty? Well, then, he need not be. Is he afraid? Well, then, he has good reason to be. Those messages are, for Percy and his islander, "news" — they have to do with their (and more abstractly, the existentialist philosopher's) "concrete predicament."

The essence of the castaway's situation or predicament is this: he is not at all aware of his origins or destiny, and he wants to know about both. He is not "objective" when he is doing so. True, he can sometimes be interested in knowledge for its own sake; but as a castaway he has his very own reason, tied to his situation, for obtaining certain information. Percy is delightful with his examples of such information, which he calls "news." For a moment he leaves aside his castaway and connects pieces of "news" to situations others have found themselves in: "Mackerel Here!" ("Malinowski's Trobriand Island fisherman announcing a strike to his fellows"); "The market is up $2.00" ("I am in the market"); "Eisenhower is elected!" ("I voted for Stevenson"). Needless to say, news has its own importance; it cannot be evaluated by the criteria of "science," of "objective knowledge"; it is, rather, information connected to a person's "condition." Thirsty as can be, I consider news of the presence of water nearby the most important information in the world. Sated with water when I hear that news, I feel it is irrelevant.

Of course, it matters that the bearer of news be believable — have a reputation, speak sense, present himself in a way that doesn't immediately turn others off. It also matters that the news be sensible. If a man brings as news something I know to be absurd or impossible — General Grant is approaching Vicksburg, Mississippi, in late autumn of the year 1973 with five million Union soldiers — I wouldn't quite get excited, even if I lived in that city and worked for the police there. Yet a certain degree of vagueness, even mystery, is tolerable, depending upon which person in which concrete situation is approached by whom with what "message" or piece of news. Here is an aside Percy takes — in a brief move from the island back to his "man on the train": "Two men are riding a commuter's train. One is, as the expression goes, fat, dumb, and happy. Though he lives the most meaningless sort of life, a trivial routine of meals, work, gossip, television, and sleep, he nevertheless feels quite content with himself and is at home in the world. The other commuter, who lives the same kind of life, feels quite lost to himself. He knows that something is dreadfully wrong. More than that, he is in anxiety; he suffers acutely, yet he does not know why. What is wrong? Does he not have all the goods of life?

"If now a stranger approaches the first commuter, takes him aside, and says to him earnestly: 'My friend, I know your predicament; come with me; I have news of the utmost importance for you' — then the commuter will reject the communication out of hand. For he is in no predicament, or if he is, he does not know it, and so the communication strikes him as nonsense.

"The second commuter might very well heed the stranger's 'Come!' At least he will take it seriously. Indeed it may well be that he has been waiting all his life to hear this 'Come!' "

All of this, the difference between objective knowledge and news, and the way either is tied to the particular life of a person — the man in the laboratory, the castaway, the contented commuter, the "alienated" one — has for centuries been at the heart of philosophical inquiry. For St. Thomas Aquinas "the act of faith consists essentially in knowledge and there we find its formal or specific perfection." And others of us, less assertively, go along: *prove* that God exists; *show me* how you came to hold this faith of yours; I want the evidence; I'm no atheist, just an agnostic who wants a good, logical argument made. For Kierkegaard, however, it was quite different: "Faith is not a form of knowledge; for all knowledge is either knowledge of the eternal, excluding the temporal and the historical as indifferent, or it is pure historical knowledge."

Kierkegaard's "knowledge of the eternal" is for him a distinct category, not subject to the verification of logic or analysis. For many who live on the castaway's island, historical knowledge is all they ever have sought or will require. Percy takes pains not to equate such people with his "fat, dumb and happy" train rider. Nor is he writing in the apologetic tradition: he does not, for example, want to proclaim the Christian "message" — Christ's "good news" brought here for all who would like to hear and rejoice in it. Rather, he wants to demonstrate that for a castaway, a man who is a stranger in the world, however "integrated" he is in however "developed" a culture, there is a hunger for a certain kind of news, and that Kierkegaard was correct in disavowing the hope that one or another kind of "knowledge" (Hegel's, Kant's, anyone's) would satisfy such hunger. The only moralistic remark in the article is this, said of the castaway: "He should be what he is and not pretend to be somebody else." Despair, sometimes cloaked in elation or indifference, is the price a castaway pays for denying his situation: I may have come here under strange circumstances, but so what — there is a wonderful party tomorrow! The castaway is a seeker: "To be a castaway is to search for news from across the seas." No news from a nearby laboratory, or from a sharp reporter who lives in the next town on the island, will suffice.

For Percy the Christian faith is the news from across the sea that a castaway craves. It is "news" which, however, the castaway may not always find believable. It does require an act of faith. The act may be seen as extreme: *credo quia absurdum est* — in Kierkegaard's words, an embrace of "the absolute Paradox."

It is one of Percy's intentions in this essay, though — for all the affection he feels toward Kierkegaard, and the debt he owes him — to take issue with that phrase of his, as well as this sentence: "No knowledge can have for its object the absurdity that the eternal is the historical" *(Philosophical Fragments).* He believes that the very use of the word *absurd* on Kierkegaard's part was a needless bow to the Hegelian, or in our time, the "scientific" view of things. Percy, it has to be said repeatedly, is not at all anxious to launch an assault against science. If there is a "wasteland" he wants to criticize, one doubts he will ever do so through resort to a "counterculture." For him a hippie or a poet consumed by Blake's vision is also a man in jeopardy, even as the "man on the train": tempted by pride and self-centeredness, and inevitably capable of hurting his fellow man. That is to say, Percy has a Christian's view of human nature. He sees flaws, imperfections, *sins* to be inevitable and, to a degree, ineradicable. He is anxious to show that there are some questions "science" was never meant to answer. Jaspers saw man as one shipwrecked; and again, Heidegger used the image of the castaway. Such a situation generates a hunger for news; and so when it arrives, brought by a Christ, it is not at all "absurd" or "paradoxical" in nature but right to the point — in the Quaker phrase, it is news that "speaks to the condition" of the castaway.

Percy conceives such "news" to be exactly what Kierkegaard (in *The Present Age*) described when he made reference to "this little advertisement, this *nota bene* on a page of universal history — 'we have believed that in such and such a year God appeared among us in the humble figure of a servant, that he lived and taught in our community, and finally died.'" Christ's "good news" happens to be the "message in the bottle" which Percy happens to find most responsive to his situation. But he wrote the article not so much to indicate his own religious beliefs as to show through an extended image (the parable) what it is that separates the philosophers who have influenced him (the so-called existentialists, and not all of them have been

Christians like Marcel or Jews like Buber) from the assorted behaviorists, logical positivists, empiricists, semanticists, and philosophical idealists (from Kant on down) who have been so influential in recent Western history. Not for a moment does he want to forsake the "science" these latter value so highly. It is, quite simply, a matter of saying this: I have something to search for outside the laboratory or the seminar room, and without hard feelings I am going to do so.

Of course, a seeker does not have to be totally solitary; he can occasionally try to influence others, perhaps as a means of telling himself something. In "Naming and Being," published in *The Personalist* (spring of 1960), and in "The Symbolic Structure of Interpersonal Process," published in *Psychiatry* (February, 1961), Percy again wrote carefully thought out essays of a philosophical nature — directed, respectively, at liberal humanists and the various social scientists who read the latter journal, one of small but influential circulation. Both articles aim to educate rather than argue; in fact Percy is never polemical. In his early articles he wanted to declare a position; in these last two articles, as in the parable that preceded them, he wants to emphasize for those apt to be interested, if not sympathetic, why a given point of view deserves more than a passing nod: oh, yes, existentialism — a postwar philosophical "development" (and fad) that held sway on the Left Bank of Paris and such places; or a preoccupation of a few hard-to-fathom German scholars.

Percy knew that if anyone is given to "naming" it is educated, secular liberals — and a seer of sorts for many such people is the social scientist. We hunger for information, and often confuse what we find with final explanations of the very meaning of life. There is nothing wrong with probing the world (or the human mind) with a view to reducing the apparently obscure to the "lowest common denominator": the molar becomes the molecular, or puzzling behavior becomes an Id erupting, a Superego restraining, an Ego adapting. But Percy continues to insist that "naming" has its limits: the self defies naming, cannot be explained away mechanistically, behaviorally, psychoanalytically.

Sometimes the issue is not who is right or wrong, but how different people choose to look at the same phenomenon. Freud believed anxiety to be a symptom of a disorder; Kierkegaard looked upon anxiety as a companion on a person's journey toward self-discovery. Perhaps that is a bit of a simplification. Toward the end of his life Freud had become rather "philosophical" himself; he saw anxiety as much more "basic," as far harder to explain away (the result of conflicts or threats) than he had once thought. Nor was he so confident that anything he had discovered (or that others, standing on his shoulders, might someday discover) would make the difference: at last, a life without anxiety. There is, though, in twentieth-century psychiatry a tendency to regard man as an organism, ultimately to be fully explained through closer and closer examination, by the most precise of analytical constructs. Freud's man is, more than anything else, *homo natura*, the man natural scientists had been quite properly trying to understand.

Yet, Freud also gained distance on that man; he wrote about him, described him at length and unforgettably. Again and again philosophers like Buber or Heidegger or Ludwig Binswanger had emphasized that man has will, choice, freedom, a degree of leverage on himself and the kind of life he lives that cannot be reduced to mechanistic variables. The whole is, again, more than the sum of its parts. Ludwig Binswanger, a longtime friend of Freud's, and a Swiss psychiatrist and philosopher, approached the nub of the problem in his book on Freud and in a fine essay he wrote, "Freud and the Magna Carta of Clinical Psychiatry." Once the two men met and exchanged observations: how does one work with various kinds of patients? Especially vexing for both psychiatrists were the men and women who probably make up most psychoanalytic patients: mildly "obsessional" people, not too disturbed, intelligent and well meaning, yet locked in by a range of inhibitions and fears. The analyst struggles with them for years; among clinicians one often hears the expression "free up": if only those patients could become a little less uptight, a little more relaxed about themselves and others. Often such individuals are prone, in Percy's words, to " 'scientific' concrete experience"; they pin labels on human experience — their own, never mind that of others — and forget that words are only as valuable as the intent of the speaker: to convey and affirm to another, or to surround oneself with terms, thereby cutting out the possibility of another's presence. (Buber's I-Thou becomes I-It.)

During their meeting Binswanger pushed Freud hard: why don't such patients eventually "break through," become able to demonstrate more openly and directly their personal freedom — their capacity to relinquish the rituals and constraints of mind and heart which brought them into analysis in the first place? Freud surprised Binswanger by refusing to fall back upon "insight": to insist simply that more of it was needed, and eventually the patient would "see," really see, and then become "better," or at least different. Instead, Freud remarked: *"Ja, Geist ist alles"* — yes, spirit is everything. He went on to say that he had merely tried to explain some biological and psychological phenomena, but was not about to equate his observations with the sum and substance of man's nature. For Binswanger the remark about "spirit" was right to the point — not some vague, mystical talk, a lapse of sorts on the part of a usually tough-minded natural scientist, but the considered response of someone who had put in a lot of time with patients, done a lot of introspection, too, and realized full well that the rational method, cause-and-effect inquiry, was only one of several approaches to an understanding of human behavior.

For Binswanger and for Percy, who refers to him in his article in *Psychiatry,* "treatment" has to do not only with verbal explanations ("insight") but the important matter of common understanding on the part of the analyst and patient — not something to be confused with words like *transference* and *countertransference.* True, distortions take place between people as they spend time with one another and get to know one another — distortions based on earlier experiences each of us has with mothers and fathers, brothers and sisters, childhood friends and teachers. But we also are capable of something else, something independent and continuing, not to be traced back, derived from various antecedents, explained through *origins*. "Spirit" is admittedly an elusive term for what it is we have and summon as we struggle to affirm ourselves, but the word may indeed be useful, a means of indicating an "element" of character that prompted a brilliant and ambitious turn-of-the-century Viennese psychiatrist to become exactly the "conquistador" he once described himself as being.

A French social critic, Roland Dalbiez, has commented that "psychoanalytic investigation does not explain the philosophical aspect of philosophy, the artistic aspect of art, the scientific aspect of science, the moral aspect of morality, or the religious aspect of religion. The specific nature of the spiritual values eludes the instrument of investigation which Freud's genius has created." It may indeed be that the thrust of Freud's activities falls under that limitation. One can speak of his "creativity" or of the capacity his "ego" had for "synthesis," but soon enough we recognize that the mystery of his achievements, like those of countless artists and writers, continues to defy us. Percy wants to come as close to the "mystery" as possible, not by using words which, in essence, beg the question, but by indicating not only how unique Freud was, but all of us are. He draws upon Binswanger's use of *Welt* and *Umwelt*, shows how his own way of looking at human relatedness (it can be called) is very much like Binswanger's: "The greatest difference between the environment *(Umwelt)* of a sign-using organism and the world *(Welt)* of the speaking organism is that there are gaps in the former but none in the latter. The non-speaking organism only notices what is relevant biologically; the speaking organism disposes of the entire horizon symbolically. Gaps that cannot be closed by perception and reason are closed by image and myth."

To Percy it is crucial for psychiatrists and patients, indeed, all of us, to understand what it is, at rock bottom, that makes us distinctively human; but he does not want to hand down yet another classificatory system. It is not a matter of science *versus* intuition, or the objective *versus* the subjective, or Freud's theories as against his recognition that at a certain moment "spirit is all." It is possible to discover by direct and careful observation (the *sine qua non* of empirical science) that what Heidegger claims to be the very essence of man is every day affirmed by individuals — a factory worker, a patient, a psychoanalyst — all of whom certainly respond to signals and get ' driven" by various biological or social imperatives, but say those things, ask those questions which suddenly mark a shift: from the flow of life to a position wherein one beholds the world. It can even be said that psychoanalysis is nothing if not a sustained effort to gain such distance, in the hopes that vision repeatedly had will be vision reliably kept, because it will have become very much part of the person, not something spoken, heard, and forgotten. One therefore remembers not only the past of a childhood but so very much that has been happening recently in a certain office, where words (the "symbols" Percy speaks of) repeatedly become bonds between two people: an "interpretation" heard and understood is a shared affirmation, a measure of high ground, it can be called, jointly achieved by two people — and needless to say, a doctor wishes for his listeners even as patients speak in hopes of, at long last, being heard.

Dr. Percy, the essayist, wished for listeners, but worried all during the 1950s that he was not quite able, in his various articles, to spell out his particular, American, and Christian existentialism. He tried and tried; he put the words into sentences, paragraphs, short or long statements. But he was searching for a way to bring home, tellingly, to his listeners (readers) what has happened to them — to him, of course, as well: spiritual homelessness. With each essay he explored a facet of that "problem," that "condition." But he sensed himself in a maze: how to make his "message" come closer to the lives of others — connect with their human sensibilities. By the late 1950s, he had come upon an answer: escape the maze, leap over the wall, write novels.

THREE

The Novels

WALKER PERCY IS KNOWN to many as a novelist, yet his first novel, *The Moviegoer,* appeared in 1961, after some thirteen of his philosophical essays had been published, in addition to essays about the racial struggle that was growing more intense by the year. In those articles he approached social and political issues just as he did the more speculative matters he discussed in his larger pieces, drawing once more on the theological and philosophical polarity of immanence-transcendence: God as indwelling in the ordinary life of the world, in contrast to God as beyond the world, the exalted one. Though Percy doesn't draw upon that distinction explicitly, he uses it or applies it when he writes about his native region. He refers to the South that was and is and even now still fights to be — the old South, the segregationist South; and he dreams of the South that someday might be, given the many, many acts of courage and decency which men and women, both black and white, will prove able to demonstrate. The former is the immanent South; the latter a dream — the transcendent South, for which many are struggling. Percy will not turn on his people and their lives in such a way that they become caricatures of human beings. Day in, day out, they don't for the most part sit and calculate how to be bad, wrong, malicious, or uncaring. Like "alienated commuters," riding trains through Westchester County or the suburbs north of Chicago, Southerners wake up, go through the motions of life, come home, and rather soon are ready for bed — and maybe for dreams which show sides to their minds not otherwise in evidence: a man who mouths hateful pieties can cry for, or lust for, those he denounces under threat of social ostracism.

Sometimes, however, a historical moment makes everyone's life "different." The immanent is challenged directly and massively by the transcendent: in our everyday lives a great ideal and its demands confront us. So it went for Percy and those like him after the Supreme Court ruled school desegregation unconstitutional in 1954. The decision was but the start of a long regional struggle, and the "news" which the rest of us read was only the most public manifestation of that struggle. In the lives of individuals, millions of them, the struggle took on a less dramatic and more persistent life — as particular men and women suddenly began to think about issues hitherto ignored. Upon occasion those men and women became people they themselves had trouble recognizing. They did things which surprised them. They became more (or less) than they or others thought possible. Percy knew that for people like himself "the traditional world-view of the upper class white Southerner" was simply no longer "adequate to the situation." He had said so in *Commonweal* in 1956, and he kept saying so year after year — until the 1960s arrived, with the sit-ins and freedom rides, to make the point rather obvious.

If he could be scornful of nearby racists, he could also refer to "the cruising social critic," the man who has something to say about everything and everybody, certainly including the South and its people. But from what position or, as it is put, "frame of reference"? "Popular sociology" is his answer, and he is quick to object: "The objective posture of the social scientist," he wrote in a 1959 issue of *Commonweal*, "is to be turned into a superior vantage point from which negative judgments are pronounced upon society in the guise of objective observations." Percy is wary of supplying "solutions" or heroes, and distrustful of both when they come his way from others. Because he looks upon all men as more or less caught up in their particular version of "everydayness," he is unwilling to become self-righteous.

On the other hand he is a man who has heard and come to believe the Christian message — as he puts it: "the sacramental and historico-incarnational nature of Christianity," or, with a lighter touch, "all that business about God, the Jews, Christ, the Church." He believes that man is here to be saved, not fulfilled with respect to his "needs" or applauded as a "model citizen," a "true patriot," or one possessed of excellent "mental health." The entire direction of his thinking, as it had developed for nearly two decades, comes across in an article on America's "culture critics," its various social observers, written in 1959: "It is no doubt legitimate, for sociological purposes, to speak of a member of the upper-middle who has his house done over in Early Federal with decorator's Picassos as status symbols. But let us not forget that this same class-member may have saved a comrade's life in battle, suffers from sinusitis, has a sick wife, and works like a dog to pay his debts. He cannot really be understood by a sociology of motivations but only by a larger view of man which takes account of what a man is capable of and what he can fall prey to. There is not really such a thing as a consumer or a public or a mass man except only as they exist as constructs in the minds of sociologists, ad men, and opinion pollsters."

Philosophically the words are the "existentialist's"; they are also the words of a man who had increasingly been drawn to the novel, with its concern for the particular, the man or woman who has a certain kind of character and meets up with others, with situations, and not least, with the hand of fate. In the middle 1950s he had tried a novel, which he called "The Charterhouse." Its subject matter was familiar to those who have read Percy's published fiction: the country club as setting — and as the twentieth-century replacement of the medieval church. Where else to go on a Sunday? What else to do but swim, play tennis or golf, be near one's neighbors or friends for lunch or dinner "at the club"?

The book was sent off to several publishers and promptly rejected. Allen Tate saw it and called it "dreadful"; he told the author that action was needed to replace long stretches of diffuse talk or comment. Caroline Gordon, then Tate's wife, was interested enough to send the author no fewer than thirty pages, single-spaced, of comment and suggestions. He absorbed them, but put aside the novel. Soon thereafter he started a new one — now about a pathologist who does autopsies on the tuberculosis patients who live in a place like the sanitarium at Lake Saranac. Percy never even sent that manuscript to a publisher. He could not, however, stop trying to construct a novel, even as he became his own strong critic after he finished the writing. By 1959 he had begun another book, and this time he was determined to tie his philosophical ideas firmly down; give them the life that a novel can offer.

He stopped writing philosophical articles, slowed down his hitherto steady flow of essays or book reviews for *Commonweal* and *America*. The matters which continued to concern him, which he had written about analytically or as a commentator, now became challenges for the novel he was working on: how to indicate the enormously complex and sometimes tortured viewpoint of Kierkegaard in a story — without turning out a thinly disguised exercise in philosophical or theological exposition? By early 1960 Percy had finished the first draft of a novel which he titled "Confessions of a Moviegoer." He sent it to a literary agent in New York City, Elizabeth Otis, and she in turn sent it to Stanley Kauffmann at Knopf. Kauffmann well remembers his reactions as he went through the manuscript: "It needed work. I knew that right off. But it had some wonderful sections — as original as I'd seen in a long time. I didn't think we should immediately offer him a contract; I felt there were important revisions to make. But I also knew that the chances were that if the manuscript were sent to another publisher, he'd be signed up immediately." Kauffmann gambled. He decided that the man who wrote that novel — obviously a sensitive and thoughtful person — was an artist, and that he wanted to perfect what he had done, rather than see it rushed into print. And he had been told as much by Elizabeth Otis: Percy was a doctor; he wrote philosophical articles; he had no financial pressures on him, so was not out for big advances, quick publication, a splash of hyperbolic advertising. The manuscript went back and forth four times. "Each time," Kauffmann remembers, "it came back not only 'improved' but more brilliant, more comic, more delightful. I never met him. I never talked with him on the phone. It was an old-fashioned relationship: polite letters back and forth, each of us putting down on paper what we thought. And each time I felt he'd run the manuscript through his head, not the typewriter; even when I knew it was a wonderful novel, and ready for publication, I wondered what might happen if he went through another revision." From Mr. Knopf Kauffmann obtained the modest sum of three hundred dollars as an advance to Percy: "Let me put it this way: Percy was a middle-aged, unknown novelist, and the head of the publishing house had the work of many famous writers on his mind."

The reviews, to repeat, though not extensive or long, were respectful. Percy was quickly described as yet another of that strange breed: the Southern writer. He was credited with a sense of humor, and with a shrewd social eye. He was described as a "medical doctor," and his interest in psychiatry was remarked upon: "the way he probes at the mainsprings of his characters" — as if someone with such an intent has to have an interest in psychiatry. As a Southern writer, of course, he had to offer his predominantly Northern readers something "regional," and he did, or so it was claimed: a glimpse of New Orleans, that interesting old port city, full of whiskey and French cuisine, which so many tourists enjoy. Is the novel about "identity," a critic or two asked — a Southerner's effort to find it?

The author of the novel was pleased to be favored with the brief attention he received, and even more pleased to receive the National Book Award in 1962. Perhaps more than anything else, though, he has been fascinated by the reactions he has received from those who have read the book. "Dear Dr. Percy, I have read your novel, and thought it was interesting. I go to the movies myself, and once I went to New Orleans, which has to be one of the real knock-outs of American cities. What I want to know is this . . ." People tell him about their intensely personal longings, frustrations, doubts, hesitations; and then he is asked a question: what ought I to do — being this person, living this life, and faced with this kind of future or dilemma? "I'll get a call — or I did, before I had to get an unlisted phone, I just *had* to — and someone is in Arizona, and he's run out of money. He's going to California, and you know, his whole life depends on it; he wants to get there and find a new life for himself. I send the money. Of course, you can't just keep doing that." When he tells of the incident he isn't quite sure that, in fact, it wouldn't be a fine thing for him to do with his life: keep on responding to the S.O.S. messages which various individuals try to send him — a measure, perhaps, of his ability to recognize the many kinds of despair about him.

No wonder a number of readers have not only written to Percy about his novel, but have published strongly autobiographical essays on it. "I first read *The Moviegoer* on a familiar train journey from New Orleans to Chicago in 1961," says Scott Byrd in a fine piece ("The Dreams of Walker Percy") written for *The Red Clay Reader*. And no wonder, too, that an increasing number of readers or critics, ranging from Alfred Kazin to a host of undergraduates, graduate students, and interviewers for various anthologies or literary quarterlies *(Shenandoah, Georgia Review, Southern Review)*, have made the trek to Covington, Louisiana, some twenty-five miles north of New Orleans, on the other side of Lake Pontchartrain, in order to catch a glimpse of the man whose novels are so funny and full of satire, yet so completely serious: *unnerving* and *disquieting* are words often used to describe them.

It is certainly unnerving for one to try to summarize the plot of *The Moviegoer* (just as Camus's *Stranger* also defies the familiar précis: it is "about" an ordinary man who lives in Algiers and tells us what befell him — his mother's death, the trip to pay respect to her memory, the daily routines that followed, a sudden encounter with strangers, a pointless murder, a trial, a prisoner's attitude toward impending death).

Binx Bolling, the narrator and among other things a chronic moviegoer, begins by telling us, "This morning I got a note from my aunt asking me to come for lunch."

Binx Bolling is a twenty-nine-year-old stockbroker who has taken himself to Gentilly, a suburb of New Orleans located on its eastern edge. It is an interesting suburb — less under the city's French influence, architecturally and culturally, than other sections. It is more American, yet one enters it, coming from the east out of Mississippi, through a boulevard with the unusual name of Elysian Fields, off which run streets with names such as Humanity, Pleasure, Abundance, and Treasure. Binx comes from a well-to-do, socially prominent family. He doesn't "belong" in Gentilly, but then, he doesn't belong anywhere. He is confused, suffers from "loss" — the "malaise." What is the "malaise"? Binx calls it "the pain of loss." When things get bad "the world is lost to you, the world and the people in it, and there remains only you and the world and you no more able to be in the world than Banquo's ghost."

Binx may be peculiar, but he can also get up and go to work, make money, live the pleasant, comfortable life of a 1950s bachelor-swinger. He takes his girlfriend Linda to the Blue Room of the Roosevelt Hotel. They dine and dance. Linda loves him for giving her such a good time. Binx, in turn, enjoys her good humor. He is no secret critic, anxious to judge others "superficial." Linda "feels exalted" in the Blue Room, and why not? The problem, Binx knows, is himself; he likes Linda, but he can't stay with her or, it seems, any woman for too long. Black skies get to him. The wind makes him feel fragile. He gets vague sensations of apprehension: his heart gives a "big pump," his neck prickles. So, back to his room, or quick, find a movie to see. Soon enough Linda gives way to Sharon Kincaid.

Binx lives in a basement apartment; the owner is Mrs. Schexnaydre, a fireman's widow. We learn from him that he manages a branch office of his uncle's brokerage firm. His aunt lives in the Garden District. He lives a bit below the street level, but he is not quite Dostoevski's "underground man," or at least not so in the first part of the novel. Percy wants to draw us close to Binx, make us, it can be said, feel at home with him and his kind of living: oh, yes, the still young man who has a good job and a promising career, who is attractive and charming, a good catch for some lucky girl; he does at times seem a little strange, but that will go away, once he settles down, and anyway, one doesn't want someone *too* ordinary; this fellow has a touch of the mysterious to him, and that is always exciting.

The novel's tone is all-important. Binx speaks in a matter-of-fact way, and is only gently given to satire: "In the evenings I usually watch television or go to the movies. Weekends I often spend on the Gulf Coast. Our neighborhood theater in Gentilly has permanent lettering on the front of the marquee reading: Where Happiness Costs So Little." Or, at another point: "What satisfaction I take in appearing the first day to get my auto tag and brake sticker! I subscribe to *Consumer Reports* and as a consequence I own a first-class television set, an all but silent air conditioner and a very long lasting deodorant." Binx can wryly tell us that he pays attention to all those spot announcements: try to "achieve" mental health; watch for the various "signs of cancer"; drive safe, lest you do away with yourself. But he stops after a while, stops rubbing in his detachment, stops telling about all the ironies and absurdities of so-called civilized life — identity cards, credit cards, and all those certificates, diplomas, deeds, passbooks, and God knows what else that we stick in strongboxes: they are, in a way, us. Suddenly we are told: "The fact is I am quite happy in a movie, even a bad movie." Binx's despair is kept under wraps.

A good deal has been made by critics of the "meaning" of the movies, their "purpose" in this novel. They have been considered to be a reflection or "mirror" of "reality," a means of social observation and comment: what they "picture" is the dreams we have, or the kind of life we live, or would like to live — and on and on. Percy unquestionably uses the movies that way; they provide, as with "Pepper Young's Family," an entry into the complexities of existentialist philosophy, a series of illustrations which make Kierkegaard and Heidegger become as familiar as — well, William Holden, John Wayne, or Orson Welles. But through the movies he also makes *Binx* familiar; he is not Dostoevski's "sick" man, "spiteful" man, unattractive man, and he is not Kafka's K, wandering about mysteriously, never recognizable to anyone; nor, again, is he Meursault, who seems so apart from others, so driven — by what or toward what he knows not. Certainly Binx is not going to sit down, like Roquentin, and write a diary full of intense, weighty speculations: "Will it not still be existence, variations on existence?" or "Existence is what I am afraid of."

The movies enable Percy to let Binx reveal rather a lot about the condition of his soul, but to do so with a light, engaging touch. When he recalls the time "John Wayne killed three men with a carbine as he was falling to the dusty street in *Stagecoach,* and the time the kitten found Orson Welles in the doorway in *The Third Man,*" he reminds us that we have all gone through similar experiences; the movies by now have become part of the "collective unconscious" of Americans. Yet, Binx is different: it is for others to have "a sweet and natural relationship, as they say in books," with a nice girl they have met by chance, or been introduced to formally at a dinner party. He has his secretaries, none of whom he stays with very long, and Kate, who was even at age ten a source of worry to her stepmother. An obedient girl, who did well in school, she was solitary and when confronted with people exceedingly shy. Before we meet her as a grown-up woman of considerable anxiety — at times she seems the incarnation of Kierkegaard's "fear and trembling" — we get to know Binx and his women friends, each of them so cheerful, bouncy, giving (but also self-protective). The women ask no questions about "life." They love Binx's M.G. They love his position in the world. They would like to have one of those "relationships," "meaningful" at first and then permanent: marriage, children, a move from Gentilly to, say, Metairie, where New Orleans' upper-middle-class business and professional men live after they've had their fling in bachelor apartments and are ready to settle down.

Binx can't seem to "settle down," though. I suppose it can be said that the novel is about a man who gets seized by waves of restlessness, as a result of which he resists the tug to the altar, a nice house, a slow rise up the "socioeconomic scale," and on and on. But it has to be emphasized that he does not come across as "neurotic." Nor does he filter the world through clinical eyes. Kate, yes; she is in "treatment." She has been dangerously suicidal. But Binx (and the novel) will move toward her and her difficulties only after quite another kind of difficulty is explored — Binx's particular effort to break out of "the everydayness of his own life."

Once so freed, he is able to start out on what he calls "the search." Negatively, the search is what "anyone would undertake," if he were able to get beyond the daily absorption in routines and habits. The search begins when for one reason or another a man "comes to," suddenly looks closely around, and notices just about everything — the "background" of life (in the form of persons, places, things) we all take for granted as we move along: eight hours at work, an hour on the freeway, supper, television, and to bed. For Binx the search began in 1951. He was a soldier in Korea, and one day he found himself lying on the ground injured. His shoulder "was pressed hard against the ground," as if somebody were sitting on him. He did not think about his situation, though. He stared at a dung beetle six inches away. As he watched that beetle he felt himself "onto something." If he got out of the fix he was in, he told himself, he "would pursue the search."

Exactly what happened over there in Korea to Binx? Or what is it that happens to him when he is driving, and suddenly he no longer listens to somebody next to him, or if he is alone, no longer lets the radio hypnotize him? We are never told directly. Binx never comes up with clear-cut formulations about himself or others. He is an intent observer, and maybe that is enough to explain his reactions. He watches others as they drive, observes how invisible they have become: they glare at each other's fenders, and for all the world there could be no one inside, so long as the fenders keep moving. Or he is walking down Royal Street in the French Quarter, on his way to Canal Street, and who should he see but William Holden, in the flesh. To be a seeker, of all things, is to keep one's eye on both Holden and those who, one by one, recognize him. Percy has a fine time setting the scene for Holden's walk by describing the tourist-filled French Quarter.

Holden walking down the street becomes twentieth-century America — our values, our idols — exerting itself upon a number of men and women, most of whom do the predictable: become awestruck, surrender whatever authority they may on other occasions possess. But Percy has a young couple resist the inclination to surrender. When they spot Holden they, too, are excited; but the young man keeps his cool, and when Holden asks others for a match, and they are too flustered even to reply, let alone respond, the youth "holds out a light, nods briefly to Holden's thanks, then passes on without a flicker of recognition." Holden won't let that end it, though. He catches up, talks briefly with them, comments on the weather, and then they separate. "The boy has done it!" Binx exclaims. What has he done? A little more than meet William Holden, or even help the man out in the nonchalant manner: "He has won title to his own existence, as plenary an existence now as Holden's, by refusing to be stampeded like the ladies from Hattiesburg."

Binx has nothing against those "ladies"; they clearly lose out, but it is a struggle for him, too: the only way he can claim "title" to himself, to his existence, is by keeping his distance, keeping an eagle eye on what others do, in films and on the streets. And inevitably, he slips: becomes part of many stampedes — into the bus, out of it, into automobile traffic, out of it, up with the phone, down with the phone. To draw upon a factory worker of my acquaintance rather than on Binx: "Sometimes I'll go through a whole day, and I can't even remember what I did. I could have been a robot. The only reason I even try to remember, once in a while, is because my daughter will come in, and she's a teenager, you know, and she asks me these damned questions: 'What's it all about, Dad?' Well, you get a line-drive like that, and you try to catch it, and you're no longer in a daze, no sir." Binx refers to the "aura· of heightened reality" that accompanies William Holden. It is, he further muses, a "peculiar reality." For a second people are taken off guard. But usually they lose their chance, it can be called, and move out of one daze and into another: from tourist to movie fan to gawker.

The articles Percy had been writing come to mind constantly as one goes through *The Moviegoer*. His philosophical preoccupations are enacted by Binx. There is Kierkegaard's "aesthetic stage" — not necessarily a sensual life, but one that moves along from "experience" to "experience," a rotation here, a moment of nostalgia there, a flash of excitement in the presence of Bill Holden or Mayor A, Senator B, and, eventually, the last breath. However, some move into quite another kind of life: "the ethical stage." Such people gain enough "title" to themselves, as Percy would put it, to be capable of sustained direction: they may not be sovereign lords of their entire household (Kierkegaard uses the image of the house), but they are not in and out, strangers at their own address. They have settled down; rather than wander over highways and byways, they go from room to room, trying to figure out what the house might best be used for.

To all outward appearances they might well be mistaken, Binx knows, for ladies (or gentlemen) from Hattiesburg. But they have a firm sense of place (their place in the universe) and they feel a firm commitment to live up to the responsibility of a good householder: respect and love those who share a domicile with them; be ethically bound to others — the near and not-so-near neighbors. Binx well knows that for such people "everydayness" is still present — in Binx's words, "a fog of uneasiness, a thin gas of malaise." William Holden may for a moment even shake up the Hattiesburg ladies: what must it be like to live his kind of life, they ask themselves after he has left — and what kind of life are we, in contrast, living? But soon they have lost even that tenuous hold on themselves. The fog blinds them. The gas gets to them. They are utterly unconscious, though by every medical or psychiatric criterion they are thoroughly conscious: "Ah, William Holden, we already need you," says Binx, a few moments after the actor has vanished.

The man who is able to see and talk to himself as Binx does is in more jeopardy than he himself, or the reader, may realize. Binx has taken an implicit satisfaction in noticing others, keeping track of the foibles, the deception and pretense those others demonstrate, the thick web of illusions they spin for themselves. But the canny, knowing outsider, the aware observer, the ironist, the man who uses the "everydayness" of others as a means of getting a rotation or two himself, can also be the man who has nothing of his own. If others are blind, he has only the vision of their blindness. In a luminous moment Binx observes: "My exile in Gentilly has been the worst kind of self-deception." It is a thought buried in the exile's narrative. We are apt to glide over it, hungry for more of his sharp appraisals — in the case of Eddie Lovell and his wife Nell, the "bright texture of investments, family projects, lovely old houses, little theater reading and such."

Percy is wonderful at portraying knowing observers; at times he has one of them regard another. Eddie Lovell, like others who now and then enter Binx's life, is not a "man in the gray flannel suit"; rather, he is himself a complex and sensitive man, and if the author, through Binx, is willing to show us the vanities or vulnerabilities of such people, he is not without admiration for them: "Yes! Look at him. As he talks, he slaps a folded newspaper against his pants leg and his eye watches me and at the same time sweeps the terrain behind me, taking note of the slightest movement. A green truck turns down Bourbon Street; the eye sizes it up, flags it down, demands credentials, waves it on. A businessman turns in at the Maison Blanche building; the eye knows him, even knows what he is up to. And all the while he talks very well. His lips move muscularly, molding words into pleasing shapes, marshalling arguments, and during the slightest pauses are held poised, attractively everted in a Charles Boyer pout — while a little web of saliva gathers in a corner like the clear oil of a good machine. Now he jingles the coins deep in his pocket. No mystery here! — he is as cogent as a bird dog quartering a field. He understands everything out there and everything out there is something to be understood."

Binx keeps demonstrating the maneuvers Percy has described in his articles — the ways we find distraction, a moment of suspense, an escape from the tedious or the merely ordinary. Binx also acquaints us, indirectly, with a number of "concepts" a longtime student of various philosophers had mentioned, but never gone into as he wrote his various essays: the role of a "crisis" in lives; the circumstances under which individuals "come to," try to make the "search" Binx keeps speaking of. And the obstacles that crop up to hinder that search, especially the temptations a finely honed intellect, given to verbal fluency, can offer. Binx is not helped on his "search" by his ability to "take in" people and come up with all too accurate descriptions of them. They become items for him;

they are abstracted by his quick mind. He has moved all that closer to the world he dreads.

The "search" requires that Binx not only look squarely at his aunt's assumptions, or those of her black butler, but also face quite frankly the mischievous, self-congratulatory behavior of his that accompanies such an effort. None of this gets "spelled out," only worked into the easy flow of a story which is both entertaining and highly serious. Here is the butler, spared nothing by Binx, even as rich, white businessmen aren't: "Mercer is a chesty sand-colored Negro with a shaved head and a dignified Adolph Menjou mustache. Behind the mustache, his face, I notice, is not at all devoted but is as sulky as a Pullman porter's. My aunt brought him down from Feliciana, but he has changed much since then. Not only is he a city man now; he is also Mrs. Cutrer's butler and as such presides over a shifting menage of New Orleans Negresses, Jamaicans and lately Hondurians. He is conscious of his position and affects a clipped speech, pronouncing his *R*s and *ing*s and diphthonging his *I*s Harlem-style." As for Mercer's place of work and his employer, Binx's aunt: "The room is a beautiful room and by every right a cheerful room, with its walls of books, its bokhara glowing like a jewel, its blackening portraits. The prisms of the chandelier wink red in the firelight. Scattered over the satinwood table is the usual litter of quarterlies and rough-paper weeklies and, as always, the great folio *The Life of the Buddha*. My aunt likes to say she is an Episcopalian by emotion, a Greek by nature and a Buddhist by choice."

At certain points in the novel Percy's didactic intentions appear, but never disruptively. The reader is free to glide through and beyond, simply enjoying a witty and charming Binx as he recalls his past or makes his clever appraisals of others: "Until recent years, I read only 'fundamental' books, that is, key books on key subjects, such as *War and Peace*, the novel of novels; *A Study of History*, the solution of the problem of time; Schroedinger's *What is Life?*, Einstein's *The Universe as I See It*, and such. During those years I stood outside the universe and sought to understand it. I lived in my room as an Anyone living Anywhere and read fundamental books and only for diversion took walks around the neighborhood and saw an occasional movie. Certainly it did not matter to me where I was when I read such a book as *The Expanding Universe*. The greatest success of this enterprise, which I call my vertical search, came one night when I sat in a hotel room in Birmingham and read a book called *The Chemistry of Life*. When I finished it, it seemed to me that the main goals of my search were reached or were in principle reachable, whereupon I went out and saw a movie called *It Happened One Night* which was itself very good. A memorable night. The only difficulty was that though the universe had been disposed of, I myself was left over. There I lay in my hotel room with my search over, yet still obliged to draw one breath and then the next. But now I have undertaken a different kind of search, a horizontal search. As a consequence, what takes place in my room is less important. What is important is what I shall find when I leave my room and wander in the neighborhood. Before, I wandered as a diversion. Now I wander seriously and read as a diversion."

In that paragraph one finds allusions to Kierkegaard's life and "thinking"; a bit of self-representation on the part of the novelist; and a significant movement forward for the novel, all tucked into the charming flow of Binx's narrative voice: folksy, sly in its humor, serious as can be, but never portentous. Before Kierkegaard, before Christ, there were the Stoics; and before Binx there was his stoic aunt, actually his great-aunt, who is sixty-five, and clearheaded, farsighted. Binx remembers her words, her testimony, really — an inheritance he is asked to accept and pass on: "I don't quite know what we're doing on this insignificant cinder spinning away in a dark corner of the universe. That is a secret which the high gods have not confided in me. Yet one thing I believe and I believe it with every fibre of my being. A man must live by his lights and do what little he can and do it as best he can. In this world goodness is destined to be defeated. But a man must go down fighting. That is the victory. To do anything less is to be less than a man."

Aunt Kate's world has collapsed. Binx's world is elusive. What *does* he believe in: the pursuit of pleasure; the power of positive thinking; hard work and to church on Sunday? He listens half seriously to a program that goes on at ten o'clock every night: *This I Believe.* Those who appear reveal how devastating the collapse of the old order was. If Aunt Kate exhibits detached pessimism, balanced by a sense of duty, others utter the banalities Binx can't help finding interesting as well as funny: "Everyone on This I Believe believes in the uniqueness and the dignity of the individual. I have noticed, however, that the believers are far from unique themselves, are in fact alike as peas in a pod.

> I believe in music. I believe in a child's smile. I believe in
> love. I also believe in hate.

This is true. I have known a couple of these believers, humanists and lady psychologists who come to my aunt's house. On This I Believe they like everyone. But when it comes down to this or that particular person, I have noticed that they usually hate his guts."

Under the shadow of such a "cultural inheritance" Binx conducts his "experiments." He angles roguishly for relief from his boredom. He experiences disgust with the superficiality, the phoniness, he sees everywhere. He tries to do something quite complicated and ambitious — not only rid himself of the world's ugliness, including his particular contribution to it, but find an alternative that his own scrutinizing, occasionally cynical or corrupted, eye will not immediately reject. Percy is no student of the film, but he knows what movies can become for a person, even as he uses them as an instrument in his principal character's "search." Binx would no doubt smile knowingly at what Stanley Cavell writes in *The World Viewed: Reflections on the Ontology of Film,* published a decade after *The Moviegoer:* "What we wish to see in this way is the world itself — that is to say, everything. To say that we wish to view the world itself is to say that we wish for the condition of viewing as such. That is the way we establish our connection with the world: by viewing it, or having views of it. Our condition has become one in which our natural mode of perception is to view, feeling unseen; viewing a movie makes this condition automatic, takes the responsibility for it out of our hands.

Hence movies seem more natural than reality. Not because they are escapes into fantasy, but because they are reliefs from private fantasy and its responsibilities."

Binx certainly has fantasies. He is struggling throughout the novel to assume responsibility for them — turn them to some account in life, rather than run from them or flirt with them intermittently. He shuns personal possessions. He distrusts everyone, especially himself. He uses the streets of New Orleans, the homes he visits, his office, and of course the movie houses as endless sources of distraction. The man who wanders, wonders, worries; who seems to slip away from any sustained involvement, yet be ever watchful of people, will allow only two Currier and Ives prints of ice skaters in Central Park to hang on his walls. The figures are fragile, for all the joy they presumably are experiencing; they are alone against the background of the city. Who knows where they live, where they are headed? Maybe the ice will give way, and all the cheer suddenly turn to naught. Binx is inclined to have just such thoughts. He is willing sometimes to call himself "depressed" — yet, perhaps like the skaters, he keeps moving, goes around and around like them, or like the hands on a clock: "So ended my thirtieth year to heaven, as the poet called it."

By the time Binx says that, Carnival week is over, Lent is begun. And the reader has been witness to a journey. The guide has been genial, his language attractive, sometimes dangerously seductive — to the point that one wonders why he is so slippery, so noncommittal, so quick to observe then leave for the next scene, the next appraisal, the next car ride or movie. When will this man "settle down"? But by the time we ask that question we have been educated by Binx and his creator: to settle down is to face a new set of temptations, dead ends, pitfalls. However, Binx's posture of self-indulgence, occasional hauteur, and delightful social resourcefulness is no less futile than the rat race which, in its many versions, he both regards closely and flees. The couple he describes as spending twenty years worrying about whether their sons will "make Princeton" has a right to ask how many movies and M.G. rides a man can treat himself to, even if he does make a point of being openly self-critical and given to the most serious and introspective of thoughts.

Alienated commuters may be doomed, but sooner or later the search Binx refers to can disintegrate into a romantic's various escapades. At one point Binx sees a college student on a bus and recognizes himself in the shy, lonely youth: "He is a moviegoer, though of course he does not go to the movies." The line is the only one in the book that gives us an explicit clue to what Percy has in mind with a particular symbol; the rest is done by implication. Definitions and explications offered the readers of various scholarly or literary journals now appear in a paragraph like this: "Tonight, Thursday night, I carry out a successful experiment in repetition. Fourteen years ago, when I was a sophomore, I saw a western at a movie-house on Freret Street, a place frequented by students and known to them as the Armpit. The movie was *The Oxbow Incident* and it was quite good. It was about this time of year I saw it, for I remember the smell of privet when I came out and the camphor berries popping underfoot. (All movies smell of a neighborhood and a season: I saw *All Quiet on the Western Front,* one of my first, in Arcola, Mississippi in August of 1941, and the noble deeds were done, not merely fittingly but inevitably, in the thick singing darkness of Delta summer and in the fragrance of cottonseed meal.) Yesterday evening I noticed in the *Picayune* that another western was playing at the same theater. So up I went, by car to my aunt's house, then up St Charles in a streetcar with Kate so we can walk through the campus."

Kate is for Binx more than a relative or a friend; she is distraught, and in a sense more honest than he, not because he lies and she tells the truth, but because she is not at all devious and he is enormously agile and spirited. His despair is the unwitting kind Kierkegaard mentioned — hence the quotation that precedes the novel. Kate sees Dr. Merle Mink, the first but not the last psychiatrist Percy would smile at with mixed respect and skepticism. Kate clearly needs the man's assistance, and gets it; yet, there is a limit to what office visits can do. Anyway, Kate is fine when she is talking to the doctor, and fine when there is a tangible difficulty to face. Her despair comes in response to those interludes between emergencies. If nothing at all is "wrong," if there is only today, tomorrow, the next day, each pleasant, ordinary, and unremarkable, then Kate is likely to think of suicide. And Binx, all he need do on days like that, when he feels himself sinking, is remind himself that suicide is a possibility. It is good when a "suicidal impulse" comes to the mind's surface: he is alive, after all. He is "free" to end his life. We are reminded of Camus's essays on freedom, choice, suicide, or Sartre's somewhat similar preoccupations.

The mind can trick itself with endless diversions; it can, for instance, muster up a formidable array of ideas, propositions, theories and use them rather as the alienated commuter does — to convince himself that he has a "valid purpose" in life. Binx diverts himself by smiling indulgently at, or running away in panic from, the goings-on he witnesses. In contrast, Kate is almost completely self-absorbed. Her seriousness is edgy; at any moment she might throw up her hands and call it quits. But at least she does not pretend to a search. She is buffeted by the dreary small things of life, and has never thought to move away from them. When they are suspended by a disaster, she is in fine shape. When they bear down relentlessly on her, she begins to crumble. She hasn't become "alienated," but neither has she felt the need for rotations or repetitions, for hilarious or antic excursions, for cleverly self-indulgent philosophical ruminations. She has not taken to scribbling her thoughts down in notebooks, as Binx occasionally does, and certainly she doesn't take herself through his phenomenological paces, however disguised or dramatized. When he self-consciously tells her about his "search," he becomes revealingly didactic. One learns things. There is excitement. When she asks how or why, he becomes self-confident: "As you get deeper into the search, you unify. You understand more and more specimens by fewer and fewer formulae. There is the excitement. Of course you are always after the big one, the new key, the secret leverage point, and that is the best of it."

But the man who sees the vanities of others, the guile and

self-deception they endlessly practice, always in the name of "living," making an "adjustment," doing the best one can in a "tough world," is himself subject to the temptation of pride, and all that goes with it: smugness, immodesty, arrogance — and ultimately, self-deception. Binx is wonderfully adept with Kate, with everyone, in fact. Others are blunt, demanding, upset, at the brink of tears or strained laughter or bluster. Binx is ever the knowing listener or speaker. And when Kate strikes out or moves near tears or worse, he measures his responses like a master, and puts it across like the best of the actors he watches: "Therefore I take care to be no more serious than she." For too long he escapes realizing not only the presumptuousness of his intellect, but the mortal danger his deftly resilient, and occasionally exuberant, manner places upon him. Kate is *there*, vulnerable as each day is: soon enough, the night. Binx is in danger of being everywhere and nowhere; he is fast of foot, and quick on the draw, to the point that he escapes from not only all the lost souls he is so good at diagnosing, or the decent ones he recognizes as worth saving, but himself. If others don't quite know what to do with this earnest, funny, adept man, so hard to pin down or figure out, he manages more often than not to accomplish on the minor scale of his own life Hegel's feat: everything is figured out, except how he himself is to live a life.

Now and then Binx briefly catches on to himself. He not only asks himself a shrewd question or two ("Does a scientifically minded person become a romantic because he is a left-over from his own science?") but stops and points a finger at himself: "I accept my exile." And goes further: "For some time now the impression has been growing upon me that everyone is dead." And further still, now with a lurch: "It is not a bad thing to settle for the Little Way, not the big search for the big happiness but the sad little happiness of drinks and kisses, a good little car and a warm deep thigh." With that knowledge, he moves nearer to Kate, but also nearer to all those others whose lives he has scrutinized and by implication criticized so well: "The closer you get to the lake, the more expensive the houses are. Already the bungalows and duplexes and tiny ranch houses are behind me. Here are the fifty and sixty thousand dollar homes, fairly big moderns with dagger plants and Australian pines planted in brick boxes, and reproductions of French provincials and Louisiana colonials. The swimming pools steam like sleeping geysers. These houses look handsome in the sunlight; they please me with their pretty colors, their perfect lawns and their clean airy garages. But I have noticed that at this hour of dawn they are forlorn. A sadness settles over them like a fog from the lake."

Best, perhaps, to stay away from the lake, and from himself, too. The tension in the novel is the tension in Binx's life, as he moves along on a search which at the same time he wants to undercut, or worse, size up all too exactly — and thereby thwart. His evasiveness is fueled by his perceptiveness; psychiatrists could want no keener "level of awareness." The nearer he comes to the most important step a person can make — decide to exercise his freedom, make choices, and stand by them with commitment and intelligence — the more evasive he becomes: a cagy mind fights hard, perhaps unable to believe that, seeing so much, it can survive. The alternative to that step is obvious: hold back; keep the world at a distance; continue the endless, sophisticated analysis of things; smile to oneself often; watch Gregory Peck pull his stunts on the screen, and watch the people on either side of him get their kicks; the relief that is no relief at all, a shot in the arm that is gone in no time. And if the movies don't always work, there is always the public library: "Down I plunk myself with a liberal weekly at one of the massive tables, read it from cover to cover, nodding to myself whenever the writer scores a point. Damn right, old son, I say, jerking my chair in approval. Pour it on them. Then up and over to the rack for a conservative monthly and down in a fresh cool chair to join the counterattack. Oh ho, say I, and hold fast to the chair arm: that one did it: eviscerated! And then out and away into the sunlight, my neck prickling with satisfaction."

Binx has a half-brother named Lonnie, who is fourteen, quite small for his age, and in a wheelchair: sick, deformed, in many respects not only vulnerable but helpless. Ironically it is Lon-

161

nie who brings out Binx's vulnerability. They are comrades, as well as brothers. There are elements of both Dmitri and Ivan Karamazov in Binx, though he is never as haunted as Dostoevski's characters; maybe it is too late for that, or maybe Americans have their own ways of being haunted. But Binx can be hungrily sensuous, and he can be very much the philosopher-theologian. He does not shake his fists at the universe; but sometimes a sneer, a smirk, or even a daring wink will do. The third Karamazov, Alyosha, lacked Dmitri's cunning, his male power and drive; he also lacked Ivan's capacity to see and analyze in a formal or argumentative way; all he had was a deep reverence for God and His creatures which never came across as mawkish or pietistic, hence was frustrating or incomprehensible to many who encountered him. Percy has told interviewers (for example, John Carr in *Kite-Flying and Other Irrational Acts: Conversations with Twelve Southern Writers*) that he had Alyosha in mind when he constructed Lonnie — a minor character, entirely without the ego or the desperation that major ones so often possess.

Lonnie has no interest in fooling himself or anyone else. He is not an unfamiliar figure in fiction — the person who is childlike in a special way, regardless of his or her age. From a position of relative "helplessness" such a person looks at the world without any stratagems at all: it is for God to know the answers, for man to await His summons, not passively or actively, not blindly or knowingly, not naïvely or with the utmost of sophistication, but out of an insistent trust that is sure enough of itself to require no words, no acts, no ploys. Kierkegaard wrote of "the leap of faith": one is ready to make any sacrifice — not in order to placate or win over God, but out of faith. One doesn't complain, one sets about today's tasks, and then the next day's, and if they involve the largest of risks, then so be it. Lonnie is no Abraham, ready to give up his own son if that is the Lord's Will — Kierkegaard's "teleological suspension of the ethical" — and he is not enough portrayed by the author to warrant the characterization "Alyosha-like." In a religious age he would be considered an "instrument of the Lord's."

We meet and know Lonnie through Binx. Lonnie brings out a certain joy in Binx; they do not need words to "communicate." Marcel would declare each able with the other to "pass beyond the limits of the ego." The Binx who is struggling so long and hard on his "search" is Heidegger's kind of young existentialist — fiercely independent, because anxious to use what freedom he can find in himself to affirm himself, so that he no longer is at the mercy of thoughts, actions, habits imposed arbitrarily or gratuitously from outside. The "authenticity" Heidegger analyzes is achieved by *a* person fighting a hard battle against odds which, in fact, make up what we tend to call "life." A factory worker or an office worker (or doctor, or lawyer) might, with Binx, stop and say: "Only once in my life was the grip of everydayness broken: when I lay bleeding in a ditch." By which Percy means to say that then, and only then, was Binx able to look at himself and the world around him without the constraints that go with immersion in the so-called routines of life.

Here is a factory worker saying in his own way, out of his own life, what Percy, through Binx, says: "Twice, just twice have I stopped and thought to myself: who are you, mister, and what are you doing here, and what *should* you be doing — besides what you're told by your boss and your neighbors and everyone else? It was after my father died; and it was when my little boy fell sick and he had leukemia, they thought. And for a month we stared death in the face, with him; and for a month I wasn't the same person I usually am. Then they decided he didn't have leukemia, and he'd be all right, and I told my wife I'd never lived like that before — all the wondering about the world, all the questions I asked. I don't mean that my questions were so good. And I know, everyone asks questions sometimes. But I asked them with my whole heart, that's the only way I can put it to you."

His "whole heart" would be Heidegger's "authentic being." There is, however, a solitary quality to Heidegger's notion of the search: one has to work miracles, it seems, to find "authenticity," and implicit in the attempt is a need to shed oneself of the "inauthentic" — which is, inevitably, personified. In contrast, Gabriel Marcel regards the "search" as quite something else. He by no means overlooks the dangers that "others" present to us. The title of one of his books, *Man against Mass Society* (1952), is suggestive enough. There and elsewhere he has referred, sadly, to the *Fachmensch* of technological society: lives become property, people become things. Ideas, too, become reduced to weapons in ideological warfare; his references to the *nivellement* of individuals have to do with his belief that so very often the truly excellent — be it a product or an idea — is drowned by a flood of the mediocre, the standardized. We become detached, but not in Heidegger's sense. We become indifferent — an insouciance toward others reflects the attitude we have toward ourselves: ours not to reason why; ours but to do and die.

Marcel raged against "progress" not in order to espouse reactionary politics, but because he believed he discerned hunger in well-fed people; they have become cut off, emptied of all desire, it seems, to reach out toward others in any but the most set and conventional of ways. They are spectators; *homo spectans* is his term. If intellectuals, they take in people and situations, cough them up as abstractions. If ordinary working people, or, for that matter, members of professions or in the "business community," they have their own way of doing the same: everything becomes grist for whatever mill is being run. One weaves through traffic, attempts to bypass "them" who are competitors and rivals, or who are simply in the way along an aisle, or on the street.

I suppose Marcel can be called more "emotional" or "mystical" than Heidegger; though each man would decry such a distinction. It does seem fair to point out that for Heidegger man struggles against enormous difficulties to find *himself* — free, at last, of all the falsity around and inside him; whereas for Marcel man only finds himself through solidarity with others, through the "actualization" of his freedom in several kinds of love: a wife, a husband, friends, the person one may meet only briefly, but in a way that is honorable and kind-spirited on both sides — without false or automatic gestures.

Marcel is no impossible moralist; he knows that formalities

in and of themselves are minor evils: who can be a saint all day, every day, always *meaning* everything he says with all his heart and soul? The point is that there comes a time when minor "necessities" (the need we have to get through a day without exhausting ourselves in endless encounters, confrontations, moments of pure and unashamed honesty) can become a whole way of life, so that even at home with our wives or husbands and children, we say things that are all too predictable, and reflect the boredom, the "death" that has fastened itself on every part of our lives: Sartre's "nausea," Binx's (Percy's) "malaise."

What has Lonnie to do with all of that? When Binx drops in on his mother and her children, one of whom is his half-brother, Lonnie, the reader has gone through over half of *The Moviegoer* and may well be wondering whether there is any hope at all for Binx. Only when he is with Lonnie does Binx's guard come down. They love one another, though not in any insistent or demonstrative way; their affection is mutually understood, therefore needs no repeated avowal.

They can go to see *Fort Dobbs* at "The Moonlite Drive-In," back of the old Route 90, a few miles up from the Gulf Coast, in deserted, moss-covered, swampy pine country, and enjoy not only Clint Walker riding alone under the enormous Western sky, but each other's company. One of Binx's girlfriends is there, and he likes being with her, too; but it is clear that Lonnie is the one who draws him out, makes him seem, for the first time, less odd, less wrapped up in himself. No one else in his family, certainly not his mother, his stepfather, his other half-siblings, or, on his dead father's side, his great-aunt, seem able to reach him, though from behind the protection of his polite, genial, obliging manner he misses little.

And of course, that side of him gives the author a chance to be a wonderfully entertaining observer and storyteller; we get fine accounts of a mass in a Biloxi church, an egret lifting itself into the air, the varieties of seafood that a certain kind of Gulf Coast family hankers after, or the expressions such people use ("This is your mother you're talking to and not one of your little hotsy-totsies").

At one point, Binx's mother looks at him and Lonnie and says, "Now aren't those two a case?" She can't figure out why her two sons are so strangely playful with each other. They talk about religion. They drive all over. But, most confusing to her, they kid one another. Binx pretends he is an evil marauder, going after Lonnie, who loves sitting in his wheelchair: the helpless, terrified victim, as in an Akim Tamiroff movie. "During my last year in college," Binx observes, "I discovered that I was picking up the mannerisms of Akim Tamiroff, the only useful thing, in fact, that I learned in the entire four years."

When Binx leaves Lonnie and is back in New Orleans he is more sarcastic and cynical than ever before — a clue perhaps: he is lonelier than ever, because he has left someone he really touches and is touched by. We now fully realize that he is not at all a Meursault, who is eerily calm, unfailingly detached, a man puzzled by all those who think that what they say or do matters very much. Sam Yerger, an old friend, awaits Binx on his return. By the time Binx gets through ruminating about his friend and others like him, we can see that the "malaise" has not quite consumed its victim. "There is very little sin in the depths of the malaise," Binx states elsewhere. He also observes: "The highest moment of a malaisian's life can be that moment when he manages to sin like a proper human." At that moment one at least makes an affirmation of a kind: I am a human being, and willing to take my stand as such: to sin. Meursault or Roquentin can only ponder suicide as a way of exerting their freedom, showing themselves that they do, after all, have some authority that is *theirs*. In contrast, Binx flexes himself through mischief.

By subtly changing the tone of Binx's comments, Percy makes quite clear that this man has some strong ideas, and will speak up for them — even if through a series of negatives. Thus, Binx reminds himself that Sam Yerger and his wife once lived in the French Quarter, but then moved to "the Mexican state of Chiapas, where I visited them in 1954." Then he adds that "there he wrote a novel called *The Honored and the Dishonored* which dealt, according to the dust jacket, with 'the problem of evil and the essential loneliness of man.' " Binx once went to visit Sam in Mexico, and "met this girl from U.C.L.A. named Pat Pabst." Who was she? "I looked over at Pat Pabst who, I knew, was in Mexico looking for the Real Right Thing." Binx's wicked tongue shows that he is far from lifeless. He is alone, and he clearly doesn't like much of the world around him — but at least he is full of lively, even biting, reactions to that world.

The novel moves to its climax slowly and quietly: a low-key confrontation takes place between Binx and his great-aunt, with the latter doing almost all the talking. Kate has been increasingly distracted. Binx has spent more and more time with her. They went to Chicago together. Having done so, they stand accused in the aunt's eyes. And she is right about their affection for each other. They are indeed drawing closer together, and will soon be married. The aunt lectures Binx somewhat sternly and, as she does, manages to convey her own aristocratic, stoic philosophy. She feels betrayed by someone she thought a compatriot: "All these years I have been assuming that between us words mean roughly the same thing, that among certain people, gentlefolk I don't mind calling them, there exists a set of meanings held in common, that a certain manner and a certain grace come as naturally as breathing. At the great moments of life — success, failure, marriage, death — our kind of folks have always possessed a native instinct for behavior, a natural piety or grace, I don't mind calling it."

There is more; it is the longest speech of the book. Critics have traced the origins of the aunt's philosophy to Percy's cousin and adoptive parent William Alexander Percy, and there certainly are resemblances between passages in *Lanterns on the Levee* and the speech Binx hears from his aunt. "Honor and honesty, compassion and truth are good even if they kill you, for they alone give life its dignity and worth," the aunt declares, and William Alexander Percy affirmed a similar conviction many times. A cousin of Percy's, Phinizy Spalding, writing in the *Georgia Review* ("A Stoic Trend in William Alexander Percy's Thought"), has shown how deeply rooted in the Percy family was that commitment to the "old virtues": responsibility to others, even when they seem uninterested or ungrateful, and a high standard for oneself, even if one is likely to be, at the same time, rather doubtful about the capacity of most people to respond in a similar vein. This mixture of social responsibility bordering on the sacrificial with psychological skepticism (are "people," most of them, really worth the effort?) does indeed come across in William Alexander Percy's writing, and for that matter, more indirectly, in his father's essays — for example, Senator LeRoy Percy's *Atlantic Monthly* article on the Ku Klux Klan. And Binx's Aunt Emily joins them: *noblesse oblige* — but don't at all expect to be thanked, or to see the world suddenly become a charming, dignified, decent place.

But Aunt Emily almost caricatures stoicism; at the very least, she serves to make some of its social and economic underpinnings quite explicit. At one point Aunt Emily throws caution to the winds and blurts out: "I'll make you a little confession. I am not ashamed to use the word class. I will also plead guilty to another charge. The charge is that people belonging to my class think they're better than other people. You're damn right we're better. We're better because we do not shirk our obligations to ourselves or to others. We do not whine. We do not organize a minority group and blackmail the government. We do not prize mediocrity for mediocrity's sake. Oh I am aware that we hear a great many flattering things nowadays about your great common man — you know, it has always been revealing to me that he is perfectly content so to be called, because that is exactly what he is: the common man and when I say common I mean common as hell. Our civilization has achieved a distinction of sorts. It will be remembered not for its technology nor even its wars but for its novel ethos. Ours is the only civilization in history which has enshrined mediocrity as its national ideal. Others have been corrupt, but leave it to us to invent the most undistinguished of corruptions. No orgies, no blood running in the street, no babies thrown off cliffs. No, we're sentimental people and we horrify easily. True, our moral fiber is rotten. Our national character stinks to high heaven. But we are kinder than ever. No prostitute ever responded with a quicker spasm of sentiment when our hearts are touched. Nor is there anything new about thievery, lewdness, lying, adultery. What is new is that in our time liars and thieves and whores and adulterers wish also to be congratulated and are congratulated by the great public, if their confession is sufficiently psychological or strikes a sufficiently heartfelt and authentic note of sincerity. Oh, we are sincere. I do not deny it. I don't know anybody nowadays who is not sincere."

The words could be Evelyn Waugh's — but certainly not William Alexander Percy's. And anyway, there is another side to *Lanterns on the Levee* that has received virtually no attention, and understandably so, because the book's author is reluctant to be explicit about his particular search — one for something else besides the poet's "beauty" and "truth." Often he went to Greenville's cemetery and sat there, in communion, it can be said, with his dead ancestors and himself. He could be openly, unashamedly self-critical, and admiring of people utterly unlike himself in "class," "background," or race. And he could look up to Heaven, perhaps not the way believing Christians do, but not quite as a stoic (or an Aunt Emily) does: "Here among the graves in twilight I see one thing only, but I see that thing clear. I see the long wall of a rampart sombre with sunset, a dusty road at its base. On the tower of the rampart stand the glorious high gods, Death and the rest, insolent and watching. Below on the road stream the tribes of men, tired, bent, hurt, and stumbling, and each man alone. As one comes beneath the tower, the High God descends and faces the wayfarer. He speaks three slow words: 'Who are you?' The pilgrim I know should be able to straighten his shoulders, to stand his tallest, and to answer defiantly: 'I am your son.' "

The important words are *wayfarer* and *pilgrim;* William Alexander Percy was both, and Aunt Emily is neither. Those two relatives of hers, who disappoint her so, rather quickly let us know that silence will now more than likely prevail. No long speeches from either in reply to their aunt. Once their kind of commitment has been made — it is a shared lovingkindness in the face of the obvious difficulties each offers to the other —

169

words become unnecessary, maybe misleading. Marcel speaks of the need for us to go from the concrete to the abstract *and back to the concrete:* we are in a certain situation — we want to know who we are and whither we are going; we use our heads to find answers to those questions, hence ideas get endlessly spelled out; with luck at some moment we find the beginning of an answer — a direction — then we must set out, and the journey is not to be mistaken with the maps, charts, manuals, and books that tell us about the journey.

"As for my search," Binx says, "I have not the inclination to say much on the subject. For one thing, I have not the authority, as the great Danish philosopher declared, to speak of such matters in any way other than the edifying. For another thing, it is not open to me even to be edifying, since the time is later than his, much too late to edify or do much of anything except plant a foot in the right place as the opportunity presents itself." That said, there can be only a page or two left to *The Moviegoer*. Percy wants to make sure that we connect in our mind Kate and Lonnie, so in an epilogue he has Binx tell us that with Kate, and at her behest, he went to see Lonnie before he died. The fatal disease had badly ravaged the boy, yet he was calm and loving, at peace. And Binx is at peace, too. He has no "answers," and we are given to know, quite clearly, that though he will go to medical school, he will by no means be spared the anxiety, if not outright despair, he had for so long been running from or managing not to look at. His wife upon occasion is, as Aunt Emily declared, "suicidal." He has not lost his vagueness, that disguise for the utterly precise and all-important questions he asks himself. He will, now with Kate, keep on looking and asking. As he says, he is only in the thirty-first year of his "dark pilgrimage on this earth."

One suspects the couple will, perhaps, go to the movies a bit less; and certainly Binx will no longer have the time to be quite so intent an onlooker: there is a wife to be with, a lot of work for him to do, now that, in his thirties, he has undertaken a shift of occupation. It is fairly clear that, in Kierkegaard's scheme of things, Binx is no longer responding "aesthetically" to life, but has moved to the "ethical stage." Percy himself mentions "the

Danish philosopher," and Percy's critics have taken the cue —
though Kierkegaard's categories are hard ones to use for those
who write or analyze novels: the shift from one "stage" to
another cannot be turned into an occasion for dramatic presentation or wordy explication, because in many respects the person appears the same after he has made such a shift; even "the
leap of faith" is something inward and ineffable.

Even more accurately than Kierkegaard, it was Marcel
who described Binx's fate as "realities of presence" in connection with the *homo viator,* or seeker. In a way Heidegger and
the Stoics are alike: they both gird themselves, try to be true to
themselves. Heidegger's phrase "being-unto-death" suggests
how stalwart, how brave, but how alone he would have us be as
we search out our "condition" — our fate, if not destiny. Marcel has quite another point of view. He speaks of the "gift of
presence"; it is Buber's "Thou" toward whom one must move
gladly. By an "exchange of free acts" one person nods to
another, the nod is reciprocated, and two "realities" become
joined — his "fidelity" become incarnate.

Not by any means is the result a new Jerusalem, a Zion on
the Hill, or an Eden as it originally was. Marcel's plays are full
of the conceits and deceits which plague every human being
and all those "relationships" we are so prone these days to
mention. The kind of "relationship" Marcel has in mind would
strike many a "group leader" or "therapist" as insufficient, as
not "analyzed" enough, as perhaps naïve, perhaps austere.
Binx and Kate are not falling all over each other. They don't
touch one another repeatedly and proudly. They haven't "re-
solved" their problems. One thinks of them as looking at each
other for a moment with unblinking eyes — then on to the next
obligation. As Binx notes, there is even a reconciliation of sorts
with Aunt Emily; and certainly to all outward appearance Binx
the young doctor will be going along with his aunt's sense of
duty to others. To do so requires leaving Gentilly, leaving a
basement apartment. Binx will be vulnerable as never before;
some other "moviegoer" will no doubt find it easy to twit or
poke fun at, maybe even ridicule or caricature, Kate and him.
Their vulnerability will be one of the hazards they have know-

ingly assumed on the different and still quite hazardous road they are traveling, its destination, one suspects, not clear to either of them. They only know for sure where they *were* traveling, and want no longer to be found there.

The Last Gentleman was published in 1966; the five-year interval between the first and second novels is a measure of how seriously Percy took his new profession as a novelist. In those five years he published little else: no more philosophical essays; only a piece or two about the South, and a charming review of Richard Hughes's *Fox in the Attic* for *Sewanee Review*. The result of his labor was a substantially longer novel than *The Moviegoer;* its plot even harder to describe. One can say only that *The Last Gentleman* depicts the encounter of Bill Barrett with the Vaughts, a Southern family he has met by chance in New York City, *his* Gentilly. As the Vaughts move back South, Bill Barrett follows, taking his detours. His life becomes very much tied to theirs; and in time, he falls in love with Kitty Vaught. He also becomes a continuing presence, literally and in Marcel's sense of the word, to Kitty's brother Jamie, who is dying of leukemia, and to her other, older, brother, Sutter.

Bill Barrett is not quite another Binx Bolling, but there are strong resemblances. Once again a young man seems to be adrift; this "gentleman" is twenty-five, rather than twenty-nine, but he makes up in experience what he lacks in age. Binx finds his "underground" on the other side of his native city, and while there moves from one movie house to another, recording his observations. Bill Barrett ventures farther afield. He goes to New York, by way of Princeton, from Louisiana; and before we are through, he has wandered up and down the Eastern coast, through the South, and out to New Mexico. All along he struggles with the same questions Binx could not avoid asking: there is a world out there, people and more people; I am curious about them, but why am I so disconnected from them? What to do — if anything?

Again we have as epigraph a brief familiar quotation from Kierkegaard: "If a man cannot forget, he will never amount to much." In addition there is a longer quotation from Romano

Guardini's *End of the Modern World:* "We know now that the modern world is coming to an end . . . at the same time, the unbeliever will emerge from the fogs of secularism. He will cease to reap benefit from the values and forces developed by the very Revelation he denies. . . . Loneliness in faith will be terrible. Love will disappear from the face of the public world, but the more precious will be that love which flows from one lonely person to another . . . the world to come will be filled with animosity and danger, but it will be a world open and clean."

And again, though now narrated in the third person, there is the quiet, brief, opening sentence — which can lead the reader anywhere: "One fine day in early summer a young man lay thinking in Central Park." Those first sentences mean more to Percy than they may to some writers; he labors over them at great length, and somehow they set the stage for the entire novel: "In the first sentence I establish a situation — here is a person who has had *this* happen to him, or is over *there;* now let's see what happens to him." By "happens" he means not only plot, but a metaphysical sequence — Barrett as yet another version of Marcel's *homo spectans* and Barrett, ultimately, as a man literally running fast to catch up to and be with another person. Beside Barrett in the park stands a symbol of his "condition," a large and expensive telescope. He uses it to scan the sky, to look at people. Percy's tone as a narrator draws the reader gradually toward Barrett; strange and eccentric, he nevertheless becomes a believable person who is not crazy, not bizarre, not a man who possesses a schizoid, voyeuristic "personality," not the grotesque become a moment's entertainment. He is thoroughly likable and interesting; and very important, he has a way of striking familiar chords: his moments of awkwardness or confusion remind us of similar experiences we've had.

I doubt many readers have felt very close to Roquentin or Meursault; they are only impersonally haunting. In contrast, Billy Barrett, like Binx Bolling, is funny, even cozy; he ingratiates himself with the reader — as if he wants to tap him or her on the shoulder and say: Come and hear about a few surprising moments I've lived through, and I promise not to shake a fist or shout derisively or scowl. Paragraph by paragraph, sentence by sentence, the author envelops his readers in a carefully conceived atmosphere of existentialist ideas — which, at the same time, never become obtrusive or pedantic. We learn that Barrett "had to know everything before he could do anything." We learn that until we meet him, Barrett "had lived in a state of pure possibility." We learn that he had trouble knowing what to believe; he was "a watcher and a listener and a wonderer."

Percy goes over those qualities repeatedly, working them into the fabric of a particular character's background and manner. The abstraction about "a state of pure possibility" becomes six pages later: "Like many young men in the South, he became overly subtle and had trouble ruling out the possible." Such subtlety did not just arise spontaneously: "Over the years his family had turned ironical and lost its gift for action." A proud and vigorous great-grandfather, we are told, fought the Klan, brandished a pistol, and in general had not the slightest doubt about what he would fight to the death to uphold. A grandfather was also brave and honorable, but a touch self-conscious; he worried about moral issues, and wasn't completely sure of himself. A father tried to carry on the family tradition, but was altogether more sensitive to others than his predecessors had been. Life became a constant burden: "He became ironical. For him it was not a small thing, to walk down the street on an ordinary September morning."

Barrett also found life trying. From childhood on he had experienced "spells"; they are called episodes of *déjà vu*. Percy doesn't define a clinical syndrome, nor does he really tell us why Barrett suffered those periods of distraction and amnesia. But if we are to believe Kierkegaard, this extraordinarily forgetful young Southerner was destined, even as a child, to amount to something — and in fact, upon "coming to" was often Guardini's postmodern man: solitary and lonely, very much inclined to sift through or reject existing pieties, and struggle with disarming innocence for his own psychological and philosophical territory. "What happened anyhow," the author tells us about Barrett, "was that even when he was a child and was sitting in the kitchen watching D'lo snap beans or make beaten biscuits, there came over him as it might come over a sorrowful old man the strongest sense that it had all happened before and that something else was going to happen and when it did he would know the secret of his own life. Things seemed to turn white and dense and time itself became frightened with an unspeakable emotion. Sometimes he 'fell out' and would wake up hours later, in his bed, refreshed but still haunted."

Later on Barrett had out-and-out amnesia attacks. Yet, with apologies to Kierkegaard and Guardini (and Marcel and Heidegger), here is what happened when the attacks were over: "Much of the time he was like a man who has just crawled out of a bombed building. Everything looked strange. Such a predicament, however, is not altogether a bad thing. Like the sole survivor of a bombed building, he had no secondhand opinions and he could see things afresh."

During the first third of the novel we learn to distinguish Billy Barrett from any number of others: the psychiatric patient; the somewhat "different" Southerner whose "background" and habits strike others as confusing; the person who is struggling, albeit unsuccessfully so far, "to seek emotional gratifications in a mature way," as Percy puts it. Barrett does spend a good deal of time trying to achieve that goal, but he emerges always as someone to whom "well-known books on mental hygiene" have nothing to say. His very effort to go along with what he has read and heard preached reminds him of his peculiar situation: "At these times he set himself the goal and often achieved it of 'cultivating rewarding interpersonal relationships with a variety of people' — to use a phrase he had come across and not forgotten." The result: nothing. He simply went on scratching his head, going into fugues, looking intently at the world without his eyes or with a telescope or a camera — his usual evasive self.

Percy becomes quite satirical when he portrays the sophisticated world of the Northeast. He wants to show that the worries that bring others to psychiatrists, or prompt a whole range of fads, are not those that plague this "last gentleman" of his — who can face almost any disaster or threat that comes his way, who can shrug his shoulders at whatever "neurotic problem" he and his ever-so-serious psychoanalyst, Dr. Gamow, happen to examine, but who doesn't quite know how to face "the prospect of living through an ordinary Wednesday morning." Barrett is a "humidification engineer"; like Binx Bolling he is "an underground man": Macy's basement is where his mornings are spent. But boredom is all around him, and nothing that any psychoanalyst or group therapist says can take away his openness: he sees all too clearly the same "everydayness" Binx tries through stratagems to escape; and through the *déjà vu* he does manage to find a period of release. He is transported back in time; or he simply finds himself someplace, he knows not where — with a consequent heightened responsiveness to the world. Who am I and where did I come from and where am I headed? he asks — the castaway of Percy's article as opposed to the alienated commuter, who has long since given up those questions.

Barrett is amiable, funny, charming; and at all times he seems available — the man who has freed himself of obligations, and so is able to look at the world with the least number of reservations or prior (and inhibiting) commitments. When a psychoanalyst tries — he has done so for years — to *confront* Barrett, get him to shape up and respond as other patients do, the result is a hilarious collision of two quite different temperaments. The doctor has a set way of understanding human nature, and wants to use it for the edification of his patient; thereby a "cure" will be effected. The patient remains true to Percy's characterization; he is a gentleman, so responds with deference and tact: if that is what you say and want and aim at, doctor, then fine, and I only wish I could be more helpful. The problem is that this particular gentleman, for all his evasiveness and courtliness, feels strong questions gnawing at him. Are people hollow? he wonders. Is *everything* becoming contaminated — to the point that a whole civilization is dying, even as the air is foul, the countryside not inviting but a menace? And what is worth believing — once a psychoanalysis is over, and "group skills" have been mastered? And on and on.

Polite and obliging as he is, Barrett is ready to strike out on his own. His psychiatrist refers to "ideas of reference," which he then spells out as Barrett's "hollow men, noxious particles, and ultimate truths." His psychiatrist insists upon *connections:* you say this before or after that — and I will keep on remarking upon the sequences you offer in the course of your fifty-minute visits. Barrett's curiosity, his innocent questions and his hunger for answers, his peculiarly stubborn refusal to commit himself to the modish, or even the conventional — all of that must have to do with something wrong, a streak of the psychopathological. Just before the onset of his "fugue states," for instance, he develops an especially strong craving for philosophical speculation, a need for the broadest kind of inquiry. Now Barrett may be tempted to believe that the fugue state represents an even more desperate effort on his part to look about, or, in Percy's vein of imagery, cast about from the position of an islander, who is alone and puzzled, however many people are nearby, and however self-assured they appear to be. But no, Dr. Gamow considers the fugue state an escape from "reality." Let Percy's thoroughly "well-adjusted" commuter start asking a few of Barrett's questions, let him decide to get off the train and start looking affably but persistently into the eyes of people he chances to meet — do *you*, perhaps, have some clue to the riddles I keep thinking about? — and old Dr. Gamow will move a little toward the edge of his chair, raise his eyebrows knowingly, and say that the poor fellow who left the train, like the poor fellow Billy Barrett, needs to do a little "work": something has gone wrong in his head.

Barrett had put in five years with Dr. Gamow and Macy's. The point of the novel is to pick him up as he decides to cut himself loose from that life, and embark upon a search as unself-conscious as it is persistent. Percy has a wonderful time arranging the young man's meeting with the Vaughts, then moving him along — from Manhattan through New Jersey into Levittown, then on down South through the Virginia tidewater, over to Alabama and Louisiana, and thence through Texas to New Mexico. Through Barrett's eyes (aided occasionally by the lens of his telescope), the obsessions and pretensions of mid-twentieth-century American secular society, as well as its earnest, decent side, get seen and heard. To a degree *The Last Gentleman* is the familiar novel of social observation: a character of broad sensibility, both serious and with a sense of humor, travels across a country; the various experiences he has, the accidents and incidents he encounters, enable the reader to glimpse what otherwise might go unnoticed. Percy describes Barrett as "peering into the faces of Georgians and Indianians," and further along notes that he is as "alert as a cat." Not only Barrett's mind but his body has antennae out for almost everything, it seems. His heart gives "a big bump in his neck." On other occasions "his scalp bristled." The knee may jerk or leap, there is tingling, and once "his eyes twittered around under his eyeballs." His "sole gift," we are told, is "the knack of divining persons and situations." He takes in a lot, even if he does feel confused or on the verge of a spell or a fit. And he has been granted by the author the gift of periodic release from the "everydayness" Binx Bolling fought so hard in *The Moviegoer.*

At times some who use drugs or meditate at great length feel they have become much "more" than they usually are. They feel almost detached from the day-to-day realities we know so well that in fact we don't think about them, simply submit to their demands. They feel lifted out of themselves — as if they have achieved a "moment" which is not like other moments: it is as if they are united with God, or a Universal Truth, or whatever. But individuals like Barrett, far less self-conscious or determined in their pursuit of the sacred or the divine, are also capable of transcendence. Percy wants Barrett's sustained struggle to remind the rest of us of a moment or two we have had. The workingman again: "All the time it's work; even on Sundays I'm recovering from the factory, and tomorrow I'll be back there. That's what it's like to be on an assembly line. I never really relax; on vacations there's always something to do. One time in my life I got smart. It only lasted an hour or so, but to this day, when I get low, I ask myself: why don't you go into those woods again? Of course, I'd be a fool to try to get lost in the woods. That's when it happened. I was trying to get back from a hike, and I couldn't. I got scared. I was like a kid, ready to cry. Then all of a sudden I sat down on a rock and I started talking to myself. I think I hypnotized myself: you know what I mean? I became as calm as I've ever been in my life; more calm. I looked up there, at the sky, and I talked with God: I said, if You want me, I'm ready.

"I thought back about my life, and for a second I started getting scared again, but then I felt as if I wasn't myself anymore. I wasn't going crazy, believe me: no voices and all that. I'm not very religious. It wasn't that I was praying to God. I told the priest about it later, and he said I must have been praying very hard; but I wasn't. I think it was some mood that came over me. I wasn't tied up with the usual worries; I wasn't even worried about finding my way out of that forest. I figured that I'd been going around and around in circles, so the time had come to stop and wait. For the first time I could really look at the world as though I was an astronaut out in space: there it is, down there. I've never been in an airplane, but I've always wondered if the same thing might happen if I took an airplane ride: *that's* the world, I'd be thinking, and I'm an ant, and so is everyone else, and you can't take yourself so seriously. Eventually I got myself out of that forest, and then I was back to my usual self. A couple of years ago, when I went up to the top of a skyscraper with my kids, it was no different than being at home. So, maybe I *was* a little out of my head then in the forest. Or maybe I'm just not smart enough, most of the time, to see what's really going on around me, because I'm so busy keeping up with the rat race."

Billy Barrett, in contrast, is a seer (even his doctor senses that he is one) and so has "the knack of divining persons and situations." He also seems to have all the time in the world, and no great financial worries. But when he goes to visit young Jamie Vaught, in a New York hospital rather like the Columbia-Presbyterian Medical Center a young Dr. Percy got to know so well, he is quickly "mistaken for a member of the staff." And all through the novel Barrett seems to blend into the particular situation he is also "divining." He may not be Marcel's *homo participans,* but he seems to *want* to be. He is, above all, humble; and he is quick to notice foolishness or pretense, but not quick to condemn. Through him we get to see ourselves better: "He sized them up as Yankee sort of Southerners, the cheerful prosperous go-getters one comes across in the upper South, in Knoxville maybe, or Bristol." Or elsewhere: "Rejoicing, he climbed in and held his telescope on his lap: what good fortune to be picked up by a bevy of Virginia noblewomen. Nor did he mind when they turned out to be Texans, golfers from a Fort Worth club, fortyish and firm as Indian rubber and fairly bursting their seersuckers."

Nevertheless, Barrett is no mere eavesdropper, nor is he a neutral observer of his fellow man; he is a hurt and suffering man. There is about him — and the same goes for the narrative voice that sustains the novel — none of the self-confidence and moral assurance which satirists often possess. He finds himself in love with Kitty Vaught, yet he does not know how to settle down, live a life. For one thing, there are the amnesiac attacks. But more important is his transcendence over others whose immanence he sizes up and tries to join, though not with any great success. In this regard, the Vaughts both help and frustrate him. They are there, responsive to him. But they are no match for his considerable evasiveness. Mr. Vaught is a brash, forceful, outgoing Southern success story; he sells lots of cars. Mrs. Vaught is the familiar, fading Southern belle: not for her, an independent thought; though she knows how to survive in her family's war of nerves — the bluff and counterbluff, the implicit threats, barely concealed bribes, or unvarnished lies. Jamie Vaught, like Binx's half-brother Lonnie, is eighteen and already quite ill when Barrett first meets him in New York City.

He is the one, rather than Barrett, who holds the book together. Within the Vaught family, Jamie's condition inspires what Percy refers to as "the almost voluptuous intercourse of bad news." It is not that the Vaughts or their friends are sadistic or harbor "death wishes" toward Jamie. He is lovable, another of Percy's young innocents, another descendent of Alyosha Karamazov. And he is indeed loved; loved by his parents, by his sister Kitty, by his older brother Sutter, a thirty-four-year-old physician who is not unlike Ivan Karamazov in his ability to argue brilliantly against the author himself, never mind the other characters; loved by Rita, the doctor's former wife, and by Val, an older sister, who is also a sister in the Roman Catholic Church, to which she has converted and dedicated her life. Nevertheless, people can gain rather a lot from the sight of misery and suffering, an unexpected calamity, a sudden and inexplicable disaster — when it is experienced by others. Barrett comes upon a family very much in turmoil; Jamie's impending death makes those near him stop and think about themselves as well as him. *The Last Gentleman* is a chronicle of ascent and descent: Barrett from the heights of his lofty (telescopic) vision toward the actual lives of others, among whom he finds himself increasingly located; Jamie toward the final, mysterious moment no one can comprehend in advance; Sutter from *his* heights — the loneliness of the man who uses abstract knowledge to keep himself removed from concrete involvement with others — and the rest of the Vaughts, whose humanity, in the tradition of existentialist thought, is evoked by Jamie's death.

The Last Gentleman is a continuation of Percy's ambitious effort to combine an interest in philosophical explication with the traditional requirements of the novel. The novel is well rooted in particularity.

Despite repeated protestations that, *as a novelist,* he owes little to the South, Percy has not only located each of his novels in the region, but drawn poignantly of its "atmosphere"; there are passages in *The Last Gentleman* that reveal the author firmly the realist, as anxious as Zola or Flaubert to capture a limited part of what some of us these days call "the environment": "Down flew the Trav-L-Aire into the setting sun, down and out of the last of the ancient and impoverished South of red hills and Cardui signs and God-is-Love crosses. Down through humpy sugarloaves and loess cliffs sliced through like poundcake. Dead trees shrouded in kudzu vines reared up like old women. Down and out at last and onto the vast prodigal plain of the Delta, stretching away misty and fecund into the October haze. The land hummed and simmered in its own richness. Picking was still going on, great $25,000 McCormicks and Farmalls browsing up and down the cotton rows. Bugs zoomed and splashed amber against the windshield; the Trav-L-Aire pushed like a boat through the heavy air and the rich protein smells, now the sweet ferment of alfalfa, now the smell of cottonseed meal rich as ham in the kitchen."

Anyone who has spent time in the Mississippi Delta knows how exact, how fine and right Percy's writing is. He will repeatedly tell a Yankee visitor that unlike Faulkner, Eudora Welty, or Flannery O'Connor, he has spent little time with the region's "plain folk," black or white, and has followed the example of continental novelists, from Dostoevski to Sartre and Camus. Yet Percy loves the South, and if he doesn't give us the weird, bizarre, or overwhelmingly dreary people that many of the region's other novelists have made a point of putting before us, he at the very least evokes the atmosphere, the conditions of life which surround and define the lives of those who belong to a particular region. Not that he is a committed realist, either. Naturalistic observation gives way frequently to flashes of psychological subjectivity. Humorous, beguiling comedy, in no need of any heavy symbolic interpretation, and quite pleasing to the reader, gives way to densely abstract speculation, rendered through an obvious and not especially original literary device: the notebook left inadvertently but conveniently lying about. The notebook is Sutter's, and it is quite worthy of Marcel; and Heidegger, one believes, though he would not be capable of Sutter's earthy, blunt, Rabelaisian side, would certainly recognize the ideas of this wayward, distracted, near-suicidal doctor.

The notebook is Percy's way of accomplishing what Dostoevski managed to do in the Grand Inquisitor scene of *The Brothers Karamazov*. Never has a novelist resisted his own ideological inclinations as successfully as Dostoevski did through the confrontation he established between the Inquisitor and Christ. The Christ of Scripture is touching and beautifully direct; He is the Christ who entered history and to this day puzzles men: through Him God was revealed as willingly powerless. Dostoevski's Inquisitor pounces on that weakness, exemplified not only in Christ's betrayal, arrest, arraignment, and death sentence, but in His moment of radical doubt and loneliness on the Cross — as if He knew then what the Inquisitor says at such compelling length: man does not want, cannot bear, will do anything to avoid the sight of the kind of freedom Christ offered.

Ultimately, Christ's vision of man depended on the movements of the heart, as Pascal knew and emphasized, as did Simone Weil in our time. Kierkegaard's "leap of faith" is what Christ asked, and only when *that* is acknowledged can the Grand Inquisitor even be countered. When he defies anyone to *prove* him wrong, he is well beyond refutation. Christ offered men something unconditional: be we hungry, or unconvinced by a dozen scholars, or despised by everyone important, we can still follow Him, accept Him. Some secular readers of *The Brothers Karamazov* have claimed that through the Inquisitor's words Dostoevski indirectly, and perhaps unwittingly, accedes to the arguments of his political and scientific critics. But Dostoevski never intended to argue with his Inquisitor's analysis. Here is what he wrote in a letter dated February 20, 1854: "If anyone proved to me that Christ was outside the truth, and it really was so that the truth was outside Christ, then I would prefer to remain with Christ than with the truth."

In his philosophical writings Percy had tried hard to affirm Dostoevski's position without appearing to be quite so careless of the word *prove* — that is, of the Western tradition of scientific rationalism. In those writings he had invoked the more humble and self-critical elements in that tradition — for instance, the open-minded "pragmatism" of Charles Sanders Peirce — in order to indicate how imprecise any "proof" is. Percy had also shown how the assertiveness of all too many scientists is itself derived from an illusion — if not the illusion of freedom the Inquisitor refers to, then the illusion of certainty. And he had tried to indicate that the "existentialist" viewpoint, so variously advocated by Christians and non-

Christians alike, from Kierkegaard to Heidegger, from Dostoevski himself to Camus and Sartre, need not be opposed to the empirical or rational position. For one thing, we go about trying to affirm ourselves in ways that can be observed and studied. A child learning to speak may not be Jesus Christ (or Sartre's Roquentin) but he is most certainly someone struggling with the same issue of "freedom" that has seized the attention of God and the Devil, believers and atheists. Where do I end, the child asks, and where does the listener begin? What can I do, if anything, that will not in some way affect others? Put differently, how free am I to be anything — including what I then go on to call "myself"?

Christ believed that His words, offered to man, could be what an utterly "scientific" linguist might call a "language-event" — something gets shared between two people, and behold, they are different. It is not only that information has been exchanged, but that existence has been affirmed: Percy's "that is so for you and me," another way of saying "we are." In his essay "The Message in the Bottle," Percy tries to make plain the pointlessness of so many arguments between rationalists and the religious. Maybe the man who used the image of the castaway had in mind the Grand Inquisitor scene when he took such pains to show that there are some situations which demonstrably call for "news," not facts.

Binx Bolling and Billy Barrett are also — and quite explicitly — castaways, pilgrims, seekers. Percy keeps telling us so — but of course he knows that the matter will not rest there. The man who desperately tries to obtain news is also the vulnerable man quite willing, indeed anxious, to grasp any fact, any proclaimed "expertise," as that long sought, final "answer."

The tension in Percy's article "The Message in the Bottle" turns out to be the tension in *The Last Gentleman:* Barrett is adrift, an American castaway, surrounded by land rather than water, by cities rather than island bushes and trees, but nonetheless on a search. It is the same tension Sartre describes when he contrasts a man with the objects around him. His *pour-soi* is Barrett — keenly aware of himself and anxious to know even more: "Whence do I come from, where am I now, whither am I going." Meanwhile there is the *en-soi* — a tree nearby, Barrett's Trav-L-Aire. In *L'Être et le néant*, Sartre delivers as telling a blow against various theoreticians as Kierkegaard did when he ridiculed Hegel. Only Sartre, in addition, turned upon the rest of us — even the most sensitive of us, the Billy Barretts: we are easy prey to mechanistic psychologists, behaviorists, determinists, and "physicalists" of all kinds; we crave our place in a system, a hierarchy, a chart, a series of formulations; they become objects of idolatry rather than a little help in looking at things because, as the Inquisitor said, and as Sartre (no nineteenth-century Russian Christian of passionate faith) would completely agree, we fear and want to run from what is precisely human — the openness a life can possess, the possibilities about us, the choices we can visualize and make. Man's distinctive freedom, not unqualified, but nevertheless his alone, at least on this earth, terrifies each of us. We prefer to join our very nature, the *pour-soi*, to that larger *thereness*, the fixity and certainty of the *en-soi*. Better to be a helpless or predictable "thing" in someone's scheme than to take our chances as individuals with will and the capacity to use it, with ideals and the responsibility to uphold them.

Barrett in the beginning of the novel is the "man to whom all things seem possible and every course of action open." He is an exaggerated version of everyone. Most of us necessarily make at least some decisions, thereby surrendering certain realms of the possible: I live here, not there, do this kind of work, not that. Though Barrett has a job at the beginning of the novel, he soon gives that up. He lives in the YMCA, a transient place, then gives even that up — for the Trav-L-Aire. He always seems ready to buttonhole someone: tell me anything you have to say. But he fends off suggestions, which might lead to commitments: the Dr. Gamows, the pretentious writers or religious zealots come toward him with their temptations, and respectfully, almost ingratiatingly, he says thank you, but no thanks.

Meanwhile Sutter is not inclined to abandon his freedom before any altar; Sutter is the existentialist who refuses the consolation of schools of thought, bodies of belief. He is himself, an individual — and if existentialists have anything in common (they are as unlike with respect to the particulars they espouse as Dostoevski and Heidegger, Sartre and Kierkegaard, Marcel and Camus), it is their insistence upon the extraordinary, almost defiant complexity of each individual: no intellectualized "system" or analytic construct can encompass what William James called "the blooming buzzing confusion" of the mind, let alone the astonishing subtlety of each person's situation or condition. Each day we encounter a tangle of opportunities and restrictions; and there is always "fate" with its surprises, for the good or bad, as well as the capacity we have to act, whatever the constraints upon us.

Existentialists are almost invariably obsessed with death: the ultimate choice anyone has — to end his life. In *The Moviegoer* Lonnie's impending death foreshadows Binx's commitment: I will give myself to another person, rather than keep seeing life from afar, as an inveterate moviegoer and an aloof, sardonic observer. In *The Last Gentleman* Jamie's death at the end of the novel is an intense, powerfully rendered moment worthy of any nineteenth-century novelist. As the youth struggles vainly for life in Santa Fe, a city whose very name (Holy Faith) is of religious significance, Sutter stands nearby, ready to take his own life — an intention he has mentioned repeatedly in his notebooks, read all along by Barrett. On two accounts, then, the author has confronted Barrett with the presence of death, so much with us all through life: Jamie as a dying patient and Sutter as a likely suicide. As was the case with Binx in *The Moviegoer*, Percy's main character in *The Last Gentleman* is shaken to his foundations at the end of the novel. Sutter may yet end his life, but Barrett is now chasing him, wanting to talk. Barrett's spoken "wait" is enough to make Sutter stop his car. Marcel would smile and note a moment of "intersubjectivity." On the last page of the novel Barrett finally can seek out a specific instance of what two hundred pages earlier he fled with all his might: "Naturally in such an intersubjective paradise as this," the author had commented back then, "he soon got the proper horrors. He began to skid a little and catch up with himself like a car on ice. His knee leapt so badly that he had to walk like a spastic, hand thrust through pocket and poking patella with each step."

Percy has no belief in an earthly "intersubjective paradise." He mocks encounter groups, laughs at those who, even in the name of the church or religion, talk rather too glibly about "community." Even existentialist words or ideas can become dogma for us; we are ingenious enough to take anyone's phrases and use them gratuitously or sacrilegiously: St. Paul's "the letter killeth." Every existentialist philosopher has been haunted by the knowledge that however careful he be, whatever cautions, indirections, or subtleties of language and thinking he calls upon, there is that urge for self-surrender, for immersion in Sartre's *en-soi*, in Marcel's "inauthentic," in Kierkegaard's various maneuvers (rotation, repetition). We try anything, listen to anyone, so long as we can avoid the risks that go with the exertion of freedom: a step that is our own, rather than yet another gesture of compliance.

Percy's Binx Bolling and Billy Barrett avoid decisions whenever possible, at least insofar as they are of any real significance. Barrett will leave Macy's for a trip with the Vaughts; he will lose interest in Dr. Gamow and become taken with Dr. Sutter Vaught's notebook; or for a moment he will abandon previous infatuations and appear ready to consider marrying Kitty. But until the very end of the novel he comes across as an exceedingly slippery ball; no one is really going to get a grip on him. Only in the last paragraphs does this austere, self-protective posture yield. He *decides:* I want to get to know this doctor, about ten years my elder, and I will make that as plain as is possible; so, for once I will reach actively outside myself. All his clever, circuitous, ever-so-prickly tactics are abandoned, and for a change we have action, not ploys and more ploys of the mind: "Strength flowed like oil into his muscles and he ran with great joyous ten-foot antelope bounds."

At times *The Last Gentleman* brings to mind Kafka: the prose becomes terse and enigmatic, the plot gets mysterious. Specifically, there is a strong resemblance to Kafka's *Amerika,* his only comic novel, which also portrays a search by a youth, against the background of the American landscape. Karl

Rossman is as open, innocent, and responsive to the world as Barrett. Kafka can be more brutal, more stark, than Percy has it in his heart to be; but Rossman is yet another itinerant seeker who keeps moving — always lonely, though still with hope. It will be a miracle, Kafka tells us (his "celestial spell") if the search is successful. No character of Kafka's ever escaped all that much from himself: the guilt, the relentless sense of imperfection, and, most significant, perhaps, the fatalistic resignation — that suffering is one's destiny. But Karl, like Barrett." Sutter proclaims his joke, but Acts (8:26–39) tells us that smile openly and more than briefly.

Percy himself has in retrospect realized certain similarities between his second novel and *The Idiot*. His lifelong friend Shelby Foote recalls a conversation: "He said to me, Shelby, it's *The Idiot*, that's what I've written. I told him that he'd done a good job, and so the comparison was quite justified. There are differences between the two novels, of course; but I can see why Walker would look back and suddenly realize the important similarities." It is easy, perhaps too easy, for a reader to bracket Dostoevski's Myshkin with Percy's Barrett: two Christ-like figures, whose lack of guile, gentleness, and candor cut their own kind of swath. Myshkin is one of Kierkegaard's "knights of faith": he trusts everyone, and ultimately, manages to unnerve a few people — even as Christ is the One Whom Dostoevski believed we all want to rid ourselves of, so challenging is His message. Myshkin's lack of ambition, his genuine decency, his refusal to let others offend him, his almost shameless trust in others, are matched by Barrett, who is also that most perplexing of people — the man who refuses to accept the judgments others make on themselves as the final word. For a man whose intelligence and manner can be so sly and idiosyncratic, Barrett is surprisingly outspoken and direct; like Myshkin, he won't let go of others, even when they have been rude, nasty, insulting — Sutter, for instance. And like Myshkin, he offers a redemptive kind of hope which those he encounters, however self-contained or tormented, find irresistible.

At one point toward the end of the novel Sutter asks: "Are

you Philip and is this the Gaza Desert?" As usual, the man addressed is all innocence: "Sir? No sir. I am Williston Barrett." Sutter proclaims his joke, but Acts (8:26–39) tells us that in Gaza Philip met a eunuch, told him the good news of Christ's coming, baptized him, and went on — more people to meet and similarly inform — until finally he came to Caesarea. In the end, Dr. Vaught is by no means eager to hear whatever news Barrett might have, but Barrett has made a decision; he does have news: "Dr. Vaught, I need you." Percy has tried to indicate how something exchanged between two people is quite different from a monologue — and unfortunately, all too much existentialist literature has become just that: the endless self-avowals directed, it seems, to the speaker's or writer's mirror image.

Sutter's notebooks are a case in point. They are a repository for many of Percy's philosophical ideas — to develop them novelistically would have required a novel twice the size — as well as an ingenious way for him to record the sadness and disorder which can plague a mind stubbornly turned in on itself. "I am the only sincere American," Sutter announces to himself at one point — rather a bold assertion, especially for a person who steadfastly denies himself a chance to spend time with and get to know even his next of kin. Whatever the merits of his claim, he comes up with some brilliant asides, both theological and sociological, borrowed perhaps from the notebook of a Louisiana novelist: "Main Street, U.S.A. — a million dollar segregation church on one corner, a drugstore with dirty magazines on the other, a lewd movie on the third, and on the fourth a B-girl bar with condom dispensers in the gents' room. Delay-your-climax cream. Even our official decency is a lewd sort of decency. Watch a soap opera on TV where everyone is decent (and also sad, you will notice, as sad as lewdness is sad; I am the only American who is both lewd and merry). Beyond any question, these people who sit and talk so sorrowfully and decently are fumbling with each other under the table. There is no other alternative for them."

"Even if you were right," he remarks to himself on another occasion. "Let us say you were right: that man is a wayfarer (i.e., not transcending being nor immanent being but wayfarer) who therefore stands in the way of hearing a piece of news which is of the utmost importance to him (i.e., his salvation) and which he had better attend to. So you say to him: Look, Barrett, your trouble is due not to a disorder of your organism but to the human condition, that you do well to be afraid and you do well to forget everything which does not pertain to your salvation. That is to say, your amnesia is not a symptom. So you say: Here is the piece of news you have been waiting for, and you tell him. What does Barrett do? He attends in that eager flattering way of his and at the end of it he might even say *yes!* But he will receive the news from his high seat of transcendence as one more item of psychology, throw it into his immanent meat-grinder, and wait to see if he feels better. He told me he's in favor of the World's Great Religions. What are you going to do about that?"

He then goes on: "I am not in favor of any such thing. We are doomed to the transcendence of abstraction and I choose the only reentry into the world which remains to us. What is better then than the beauty and exaltation of the practice of transcendence (science and art) and of the delectation of immanence, the beauty and the exaltation of lewd love? What is better than this: one works hard during the day in the front line and with the comradeship of science and at night one goes to La Fonda, where one encounters a stranger, a handsome woman. We drink, we two handsome thirty-five-year-olds, she dark-eyed, shadowy of cheek, wistful in her own transcendence. We dance. The guitar makes the heart soar. We eat hearty. Under the table a gentle pressure of the knee. One speaks into her ear at some length. 'Let's go.' 'But we ordered dinner.' 'We can come back.' 'All right.' The blood sings with voluptuousness and tenderness."

And finally: "Women, of course, are the natural pornographers today, because they are not only dispossessed by science of the complexus of human relations (all but the orgasm) but are also kept idle in their suburban houses with nothing to do but read pseudo-science articles in Reader's Digest and dirty novels (one being the natural preamble of the other). U.S.

culture is the strangest in history, a society of decent, generous sex-ridden men and women who leave each other to their lusts, the men off to the city and conventions, abandoning their wives to the suburbs, which are the very home and habitation of lewd dreams. A dirty deal for women, if you ask me. Don't be too hard on Rita. She is peeved, not perverted. (The major discovery of my practice: that there are probably no such entities as 'schizophrenia' and 'homosexuality,' conceived as Platonic categories, but only peevishness, revenge, spitefulness, dishonesty, fear, loneliness, lust, and despair — which is not to say we don't need psychiatrists. You people don't seem to be doing too well, you know.)"

With *The Last Gentleman* Percy consolidated himself as a writer who works on the borderline of philosophy, theology, and literature. *The Moviegoer* was proved not just an aberration, a one-time stroke of luck by a man who had been storing up ideas for a long time and needed a novel to add to the task of exposition he had set for himself. *The Last Gentleman* revealed a man of fiction who clearly enjoyed the old-fashioned virtues of the trade — storytelling, the amusement and edification of readers through the novelist's ability to use his imagination, conjure up all sorts of people, events, predicaments. But it was also the work of a man who had, perhaps, decided that if some things, as Rilke insisted, are unsayable (his *unsäglich*), a few important ideas can be given the flesh of life.

Between 1966 and 1971 Percy continued to refrain from philosophical speculation, at least in the essay or article form. "I guess I've become a novelist," he could say, with just the right amount of casual uncertainty: tomorrow night might bring a new set of circumstances, a change of tack for him. The result, in early 1971, was *Love in the Ruins*, for him a departure of sorts, and one greeted with a good deal of enthusiasm, with guarded endorsement, and with outright disapproval. The novel has been repeatedly categorized as futuristic satire with the usual dose of dire prophecy, in the tradition of Orwell's *1984*, Huxley's *Brave New World* or Yevgeny Zamyatin's *We*. The main character is Dr. Thomas More, a forty-five-year-old rather heavy-drinking psychiatrist who has had his share of personal tragedy: the death of his only daughter, Samantha, and thereafter the loss of his wife to the secular cultists — food faddism, astrology, and on and on — who have become increasingly prominent in recent years. The doctor has himself been declared crazy, hospitalized, and kept under lock and key for a good long time — depression, self-destructive behavior, a failure to "adjust," the whole litany of words and phrases that Percy finds so ironic, in view of the institutionalized madness we have come to take for granted: "I have been reading my usual late-night fare, Stedmann's *History of World War I*," More remarks. "For weeks now I've been on the Battle of Verdun, which killed half a million men, lasted a year, and left the battle lines unchanged. Here began the hemorrhage and death by suicide of the old Western world: white Christian Caucasian Europeans, sentimental music-loving Germans and rational clear-minded Frenchmen, slaughtering each other without passion. 'The men in the trenches did not hate each other,' wrote Stedmann. 'As for the generals, they respected or condemned each other precisely as colleagues in the same profession.' "

The man who does that reading does so at three o'clock in the morning. As for others, they are still, as the song goes, dancing "the whole night through." Percy indicates how much whistling in the dark goes on, despite all the "enlightenment" we have managed to come up with: trips to the moon, computers for every turn of anyone's mind. And he has a hard time persuading himself, never mind his readers, that he is looking all that far into the future. He directs forceful satire at what he once referred to as "the Western democratic-technological humanistic view of man." In this novel, more than in the other two, he bears down hard on that "view," dissecting, clarifying, indicating soft spots, contradictions, ironies, or illusions, some of the last called "reality" or "scientific knowledge." We are not at all made to feel removed from Dr. More's so-called futuristic world, but rather kinsmen of his in the here-and-now.

Just two years after *Love in the Ruins* appeared (its first chapter describes Dr. More's effort to hide from snipers in a Howard

Johnson's motel somewhere in southern Louisiana), New Orleans was virtually paralyzed (June 7 and 8, 1973) by a sniper who lodged himself in a Howard Johnson's motel. I happened to be in New Orleans at the time, visiting Dr. Percy. In his home, across Lake Pontchartrain, I read the *Times-Picayune:* snipers had started setting fires in the motel on Sunday the seventh, about the time people were going to church. Louisiana's attorney-general had declared: "I am now convinced that there is an underground national suicide group bent on creating terror in America." Percy watched the television coverage intently, sometimes turning off the sound as the cameras roamed over the hotel or the streets nearby — as if he knew all too well what would be said, and wanted to let his own mind find words for what was being shown. His dentist had just asked him if he were a prophet. The New Orleans papers had been trying to reach him: how was it that a novelist writing something about the future, writing a humorous novel, writing a projected fantasy, had so precisely anticipated such an incident?

He shrugged his shoulders. He hadn't anticipated anything: "What's happening in this country is not so hard to notice. I think as a novelist I had to bring things out some — that's my job — but I don't think it's any great secret, where we are and where we're heading. The New York intellectuals, the Southern racists, the people out in California, with a new fad every six months — they're all different in ways, but they're all part of America, and they have more in common than they'd like to believe, I'm afraid. I mean, we all live in this century, and God is dead, we're told, and what you should believe in is yourself, your 'potential,' or your neighbor, *his* 'potential,' or some social change and a few more 'discoveries.' I think we ought to explore what 'brings us together' — to use a phrase the politicians always throw at us. There are assumptions which all of us share — friends or enemies, black or white. I guess a novelist ought to try to make what he sees happening around him as vivid as possible. He tells a story. Like Flannery O'Connor said: you use every trick you can think of to get the reader's attention; you want to *show* him something, *tell* him something:

193

show and tell! But I don't think I exaggerated too much in the novel. And I'm not sure I looked so very far into the future."

There is no question that this novel offers Percy's most mordant and relentless critique of contemporary Western "culture" or "civilization." Nevertheless, the familiar Percy humor and sharp but compassionate eye for human foibles are present. There is, as usual, a plot that holds the reader, and quite enough action — all of which is to say that Percy continues to be a good novelist, whatever his other (polemical, critical) interests. Dr. Tom More tells the story — and again, despite Henry James's admonition, the first-person narrative form works out quite well. Percy's skill as a narrator is more developed than in his earlier novels. The sentences tend to be shorter, crisper, more pungent. In a few words he delivers not only good scenic description but pointed social and political sideswipes. As before, the first sentence does more than set the stage; a person is located, in all his and the world's dislocation, then set on the way to find whatever destiny seems, finally, to be his: "Now in these dread latter days of the old violent beloved U.S.A. and of the Christ-forgetting Christ-haunted death-dealing Western world I came to myself in a grove of young pines and the question came to me: has it happened at last?"

Has what happened? He is waiting for the world to end. The novel is in one sense no more "futuristic" than the Bible, passages from which, slightly modified, keep on appearing: "These are bad times. Principalities and powers are everywhere victorious. Wickedness flourishes in high places." Meanwhile, people watch and wait, not expectantly as Christians, but with the exuberant self-confidence of More's friends and associates, who proclaim, like John Reed, only not on the spur of the moment, that they have seen the "future," and it works. As for Dr. More, he indulges his comic self-centeredness, which is a mask he struggles to keep on — aided constantly by alcohol. Percy makes it quite clear at the beginning that he has his eye scanning the entire horizon — as much of America as he can fathom: "The sky is a clear rinsed cobalt after the rain. Wet pine growth reflects the sunlight like steel knitting needles. The grove steams and smells of turpentine. Far away the thunderhead, traveling fast, humps over on the horizon like a troll. Directly above, a hawk balances on a column of air rising from the concrete geometry of the cloverleaf. Not a breath stirs.

"The young pine I am sitting against has a tumor and is bowed to fit my back. I am sweating and broken out in hives from drinking gin fizzes but otherwise quite comfortable. This spot, on the lower reaches of the southwest cusp, was chosen carefully. From it I command three directions of the interstates and by leaning over the lip of the culvert can look through to the fourth, eastern approach."

Dr. Tom More is in many respects the same person we have met in *The Moviegoer* and *The Last Gentleman*. Like Binx Bolling and Billy Barrett his body registers his apprehensions: the scalp tingles; there are "prickling sensations." "Noxious particles" are on hand, omens of disaster that plagued poor Barrett, and now give Dr. More the sense that time is indeed running out. And, of course, even as Binx was going to be a doctor, and Barrett is repeatedly confronted by Dr. Sutter Vaught, this novel also provides us with a physician — one who wants desperately to mend his broken self, but who seems to have given up hope of ever succeeding, because the world around him appears hopelessly bent on destruction. Jesus Christ, physician of the spirit, healer of men, had plenty of followers but few believers; likewise, Dr. More spends a good deal of time finding out what it is that ails men (his Qualitative Quantitative Ontological Lapsometer is the wonderfully antic instrument for doing so), but as a result wins not real comrades but shrewd enthusiasts, ready in a second to develop, exploit, propagandize, utilize — all the things done in the name of "progress."

More's ancestor, the St. Thomas More of history, tried to envision a utopia. The novel's Thomas More is on hand to glimpse what has come of all that fervid expectation: the New Jerusalem which one messianic dreamer after another has promised. Mixing seriousness and comic satire in a way that no doubt has puzzled many — is the author's intention to mock or to be devastatingly accurate? — Percy gives this vignette of More: "I, for example, am a Roman Catholic, albeit a bad one. I believe in the Holy Catholic Apostolic and Roman Church, in God the Father, in the election of the Jews, in Jesus Christ His Son our Lord, who founded the Church on Peter his first vicar, which will last until the end of the world. Some years ago, however, I stopped eating Christ in Communion, stopped going to mass, and have since fallen into a disorderly life. I believe in God and the whole business but I love women best, music and science next, whiskey next, God fourth, and my fellowman hardly at all. Generally I do as I please. A man, wrote John, who says he believes in God and does not keep his commandments is a liar. If John is right, then I am a liar. Nevertheless, I still believe."

As for More's beloved Catholic Church, here is what it has come to: "Our Catholic church here split into three pieces: (1) the American Catholic Church whose new Rome is Cicero, Illinois; (2) the Dutch schismatics who believe in relevance but not God; (3) the Roman Catholic remnant, a tiny scattered flock with no place to go."

Then, there are others — the disaffected ones: "Bantu guerrillas, dropouts from Tulane and Vanderbilt, M.I.T. and Loyola; draft dodgers, deserters from the Swedish army, psychopaths and pederasts from Memphis and New Orleans whose practices were not even to be tolerated in New Orleans; antipapal Catholics, malcontented Methodists, ESPers, UFOers, Aquarians, ex–Ayn Randers, Choctaw Zionists who have returned to their ancestral hunting grounds, and even a few old graybeard Kerouac beats, wiry old sourdoughs of the spirit who carry pilgrim staffs, recite sutras, and leap from hummock to hummock as agile as mountain goats."

If such are the polyglot inhabitants of the swamp, located not far from More's home and the motel where he is temporarily lodged, in the town a different situation holds: there are "all manner of conservative folk, graduates of Bob Jones University, retired Air Force colonels, passed-over Navy commanders, ex-Washington, D.C., policemen, patriotic chiropractors, two officials of the National Rifle Association, and six conservative proctologists."

More is no moviegoer. Here is how he sizes up films and what it is like to go see them: "The most popular Left films are dirty movies from Sweden. All-time Knothead favorites, on the other hand, include *The Sound of Music, Flubber,* and *Ice Capades of 1981,* clean movies all.

"I've stopped going to movies. It is hard to say which is more unendurable, the sentimental blasphemy of Knothead movies like *The Sound of Music* or sitting in a theater with strangers watching other strangers engage in sexual intercourse and sodomy on the giant 3-D Pan-a-Vision screen."

As for America's literary and political life, neither is very hard to portray: "American literature is not having its finest hour. The Southern gothic novel yielded to the Jewish masturbatory novel, which in turn gave way to the WASP homosexual novel, which has nearly run its course. The Catholic literary renascence, long awaited, failed to materialize. But old favorites endure, like venerable Harold Robbins and Jacqueline Susann, who continue to write the dirty clean books so beloved by the American housewife. Gore Vidal is the grand old man of American letters.

"Both political parties have had their triumphs.

"The Lefts succeeded in removing 'In God We Trust' from pennies.

"The Knotheads enacted a law requiring compulsory prayers in the black public schools and made funds available for birth control in Africa, Asia, and Alabama."

Against a background of such mild extrapolations, Dr. More makes his various comments. "It is not uncommon nowadays," he says, "to see patients suffering from angelism-bestialism." The diagnostic phrase is one more way to approach the polarity of the abstract as against the concrete. Dr. Sutter Vaught's preoccupations with transcendence-immanence have now become Dr. More's observation that people come up with all kinds of grandiose generalizations (Love Thy Neighbor, Be Kind, Where the Id Was, There Shall the Ego Be, Make the World Safe for Democracy) but at the same time show themselves mean or lascivious, crude or insensitive in their specific, everyday dealings with other human beings. They love mankind in general; they are "bestial" with particular individuals, including themselves (masochism). And that is the great puzzle Dr. Percy believes ought haunt more of us — the central glaring, yet often unacknowledged, fact that every single utopian promise, whether its origin was in the natural or social sciences, in politics or in philosophical theory, has ultimately foundered on the "condition" Dr. More describes. "Angelism" gets proposed, but "bestialism" persists. Why? What does the persistence tell us about man — especially if it is a phenomenon we keep on overlooking, as century after century we proclaim new sources of salvation, yet all the while demonstrate a remarkable consistency of behavior?

This novel contains Percy's most emphatic and lengthy assault on that school of psychology known as "behaviorism." In several of his philosophical essays, Percy had indicated quite clearly how little use he had for the philosophical elaboration of conditioning and learning theory publicized by B. F. Skinner. *Love in the Ruins* is saturated with satirical frontal assaults and casual asides directed at more than the psychological or linguistic arguments Skinner and others (J. B. Watson, Clark Hull) have made in recent decades. It is a state of mind Percy wants to warn against by portraying, though with no great hope that anything he writes will avail much. He makes clear how pervasive and triumphant he believes the various manipulative and reductionist theories of social scientists are: they have become, in essence, this nation's "philosophy of life." Conservatives (Percy's Knotheads) may have different "goals" from liberals and radicals, blacks from whites, but regardless of background or persuasion those who are examined by Dr. More's "spiritual stethoscope" have learned to see "things as theories" and themselves "as a shadow." Percy has More ask "who of us now is not so strangely alone that it is the cool clinical touch of the stranger that serves best to treat his loneliness?" The lapsometer measures the sad development: "Only in man does the self miss itself, *fall* from itself."

Again Sartre's notion of "estrangement" is influential. The conservative golf player at the country club who has a "program" for himself shares with the liberal activist who is trying to "realize a potential" the notion that there is an abstract

"process" or "theory" by means of which he can be both understood and interpreted. Neither of them, in Percy's words, simply dares "reenter the lovely ordinary world." It is an important phrase, and probably the one which best explains what
happens at the end of each novel: Binx, Billy, and Tom finally,
and with little fanfare and no long-winded proclamations,
"reenter." The verb reflects Percy's point of view, most pointedly given expression by Dr. Sutter Vaught: we go into the
orbit of transcendence, become heady about ourselves, lose
touch with ourselves (endless intellectualizations about "mental function" notwithstanding), and unwittingly become things
to ourselves.

When Percy spoofs someone who talks on and on about the
"warmth and tenderness" he feels toward his wife, when he
asks, "Why doesn't he just say he loves her?" when he mocks
the expression "interpersonal gynecologist," when he does
likewise with the phrase "creative nonviolent violence" (or
"violence in the service of nonviolence"), he is not simply being
wickedly facetious. Nor is he of a mind to make one more case
against jargon, against the self-serving if not self-congratulatory slogans we all tend to find for ourselves. He is after something more ominous and, he would openly say, more sinful. A
Christian, he believes in the doctrine of original sin, *and* in the
obligation men and women have to assume responsibility for
their lives. That is to say, he believes that we are "not pigs, nor
angels." We are, he says again in this novel, pilgrims —
"wayfarers on a journey."

At one point he describes what a pilgrim, a wayfarer, a
seeker, does *not* end up as: "a self successfully playing at being
a self that is not itself." When one avoids saying directly what
one has in mind or feels, when one forfeits one's own authority
to others — phrase-makers, trend-setters, theorists who insist
on fitting all of life into their schemes — one is tricking oneself,
surrendering one's critical judgment, while all the while pre-
tending the contrary: "I am actualizing myself and achieving
good interpersonal relationships," or "working through my
oedipal conflicts," or working to "implement the 'Good Society.'" That surrender of the self is what obsesses existen-

tialists — the "inauthentic," the deceptions Sartre or Kierkegaard describe. Over a century ago Dostoevski spoke as more than a shrewd psychologist, aware how much people crave directions, explanations that at least for a while smother ambiguity and make everything crystal clear. He was at the very least a moralist, as are all the existentialists, professed Christians or convinced atheists. We are capable of standing on our own, looking honestly at ourselves and others, and we sin when we refuse to exert that capability, giving ourselves, instead, to any glib expert or leader who happens to come our way with a promise of this or that: maturity, happiness, a political or social paradise.

"Nothing is quite like it's cracked up to be. And nobody is crazier than people." Those words of Dr. More's are not just the skeptic's, the cynic's, the troubled man's — wishing for company. Pride for Percy is inevitable; as are confusion and paradox in human affairs. Those who claim otherwise, who offer one *Weltanschauung* after another, who simplify not only the complex but the ineffable do so because they are tempted by pride themselves and because they know how welcome their efforts will be to others. The result: "the deep abscess in the soul of Western man," which Percy's Dr. More wants to diagnose, and just as important, heal — at least in his own life, to the degree that he can. His lapsometer, perhaps a bit optimistically, will offer "the first hope of bridging the dread chasm that has rent the soul of Western man since the famous philosopher Descartes ripped body loose from mind and turned the very soul into a ghost that haunts its own house."

Descartes was, of course, a mathematical genius, and by his own statement, "incredibly ambitious." He was a contemporary of Pascal's, and they shared an intense scientific curiosity which heralded the end of the Catholic Church's ability to control, through condemnation and excommunication, man's interest in the world around him. The Inquisition not only stopped Galileo; Descartes held up for a number of years one essay he wrote (*Le Monde*, essentially a Copernican affirmation that the earth really did circle the sun) and modified some of his later essays and "discourses" to protect himself. Nevertheless, he was called an atheist, not necessarily by unthinking religious zealots. He dared give the mind its own authority and independence, a step as radical as Galileo's with respect to the place of the earth in the solar system. Galileo realized that we are but a small part of something almost incomprehensibly large — and by implication, beyond the ken of anyone, be he cardinal or layman. Descartes saw us as on our own, psychologically — yet another blow at that organic unity and solidarity characteristic of the Middle Ages.

For Descartes rational inquiry was more than a mere interest, or even passion; he allowed his mind to pursue "essences" without restraint. The contrast is with Pascal, who tethered himself closely to experiments, to what can be verified. Descartes' ambitiousness was more than matched by Pascal's humility; for the latter there were not only limits to speculation, but outright dangers: the thinker and writer becomes (not always consciously, or out of malice) his own God — and ideas and explanations his children, hence confused with life itself. The problem is one of reification; we treat mental constructions as if they possess more than figurative or suggestive truth. They *are;* they get defended, attacked, proclaimed, saluted, discarded gladly or mournfully. Worst of all, they become tyrants: entire lives are willingly and sometimes fiercely consecrated to the particular reality a given mental construction has become — an idea transformed into a compelling ideology.

Percy does not consider Descartes an enemy, at least not in the usual sense of the word. Like Heidegger, Percy simply wants to ask questions which Descartes left to "religious authorities," with understandable if concealed scorn, given the hostility of the Church to his kind of independent mind. They are the familiar existential questions of this century — who am I? what is the meaning of life?; and they are rather susceptible to answers which often seem both glib and absurdly ponderous: I am an interpersonal nexus, the product of a social and cultural system, and so on. Descartes wanted to explore those questions objectively, as matters of scientific inquiry — or not at all. Pascal disagreed; for him they were questions that are best deferred, in favor of this kind: what kind of person is it who asks such questions in the first place, and what does the answer to *that* question tell us about the way we might want to think about ourselves? In the end Pascal had an answer, one not always taken with the degree of seriousness he intended. We are gamblers, he said, and it is that "condition" which deserves emphasis, rather than certain facts, which we have every right to discover, but not turn into objects of faith.

A gambler may not be a castaway, but there are resemblances. Both are somewhat desperate, and are looking hard for news: what happened in the past or will happen in the future that settled or will settle my fate. Such desperation warrants recognition; and Heidegger, like Kierkegaard before him, remarked upon the irony that philosophers or psychological theorists make the broadest statements about man and the structures of his mind, yet ignore what might be called his unique characteristic: the one in the universe who is desperate — Kierkegaard's "fear and trembling." Man the gambler or castaway is desperate because he knows how little time he has to learn something — not about the relationship of his mind to his body, not about the molecular structure of astral bodies, not about the reflexes within us, or the personality traits which for various reasons we develop (all very interesting, and *not* to be cast aside in an hysterical, know-nothing exaltation of the "senses"), but rather about his prospects: am I going to win or lose, and what chance, if any, do I have to learn about the connections (past or future) between my life on this island, the earth, and all "life" on the mainland (the universe)?

As soon as Percy has Dr. More speak of the modern soul as a ghost that haunts us, he moves on to a new section, which he describes as "At the Director's office to hear the good news about my article and invention." In our world, many of the West's intelligentsia behave as if God is to be found in one or another director's office; from him "the good news" is received — and it tells about inventions, hypotheses, or programs which become for us equivalents of the daily missal. The "news" Dr. More hears is not surprising; his discovery, like everyone else's for several centuries, will be "applied," used for the betterment of mankind, the development of human potential, the improvement of society — the high-sounding phrases are numerous, and it is not easy to disagree with them as "goals." Percy's Dr. More is himself in their grip: he is a reformer, intent on changing the world so that more people "fulfill" themselves, and the world keeps moving in a "positive" direction. The Skinner box, he realizes, is an absurd failure; but his instrument, the lapsometer, might work. Certainly if he would only go along with the Director, and all the other directors around, his own news would be good: recognition, prizes, the designation of leading humanitarian, or brilliant scientist, or learned, pragmatic theorist.

He is tempted; but he is also driven to liquor, driven crazy, in fact, by his sense that the whole enterprise is a dangerous fraud, that he has fatally deceived himself, that (in other words) he is the familiar sinner, full of himself and clothed in the self-protective and self-enhancing pieties which are always available. His struggle with himself is the subject matter of *Love in the Ruins*. His ancestor of the same name was wise, thoughtful, farsighted, a martyr, whereas he readily admits to being foolish, self-indulgent, full of despair — and anxious to take advantage of whatever opportunities present themselves. Still, the two men share more than a name. The modern Dr. More can dream of utopias inconceivable to his predecessor. And he does. Moreover, he can *implement* his dreams — that important verb that civilized and progressive people have learned to use. But the crisis he goes through, the testing of his soul, reveals him to be only somewhat tempted. He may want to conquer the whole world with his mind, but the sight of a particular human being (in this instance, an old man whom the various experts and authorities, for the most "progressive" of reasons, want to do away with, because he hasn't responded to various manipulative "programs") inspires what in the Bible and in the Book of Common Prayer is called lovingkindness.

Dr. More reaches out to a kindred soul, does so honestly, persuasively; that is, a number of people are moved in response to the "authenticity" he demonstrates. In the hospital pit, defending an old man about to be carted away and disposed of, the doctor is himself and no one else. No matter what he says, of course, many laugh at him, consider him impolitic, rash, overwrought, or, in the clutch, crazy. He himself realizes that there is a shrewder, more "sensible," more "practical" way of behaving: why rock the boat and challenge the high and mighty head-on? Patience is a virtue, and so is fortitude. But Dr. More is an uncanny mixture of, on the one hand, an ambitious, messianic twentieth-century scientist who wants to make a point, prove his ideas true, and, not incidentally, achieve renown, and on the other, the self-critical, lonely, honorable man Percy keeps coming up with in his novels — deluded like the rest of us, caught in all the "traps" a given society has waiting for its various members, but also sincere and upright, and so almost without guile. Late in the novel, when we know Dr. More quite well, and the risk of turning him into a vehicle for philosophical abstraction is much reduced, he says: "What I want is no longer the Nobel, screw prizes, but just to figure out what I've hit on. Some day a man will walk into my office as ghost or beast or ghost-beast and walk out as a man, which is to say my sovereign wanderer, lordly exile, worker and waiter and watcher."

The good doctor has struggled hard with an assortment of behaviorists, and is just beginning to realize that he, like those he would like to heal, has to face himself in the radical way Heidegger had in mind when he used the word *eigentlich*. In German the word means what it does in English — genuine or authentic. But the word literally translates as "own most," and such a translation, awkward though it be, offers some protection against those who would take "authentic" and throw it around all too casually: from an authentic antique or restoration to an authentic experience or personality! For Heidegger death presents a great opportunity to the willing seeker, the confused man who wants to know before he breathes his last breath what at rock bottom he can consider his "own most," because it has been rescued from the "everydayness" of his life — the pressures, the boredom, the fearful ingratiation, the surrender of more and more personal territory in the interests of "success" or "adjustment" or practicality, or simply out of exhaustion if not despair: what is the use?

When More intervenes to prevent a man's death at the hands of those who have taken upon themselves the right to decide such matters, he is in the kind of situation Heidegger spelled out as critical: a life-and-death situation in several senses of the word. At such moments we have a chance to find out a lot about ourselves. In every Percy novel there is a death; in this one Dr. More's daughter had died, precipitating one kind of crisis, and the question of what to do with the elderly patient — kill him "for the social good," or allow him his life and dignity — becomes for Dr. More a critical issue: to go along with others or find and assert unmistakably what he himself stands for.

The novel's ending has the familiar Percy ring: brief and undramatic. Dr. More has undergone no sudden and convincing conversion. He seems to be a quiet churchgoer who has a sense of humor about the liturgy and his fellow parishioners, as well as about the priests who hear his confession. He has staked a position for himself hardly worthy of a prophet or a brilliant and discerning critic — a house amid others in an American town: "Barbecuing in my sackcloth.

"The turkey is smoking well. The children have gone to bed, but they'll be up at dawn to open their presents.

"The night is clear and cold. There is no moon. The light of the transmitter lies hard by Jupiter, ruby and diamond in the plush velvet sky. Ellen is busy in the kitchen fixing stuffing and sweet potatoes. Somewhere in the swamp a screech owl cries.

"I'm dancing around trying to keep warm, hands in pockets. It is Christmas Day and the Lord is here, a holy night and surely that is all one needs.

"On the other hand I want a drink. Fetching the Early Times from a clump of palmetto, I take six drinks in six minutes. Now I'm dancing and singing old Sinatra songs and the *Salve Regina,* cutting the fool like David before the ark or like Walter Huston doing a jig when he struck it rich in the Sierra Madre."

He has chosen Ellen; she is one of three women he has been with earlier in the Howard Johnson's motel and thereabouts. The other two, Moira and Lola, were attractive and gifted, but as Percy portrays them, they come across as victims, like Dr. More himself, of any number of trends, fads, vogues. Percy gently but persistently indicates the price a strikingly beautiful Moira pays for "her perfect oval face, a face unwounded, un-scarred, unlined, unmasked by sadness or joy. . . ." It is not just that she reads *Cosmopolitan* so faithfully; it is that she would quite willingly abandon that habit, one gathers, for anything somebody suggests. Dr. More loves her, also loves Lola, "a big beautiful cellist, [who] is a wonderful girl." But we never get to find out who she is, either — in contrast to all the other women who are big or beautiful or wonderful or musically talented.

It can be argued that their lack of "depth" represents a blind spot of the author's. Another author, perhaps a woman novelist, might not be content to let the case rest there, but rather show what a novelist better than anyone else can — the lined and scarred minds or hearts that are hidden by all that fresh and unspoiled skin. Is Percy limited in his capacity to develop women characters, or is his central character a badly hurt man for just that reason — *he* is limited: he can't for a long while seem to free himself from all sorts of vogues and clichés, from the abstract way in which he sees his women friends?

Ellen eventually becomes his second wife, and the choice is interesting. For one thing it *is* a choice; in this novel, as in its two predecessors, the central figure makes an unassuming but important decision. Ellen is a Georgia Presbyterian with a mind of her own. She, too, could profit from closer, more subtle representation, but the author does give us a good sense of her: she has standards, beliefs, a vigorous conscience, and under no circumstances will she yield to the various temptations, re-quests, pleas the doctor puts in her way. She works. She is not easily intimidated. And her protectiveness toward Dr. More does not come across as tactical or ultimately possessive. For all the love he shows toward those three young women, he has lost both a daughter and a wife, and his guard is up high right through the novel. Without making a fuss about it, Percy keeps having Ellen *there*, ready to help, tough in the face of More's weaknesses, admirable in her own limitations: the streak of Puritanism she possesses is actually a welcome relief from the panicky, showy hedonism and its reverse, a bitter and narrow prudery, which together dominate Percy's not so extended projection into the future of American life. Ellen will look after her husband not because she thinks it is "right" to do so, or because she is in any way forced to do so, but out of something "own most" in her, which the author does manage to evoke.

It comes as something of a relief when, finally, in the last few pages of the novel, Dr. More starts eating well. All that Tang and vodka he has been taking in. All those duck eggs slurped down. When he moves hungrily toward a plate of steaming grits and dry, crisp bacon, one is surprised and relieved; at last the man is sitting quietly at a table and digging in. It turns out that he is digging in more broadly. Every Percy novel ends on Marcel's theme of concreteness, Heidegger's "own most": the lapsometer and other such schemes, grand designs, brilliant projects or propositions are put aside in favor of a step toward a person and a specific kind of life (a beginning of it) with that person. No magical cure is wrought. A new kind of human being does not appear. We get no promise of a life hitherto undreamed of — which everyone will soon live. Nor does the plot suddenly generate a nicely coy and indirect message for the reader: try *this* and see how your life will go. Wayfarers continue on their way. Seekers keep looking. Dr. More is older than Binx Bolling and Billy Barrett, and so his travel, the form of his journey, may also be different. But all three appear in many respects the same to their friends and neighbors. The "changes" in them are subtle, undramatic, tentative.

It may be that Dr. More has moved beyond Bolling and Barrett, at least to Kierkegaard's way of looking at things. Percy's moviegoer at last stands firm and digs in. Barrett at last stays with a person and digs in: I'll no longer bounce about from moment to moment, making no real impression on anyone and letting no one do likewise with respect to me. But Dr. More strikes one as a middle-aged man who has long before tried just about all of Kierkegaard's "aesthetic" tricks, who has long before taken his ethical stand, only to find both himself and everyone else (well, everyone except Ellen) hopelessly cynical, greedy, selfish, or thoughtless, regardless of social position or political persuasion. Perhaps the doctor's movement toward

Ellen, so unpredictable, really, in terms of the novel, is meant to indicate that "leap of faith" Kierkegaard describes: the ethical man seems almost to reverse himself, go against his own hard-won ethical principles.

A man who wanted to know so much and save the whole world ends up tending to his lawn, his home, his wife. An abnegation of responsibility? The collapse of a "creative" man, just when he was on the brink of "self-realization"? Or a paradoxical "leap of faith" on the part of a tortured believer who once and for all has submitted himself to whatever design (including the attendant risks) that Divine Providence has in mind for him? The obligation to renounce pride, in all its varied and sometimes deceptive manifestations, is a lifelong one, More seems to have decided. He will never succeed in doing so. No man does. But he has put himself in a position to begin trying, something he had resisted doing for a long time.

With the publication of *Love in the Ruins* Percy for a while began to consider his career as a novelist suspended, maybe over. As if to indicate that one side of his mind hadn't completely yielded to the demands his storytelling must make, Dr. Percy began writing those philosophical articles again in the early 1970s. "Toward a Triadic Theory of Meaning" was published in *Psychiatry* (February, 1972) and "A Semiotic Theory of Language as Phenomenon" was written and revised in 1973, then submitted with no great hope of acceptance to various linguistic journals: "I wrote it for myself, I guess. I've been working on it for months. Don't ask me why. I've asked myself why, and can't come up with an answer."

Well before Noam Chomsky had published his first major contribution to the field of linguistic theory, "Syntactic Structures," Percy had been taking after an assortment of behaviorists. In his latest papers he continues to argue, along lines familiar to readers of Chomsky, that language is simply not accounted for by "conditioning and learning." He seems to go farther than Chomsky, who in a way throws up his hands and says that, so far as we now know, children are born with a rather specific "language faculty," presumably transmitted genetically; and that "faculty" becomes somehow activated in early childhood. Clearly a follower of Descartes or, for that matter, Plato can take satisfaction only from such an approach: the "innate ideas" of the former, the "essences" of the latter, are not all that unlike Chomsky's "faculty."

On the other hand, Chomsky won't at all give the "faculty" he refers to the famous Cartesian independence from the body. He is a twentieth-century scientist who insists that at some "level" all the mind's activity has to do with neurophysiological activity. In his long paper addressed to linguists, Percy points out that Chomsky, like so many others, has been stopped short by, of all people, little children, who have not even started school, let alone devised weighty and interesting theories, but who all the time and in every part of the world and quite without boasting or self-consciousness simply start speaking the particular language they have been hearing from day to day. Percy is delighted at Chomsky's impatience with linguists: for all the density and intricacy of their theories, they have yet to tell us how it is that a child starts talking. Chomsky correctly proposes "to shift the burden of explanation from the linguist, the theorist of language as a phenomenon, to the child, the subject under study." But Percy adds: "Chomsky's theory of language is that the child is capable of forming a theory of language."

The remark in isolation sounds more critical than it was meant to be. Percy immediately goes on to say: "Now Chomsky's abdication may or may not be justified. Perhaps in the long run it will turn out that it is not possible to arrive at an explanatory theory of language in any ordinary sense of the word and that the only 'explanation' available is that the child somehow hits on the grammar of a language after a fragmentary input." Characteristically, the author would rather be modest than pretentiously knowing. Both he and Chomsky are up against a mystery still unsolved. He goes on to define the mystery further: the child's mind makes connections between sounds and sights and somehow ends up being an agent, it can be called, of expression. The child sees a balloon. The child hears the word *balloon*. The child makes a connection, linking two "phenomena." All very simple; all enormously complicated and hard to "explain." Physician that he is, Percy draws upon recent neurophysiological studies, which indicate that in man, as opposed even to higher apes, there is a distinctive area where, presumably, such a connection is made — "the human inferior parietal lobule, which includes the angular and supra-marginal gyri, to a rough approximation areas 39 and 40 of Brodmann."

Readers of *Love in the Ruins* will recognize some of the words; in the novel Dr. More wants to locate man's very "nature" in those "gyri" and "areas" every medical student learns about. In his recent articles Dr. Percy on the one hand takes note of the neurophysiological research done, then switches to a more philosophical vein, as does Dr. More. Drawing upon both empirical and existential viewpoints, Percy tries to look at how not only children go about using words, but patients and their psychiatrists as well: "It is a matter for astonishment, when one comes to think of it, how little use linguistics and other sciences of language are to psychiatrists. When one considers that the psychiatrist spends most of his time listening and talking to patients, one might suppose that there would be such a thing as a basic science of listening-and-talking, as indispensable to psychiatrists as anatomy to surgeons. Surgeons traffic in body structures. Psychiatrists traffic in words. Didn't Harry Stack Sullivan say that psychiatry properly concerns itself with transactions between people and that most of these transactions take the form of language? Yet if there exists a basic science of listening-and-talking I have not heard of it. What follows is a theory of language as behavior."

He makes quite clear the ultimate mystery: what in the brain, what in us as human beings, enables us to take all those "parietal lobe associations" and turn them into those experiences every parent knows — a child hitherto silent, or noisy but utterly inarticulate, starts using one word, then another, and finally, sentences. By watching those children, or by taking careful note of what gets said in a doctor's office, one can come up with patterns, and maybe understand more clearly what a "preverbal" child is up to, as he or she begins to speak, or what a patient or doctor is up to as words get used in so very many ways — to indicate feelings, to tell stories, to pronounce judgment, to reach out and beckon or show interest. As he does toward Chomsky, Percy pays respect to Freud, but insists that the actual listening and speaking which go on between doctors and their patients deserve as much study as dreams or free associations. In fact, a failure to do just that puts doctor and patient both at a serious disadvantage; they are not paying attention to much of what they say to each other, because they emphasize so strongly only one element in the words that get passed between them: words as a means of confirming the validity of a particular (psychoanalytic) hypothesis.

"Freud did not have time to consider what goes on between doctor and patient," Percy observes, "nor how a technique itself can loom large as part of the intellectual furniture of a later age, much less how it could come to pass that one can fall prey to the very technique one seeks help from." If a patient comes to a doctor because he has yet to find someone *with* whom he can make sense of the world, and if that inclination is ignored by yet another person, the doctor, in whom so much hope and trust has been bestowed, then needless to say the patient is headed for further disappointment. The patient may learn a good deal about what the doctor believes to be important and "revealing," but he does not learn that it is possible for another person to understand *him*, as opposed to some of the things that the doctor prompts him to talk about because of a professional "orientation," a particular theoretical interest.

By the middle of 1973 Percy could write in a letter that he was "off linguistics" for a span of time he called "forever." He was collecting his essays, including the ones just mentioned, into a volume — *The Message in the Bottle.* He was also "gradually coming around to fiction again": "As Flannery [O'Connor] would say in her unfancy way, did say, why don't you make up another story? It may or may not work. I never know. A matter of luck and God's Providence." The man who has such a view of his own work can all too easily and ironically be fitted into the very verbal straitjacket he deplores when it is thrust upon others. The phrases are there, waiting — literary, social, cultural, geographical, philosophical, psychological phrases.

There are stoicism, Southern stoicism, and Southern stoicism forsaken for European existentialism, or the two joined in some mixture. There is the intelligent youth from the distinguished family, who in turn suffers amid the strains that family's life put upon him. There is the dramatic tragedy of tuberculosis. What Heidegger said about death as the most powerful of catalysts (confronted with it, we sometimes drop all pretenses or affectations and look at ourselves and others more honestly) surely must apply to tuberculosis when it strikes people like Simone Weil, Orwell, and Percy. Already introspective, they not only look deeper or more broadly, but as Heidegger suggested, examine life with a view to its hitherto unacknowl-edged possibilities — hence, as a consequence, Orwell's futuristic turn of mind, Weil's increasingly mystical approach to the world, Percy's shift of interests and activities, and his conversion to Catholicism. All these themes were to be found in his next novel.

With *Lancelot*, Walker Percy joins the ranks of English novelists and poets who have, over the centuries, drawn upon the legend of King Arthur and his knights, the so-called Matter of Britain — that group of stories, somewhat obscure in origin, which contain pre-Christian as well as early Christian fact and fantasy. The knights of the Round Table and their exploits, intrigues, victories, defeats have been variously described, de-pending upon the particular writer, his time, native land, point of view. No one knows for sure whether Arthur, Lancelot, Per-cival, Galahad, Guinevere, and others actually existed. It is believed that in the sixth century a certain renowned battle-leader rallied a declining, jeopardized Celtic people, and se-cured for them, at Mount Badan, a decisive victory against the Saxon hordes. Soon enough those hordes would prevail, at least for several centuries — until the ninth century, when King Alfred again rallied the English successfully. For genera-tions Arthur and his comrades served as reminders of what was and what might again be — a people in control of its own des-tiny, rather than weak and floundering.

A number of storytellers nourished the Arthurian tradition in England, but by the eleventh century the knights of the Round

Table had become celebrities throughout a Christendom very much obsessed with its own pursuits and struggles — the Crusades, the desire to affirm Christ through territorial conquest. It was Sir Thomas Malory, in the fifteenth century, who gave us the first English book devoted to the legend. Malory died a prisoner (1471), and his *Morte d'Arthur* reflects the experiences of a knight who had witnessed and been involved in much tragedy — the seemingly endless Wars of the Roses. Malory had a keen dramatic sense, a poet's ear, and he delivered the essentials of Arthurian romance to the English literature we know and read.

The list of those writers who have paid heed to one or another element in the romance would have to include Dante, who mentions Lancelot in the *Inferno;* Milton, who for a while (before turning to the Bible and especially the book of Genesis) contemplated drawing on Arthur and his companions; Spenser, Dryden, Scott, and especially Tennyson in *The Idylls of the King;* more recently, T. S. Eliot ("The Waste Land") and T. H. White *(The Once and Future King).* Tennyson's long poem was, really, a poet's lifetime obsession. "The Morte d'Arthur" was first sketched in 1833, shortly after the death of the author's close friend Arthur Hallam. Already the young poet had chosen to draw upon a legend for the mixed expression of personal statement and moral reflection that was to be so characteristic of him. Not until 1888, fifty-five years later, upon the publication of the collected *Idylls* in final form, would Tennyson be done with his Arthuriad. For Tennyson the *Idylls* were an opportunity to survey with foreboding and disapproval much of nineteenth-century England's gray and sooty industrial landscape. Even as Arthur and his knights fought bravely to stave off a given social order's collapse, Tennyson worried hard about his beloved England — so full of itself, greedy, and, in ways it did not care to consider, quite vulnerable. The ruins of Arthur's world get characterized in Tennyson's "last weird battle in the west"; but the author means for his reader to look at the belching furnaces, the mills and their humiliated, desperate inhabitants, and, most of all, the values of modern industrialism.

Lancelot ("And but for all my madness and my sin") is portrayed as a tormented, tragic hero. He has his high ideals; he even glimpsed the Holy Grail. But he was fatally self-centered, and he is brought down by pride, the sin of sins. Tennyson had taken the measure of a "civilization" gone berserk with accumulation, adornment, the social and economic climb that possessions signify. He saw the craven sensuality that Victorian propriety was meant to conceal. The author of the *Idylls* wanted the English bourgeoisie, with its faith in machines, factories, science, and, not least, military might, to look closely at a number of assumptions and illusions. He wondered what his contemporary "men of property" wanted out of life, apart from accumulated capital and a few secret vices. He saw even the best of his countrymen plagued by confusion and conflict. They were loyal to the Crown and the Established Church; they were ready to die abroad for the Empire; but they were in more psychological and spiritual trouble than they cared to acknowledge.

Yet reigning collective fantasies had a way then, as now, of persisting stubbornly. The New Jerusalem was thought to be around the corner — awaiting, no doubt, a new territorial acquisition abroad (the more raw materials, the better) and a greater manufacturing capacity at home. Tennyson saw in Birmingham and Manchester, in Leeds and Bradford, an emerging Babylon — corrupt wealth and human degradation. The rich were doomed by their avarice and brutal arrogance; the poor were devoured by the unrelenting crudities and humiliating denials of everyday life. All the while, though, illusions were necessary: progress, advancing civilization, a higher standard of living, inventions and more inventions. The plague was no more. Electricity was soon to be in widespread use. Railroads made a joke of carriage travel. It was only a matter of time before machines would take to the air — or go below the surface. The fantasies of a Jules Verne or an H. G. Wells were superficial acknowledgments of a deeper, secular faith: God apart, man was headed for greater and greater things. Darwin said so one way: evolution. Marx and Engels and Hegel in another way: history's thrust or will — the dialectic.

Tennyson had other prophecies in mind. He had no use for the refuge of excessive, escapist spirituality. In the *Idylls* the search for the Holy Grail comes across as all too consuming, exhausting, and ultimately destructive. But he believed that nineteenth-century capitalism, wedded increasingly to imperialism, would compromise fatally the people of Western Europe. His Camelot is the City of Man, with its inevitable deceits and conceits. One of the latter — every such city, perhaps, has a particular version — is the notion that *here, now, this time* it is different. Does any collapsing order really dare see what is in store for itself — except at the last, apocalyptic moment? Arthur's Round Table would eventually stand abandoned; the knights fall into rivalry, mutual suspicion, betrayal, vengeance. Always, however — even in the America of the 1960s — there has been the hope of a return. For centuries, amidst the Dark Ages, the medieval period, the English looked for a resurgence of Arthurian good fortune. The legend had promised no less. Tennyson was not about to deny his fellow citizens all hope, but he was worried, if not gloomy, about the West's prospects. On the other hand, he was a poet intent on entertaining with words as well as giving warnings or preaching. The seriousness of his purpose, the applicability of his apparent flight of fancy to the modern world, has not always been appreciated — certainly not by those who have dismissed the *Idylls* as a poet's self-indulgent, medieval escapism.

In the *Idylls*, in all the Arthuriads from early times to now, the figure of Lancelot is a dominant one. Lancelot, who sought the Holy Grail. Lancelot, who was bold, courageous, self-sacrificing, without apparent fear. Lancelot, who was not blinded by the pettiness or self-absorption of other warriors. Lancelot, who, however, could not withstand his passion for Guinevere, and cuckolded King Arthur. Lancelot, who was rendered morally suspect, spiritually weak: a sin against spirituality; a high-minded vision flawed by the body's continuing passions. Lancelot, King Arthur's first knight, his "right arm." Lancelot, Queen Guinevere's lover. Lancelot's love was a "great and guilty" one. It scarred him badly: "His mood was often like a fiend, and rose/And drove him into wastes and solitudes."

Tennyson hoped that in Lancelot he had constructed not only a conventional tragic hero, but a character whose intelligence, sensitivity, and idealistic ambitiousness would address themselves to the likely readers of the *Idylls of the King* — men and women whom England's Poet Laureate badly wanted to confront with an epic poem given over to intense moral inquiry. At what point is even evident, palpable goodwill a mere sham — a sideshow to the larger drama of covetousness? If even the best of us are stained with elements of dishonor, what hope, if any, ought be held out? Tennyson never grants Lancelot the knowing satisfaction of spiritual success. He saw the Holy Grail, but what he saw turned out to be "veiled." Yet, his torment, his inclination to anguished introspection, his madness even — signs of a sensitive conscience at war with the flesh — somehow are a collective prelude to his redemption: "So groaned Sir Lancelot in remorseful pain/Not knowing he should die a holy man."

At no point does Tennyson dare get into the theology of salvation — or as Jung, the most religious of twentieth-century psychoanalysts, would have put it, the means by which souls are "cured." God's grace is meant for sinners. Sir Galahad, so unblemished and privileged spiritually, is not really of this world. Guinevere is saved, presumably, by a certain sleight of hand on the part of Tennyson: she goes to a nunnery. Lancelot gets no such institutional haven. He is left alone, saddened, bereft, and by no means completely contrite. Tennyson has him speak in the tradition of Hamlet — as we would put it today, a thoroughly "alienated" person: "For what am I? what profits me my name/Of greatest knight? I fought for it, and have it./Pleasure to have it, none; to lose it, pain;/Now grown a part of me; but what use in it?/To make men worse by making my sin known?/Or sin seem less, the sinner seeming great?"

It is not hard to move from such a Lancelot to a burgher of the nineteenth or twentieth century: the pride in success mingled with gnawing doubt, and a conviction that all is not as perfect as it seems; the knowledge that something drastic must be done, if one is to break free of stultifying if not utterly destructive constraints, yet a lethargy, an indifference, a lack of nerve, a refusal to risk what has been won, at whatever cost, for an indefinite or hard-to-imagine alternative. The result, a man lost to himself, divided in loyalties, hard put to take a stand and fight to the finish.

Tennyson, like his contemporaries Kierkegaard and Dostoevski, had a keen sense of the paralyzing influence of mental conflict on the will. Perhaps the nineteenth-century readers were being given a prophecy: keep surrendering yourselves to the increasingly mechanistic life of a so-called advanced civilization and you will lose all say in your personal affairs.

Walker Percy's Lancelot is our very own — alive in the last quarter of the twentieth century. He is American, Southern, of "good" family: Lancelot Andrewes Lamar. The novel's plot is disarmingly simple, and suggestive. Lancelot is confined to a room in a place that is both a prison and a hospital. He is sick of mind, but has also committed a crime: "A remarkable prison! Or a remarkable hospital as the case may be." The view offers him a corner of a cemetery, a bit of the sky, a small stretch of the levee along the Mississippi and of Annunciation Street, no less. There is, finally, part of a sign visible:

Free &
Ma
B

Lancelot has been there an indeterminate length of time, a year or so. He refers to his "cell." He talks of the building as a "Center for Aberrant Behavior," or as a "nuthouse." He has had trouble remembering exactly why he is there. The novel, in its entirety, has him going back in time, recalling past events in his life, and reflecting upon what he and others near and far (we) have come to. He does so with his old friend Percival — our version of those two knights of King Arthur's. Only at the end does Percival say anything, and then one word at a time: "yes" or "no," spoken in response to a series of questions. *Lancelot* is a sustained reverie of yet another of Percy's seekers —

though the Holy Grail in this particular story is as hard to grasp or describe as the legendary one of the Age of Chivalry.

We have been given four lines from Canto XXX of Dante's *Purgatorio* as the epigraph — a distinct clue of the author's intentions: "He sank so low that all means/for his salvation were gone,/except showing him the lost people./ For this I visited the region of the dead. . . ." In Canto V of the *Inferno* Dante has mentioned seeing the young lovers Paolo and Francesca, eventually discovered and murdered by the latter's husband, Gianciotto. They are reading "of Lancelot, how love constrained him" (*"di Lancillotto, come amor lo strinse"*). But Percy quotes from the canto of *Purgatorio* which T. S. Eliot has judged to provide the most intensely personal and psychologically decisive moment in the entire *Commedia*. It is the canto in which Vergil leaves the Pilgrim, who thereby is not only on his own, but compelled to face himself without the consolations of earthly wisdom. It is the canto in which Beatrice calls him by his name, Dante — the one time that happens. Beatrice is not only a reminder of a (Florentine) woman but a divine Presence — a Vision of Christ. What Lancelot of the Arthuriads sought in the Holy Grail, Dante saw before him in Beatrice. She, like Christ, was both human and of God — and the mind cannot, really, fathom the mixture or its ultimate purpose.

The "I" in the lines of Dante Percy quotes is Beatrice; she is describing Dante's earthly lapses of honor and trust. He is a given person, and of course, by extension, each of us. There is no return to Eden, she lets him know. He is a sinner; he cannot become an innocent. No doubt, as he hurt others and himself, he held out hope for himself; he justified deeds, explained them away, overlooked their moral significance. In the thirtieth canto Beatrice is a thirteenth-century psychoanalyst with theological interests in mind. She wants to let her friend know that he has deceived himself repeatedly. If he is ever to "arrive" — every pilgrim's hope — at his destination, he must look carefully at the past, without illusions. Then, and only then, can he "forget." Waiting is the river Lethe, which washes away, upon immersion, all painful memories (Percy's Mississippi River). But first comes Beatrice's psychological summary — an effort to "save" someone through reminder, clarification, interpretation, and an emotional shock or two. Dante swoons, like many of today's analysands, under the brunt of "insight" relentlessly pressed through another's eyes and voice.

Like Dante at that point in the *Purgatorio*, the Lancelot of Percy's novel is reluctant to see himself as he was, to look candidly into his heart. He has suffered a lot, fallen by the way many times, but persisted in his search long enough to be at the point Percy has him — within sight of the Annunciation. If he could only see and comprehend fully what he has been about, his future will not be an endless repetition of outright misdeeds or moral evasions. He would, instead, be "Free & Ma B" (maybe) in sight of the Holy Grail, or God's Gracious Presence, or a Vision that is more than yet another secular fantasy of omnipotence — weak and doomed man, a fleck in eternal space, a moment in eternal time, brandishing his muscles and shaking his fists as if he were God Himself. "If a man cannot forget, he will never amount to much," Kierkegaard observed in *Either/Or*. Percy put the statement on the epigraph of *The Last Gentleman*, not because he (Kierkegaard) advocated a self-serving amnesia that sets the stage for whatever kick or fancy comes along. The point is to tame the past, so that it can be set aside, rather than endlessly reenacted. It is ironic that psychoanalysis has become for many of us an endless pursuit of memories — as if the past wins out, no matter what: formerly, by dint of the power of repressed emotional experiences, and now through the constant stress our culture puts on looking at them every which way.

This most recent generation of analysts has noticed that the vague, indeterminate apprehensions and unease of many analysands do not at all yield to interpretations of earlier disappointments or hurts. What do I want out of life, bored or disillusioned "patients" ask — and there are, understandably, prolonged silences across the room. The psychiatrist may well have been asking himself or herself the same vexing, disturbing question. He or she may even be honest enough to acknowledge that now and then a patient becomes doctor — helps that question get examined more forthrightly than might otherwise be the case. Presumably, if one has at last seen oneself without evasiveness, as Beatrice wanted for Dante, then it will be possible to move away from the past, to get on with the future — and questions like "What does life mean?" or "What do I want out of life?" are directed at the time to come, rather than the years already spent.

Percy's Lancelot, with the aid of his fellow knight and longtime friend, begs to remember so that once and for all he can forget. Percival is a priest and a psychiatrist — an acknowledgment by his creator that the psychological and the spiritual, in our time, go hand in hand. Although Dante and Tennyson may have known all there is to know about the operations of the mind, and so may generations of religious confessors, for many of us psychological understanding is to be found not in a church or an epic poem, but in an office. Maybe in a novel, too, Dr. Percy gambles. And a novel that entertains, provides action, drama, suspense, mystery, as well as philosophical analysis and religious speculation. Lancelot, who comes up with existentialist ruminations that will not surprise Percy's fans, is a strongly sexual person, a sly and humorous observer, and, in the end, a murderer. His spells of amnesia and theological meditation yield with disarming ease to the imperatives of storytelling. This is Percy's shortest, most dramatic and sharply focused novel. Those who have basked in his extended cultural criticism and social satire will have to be content with brief moments here and there. When they do arrive, however, they are unmistakably his particular words: "In New Orleans I have noticed that people are happiest when they are going to funerals, making money, taking care of the dead, or putting on masks at Mardi Gras so nobody knows who they are."

The man who thus remarks upon the personal desperation of others is a forty-five-year-old lawyer who, like the central character in each of Percy's novels, hasn't been able to figure out how to live a life. At times he was idealistic, highly ethical: civil rights and civil liberties work. At times he was wantonly, brazenly pleasure-bound. He became a man indifferent to his work, not especially concerned with his children, but intent on plenty of sex, good food, a comfortable life at the lowest possible cost of mental or physical exertion. There is always tragedy — a fatal disease, or is it dis-ease? — in a Percy novel. Lancelot's first wife, Lucy, had succumbed to leukemia, leaving him with a son, a daughter. He was hardly the father to lose himself in their needs and struggles. This Lancelot, like his predecessors in other novels, found it hard to reconcile the obligations of an honorable person with a self-centeredness that demanded its own satisfactions.

Pride is the old-fashioned Biblical word for that self-centeredness. From St. Augustine to Kierkegaard theologians have centered the Christian drama on pride and its vicissitudes. Faith is constantly jeopardized by pride. Even piety can be pride concealed. In fact, piety, insofar as it becomes self-righteous, is an especially virulent kind of pride: "Let him who is without sin cast the first stone." In the Arthurian romance, Lancelot's adulterous relationship with Guinevere, in and of itself, is not so remarkable, and as Percy notes in his *Lancelot*, "Dante was downright indulgent with sexual sinners." It was the particular adultery of the knight Lancelot — so agile and competent, so insistent on leading others, telling them what to do and how to do it — that enraged other knights. Some of them were themselves small of mind, all too grateful for·the occasion of intrigue, rivalry, and gossip. But they were also enraged by the self-assurance of this knight — that *he* should have the nerve to seek the Holy Grail and demonstrate over and over again what a leader he was. There is in King Arthur and Galahad a Christ-like purity; they are remote from the rest of us in their innocence and unqualified goodness. Lancelot is good, too — but flawed. But his pride won't permit him to acknowledge the inconsistencies, if not duplicities, of his life. His nobility, proven again and again in the field of action, becomes for others a form of moralizing piety. How can one affirm one's faith, even flaunt it through bravery and courage and skill, while at the same time persisting in a liaison with the Queen?

In Tennyson's *Idylls* such a paradox becomes psychological

rather than religious; Lancelot can't give up his passion, *yet* he insists on reminding others of his high-minded, thoughtful, considerate side. He is blind to himself, for all his introspective moments. Long before Freud spelled out narcissism as a central, and perhaps ineradicable, source of human discontent, and Paul Federn described madness as one of "the narcissistic disorders," Tennyson gave us a not altogether pitiable Lancelot. We feel sorry for him, but we also get impatient with him and wonder whether, at the very least, the irony of his situation hasn't occurred to him: such a respected and even idealized figure not only with feet of clay — surely no surprise in the case of anyone — but still intent on being admired, hence lording it over others. Lancelot the "tragic hero" is, in fact, Lancelot the cleverly, insistently self-absorbed man of overwhelming pride.

Percy's Lancelot demonstrates his pride in another way. He is not the man who betrays another by taking up with his wife, but rather he is a cuckold. The central drama of the novel is his discovery of that fact, and his determination to exact murderous vengeance — as remembered and told to the "priest-psychiatrist" Percival. The first section of the novel gives us the somewhat eccentric, befuddled, cannily observant Lance, a familiar Percy figure. He is sensitive, has been hurt by life, at times becomes morbidly introspective, but has constructed a seemingly unassailable protection for himself in light humor. He can banter with anyone. He can manage a droll insouciance that signals an unmistakable message: stay away from me — the "real me," which I myself am quite anxious to avoid. He is comfortable with his family's mansion, which has been converted into a tourist trap of sorts — showing it off is a pleasant, effortless way to make a living. The visitors pay well, and he is invulnerable to them. He even feasts on their presence. Their banalities and crudities and voyeuristic greed confirm his sense of superiority: the detached and knowing social critic of "good stock" who looks with tolerant amusement at the various proletarians who are smitten with the emblems of the fading gentry. The pride in such a posture is kept implicit in Percy's evocation of Lancelot. The author does not want to give his readers a snob, a dilettante, or a calculating sybarite. As with all of Percy's anguished pilgrims, the tone of the writing is what distinguishes them from fools, madmen, socially elite ne'er-do-wells. And the tone of the writing is what makes them more accessible to the general reader. Percy has a philosophical and theological agenda on his mind in this novel, as in his others, but he does not want his readers to feel all that distant from the characters he creates, however peculiar some of their thoughts, however poignant or incisive the wisdom they only gradually acquire in the course of the various novels.

Lance, as he is called by his second wife, Margot, and his friends, takes pains to describe himself as a youth in such a way that we realize he stood out, even then, only so much from others. Surely he is an altogether new version of the Arthurian figure: "I was . . . the type who reaches the peak of his life in college and declines thereafter: prominent on campus, debater, second-string all-S.E.C. halfback, Rhodes scholar, even 'smart,' that is a sort of second-echelon Phi Beta Kappa. Being 'smart' on the football team meant that you read *Time* magazine and had heard of the Marshall Plan." There is arrogance and condescension there, but the target is the speaker, whose distance from himself is clear. Percy's upper-class, existentially haunted characters are as aloof toward themselves, as sardonic about their own situations, as about anyone else's. No one who fits the description Lancelot gave to his youthful self need fear him or the author behind him. Those who read obscure quarterlies and know every detail of the SALT II negotiations have also had a comeuppance or two in the Percy novels, which are not without a running seam of amused skepticism with respect to intellectuals and their various pretensions.

Gradually Lancelot's skepticism toward himself unfolds, as he talks to his old friend. The friend is obviously a more reflective person — always has been, since they both were children, growing up together. Lancelot reveals the self-deprecating side of himself as he defers to Percival, though not without a probe or two: what are *you* up to? We are given no response. Percy is able to make a one-sided conversation the novel's central plot. At first Lancelot is even cool and collected when he recalls the first knowledge he had of his second wife's adulterous behavior. Why be so upset, anyway, he wonders. "As a physician," he asks his friend, "wouldn't you say that nothing more is involved than the touch of one membrane against another?" And more succinctly: "Cells touching cells." So much for biological knowledge, the microscope, and one version of modern psychological insight. Lancelot has what we call "perspective." He knows full well that sexual infidelity in twentieth-century America is not rare; that sexual promiscuity is even celebrated by various authors or "experts" — one more source of "joy," or "happiness." Why should he be so surprised or offended by a relatively commonplace occurrence? He may spend his time in a tower of sorts, a pigeonnier his wife has made into a study, but he has immersed himself over the years in "bad dirty books" as well as "great dirty books," and he seems so sophisticated and wry and *au courant* that one wonders whether anything has ever really bothered him.

At one point Lancelot says this to his friend: "You would think, wouldn't you, that the new cuckold would respond with the appropriate emotion, shock, shame, humiliation, sorrow, anger, hate, vengefulness, etc. Would you believe me when I tell you that I felt none of these emotions? Can you guess what I did feel? *Hm. What's this? What have we here?* Hm. What I felt was a prickling at the base of the spine, a turning of the worm of interest."

But there is another side to Percy's thinking, and to his characters. Lancelot, like his predecessors in *The Moviegoer, The Last Gentleman,* and *Love in the Ruins,* is on a search, almost at times in spite of himself. His closest friend is a priest, after all. The two have been exchanging ideas for years — about books, the world around them, and "life." Lancelot puts important philosophical questions to his listening friend, and no doubt received answers, though they are not given us. ("Are you then one of the new breed who believe that Satan is only a category, the category of Evil?") And for all the "flatness of affect" he tells his psychiatrist friend of, Lancelot rejoices in New Orleans — its "vital decay," its "lively fetor." He insists to Percival that "it's not it, your religion, that informs this city, but rather some special accommodation to it or relaxation from it." He goes on this way: "This city's soul I think of as neither damned nor saved but eased rather, existing in a kind of comfortable Catholic limbo somewhere between the outer circle of hell where sexual sinners don't have it all that bad and the inner circle of purgatory where things are even better. Add to that a flavor of Marseilles vice leavened by Southern U.S.A. good nature. Death and sex treated unseriously and money seriously. The Whitney bank is as solemn as the cemetery is lively. Protestants started Mardi Gras, you know. Presbyterians take siestas or play gin at the Boston Club. Jews ride on carnival floats celebrating the onset of Christ's forty-day fast."

The city's soul gives us a hint about Lancelot's. He is a religious knight who has to contend — as did Kierkegaard's "knight of faith" — with the contemporary, agnostic, bourgeois world; and has done, so, rather often, by looking down from the high vantage point of his pigeonnier-office. He, too, is in a limbo — a cell, where his friend is helping him sort things out. Lancelot presses details of his past life upon the friend, and thereby provides us with stories within the larger story. We learn that Lancelot's second wife came from Odessa, Texas, the daughter of a wealthy oil man. We learn that they have a daughter, Siobhan, who seems largely in the care of her maternal grandfather. We learn that Margot was glad indeed to marry "up," that she helped remodel and furnish elegantly Lancelot's old family home, that she was an actress of sorts, and was in the midst of making a movie, directed by two men, Merlin and Janos, each of whom turned out to be a lover of hers, when Lancelot found out about her sexual life. He did so almost by accident; he noticed his daughter's blood type, and figured out that he could not possibly be her father. Much of the novel's action has to do with his effort to find out the exact nature of his wife's involvement with Merlin, not to mention his older daughter's involvement with a film actor.

The novel moves along with verve, humor, and, for Percy, a surprising amount of sex. Not that he is a Henry Miller. He still tends to slip into scientific language — the words he learned in anatomy at medical school — when describing passion. But he does even that with a touch of humor. On the whole, there is a

balance of prudishness and sexual suggestion that makes this
the least self-conscious of his novels with respect to what he, at
one point, calls the "carnal." He sends the black family re-
tainer's son, Elgin, spying on his wife and daughter, is told
what he already knows, and thereupon finds himself feeling not
so much vengeful as alive. Suddenly his life seems to have a
purpose. In an important moment of the novel, Lancelot tells
his friend of the reaction that took place: "How strange it is
that a discovery like this, of evil, of a kinsman's dishonesty, a
wife's infidelity, can shake you up, knock you out of your rut, be
the occasion of a new way of looking at things." A little later on
he connects his wife's sexual escapade to a momentous revela-
tory experience: "I discovered my own life."

The assertion of a man for whom a negative has a positive
meaning. Lance had been drifting and without much sense of
purpose. In fact, he had been in a daze. He had lost all touch
with himself. He lived in a kind of trance — the habits and
routines that fill up time. He had lost his earlier idealism: no
more legal briefs for the NAACP. He was "practical," in the
way someone is who has become a slave of rituals: they and
they alone demand attention; anyone who asks for freedom
from them is a fool, and a threat, too. The existentialist
philosophers have emphasized the tyranny of such a state — an
abdication of what is most preciously human: consciousness.
No wonder behaviorism, a psychology that emphasizes stimuli
and responses, reflexes and "conditioning," has become so
influential in contemporary America; a psychology that suits
our lives, which are spent conforming to the dictates of the
assembly line, the time clock, the deadline. But even the quite
comfortable Lance, a relatively "free agent" by virtue of his
social and economic position, could not for years allow himself
to stop and look around and take stock of his situation, or that
of others around him.

Suddenly something happened. Suddenly a man was aware
of himself, felt inclined to stop, look, listen — hear the beat of
his own heart, pay heed to the thoughts that formerly had
crossed his mind in quickly forgotten dreams, or fantasies considered peculiar, if not crazy. In Percy's words: "Five, six, seven

years of unacknowledged idleness (it takes work to be idle and not acknowledge it), drinking and watching TV, working at play, playing at work — what does it do to a man?" Once someone starts asking questions like that, he is in jeopardy. He is free, in the sense that he had dared open his eyes to — himself, his situation in this world, his "nature and destiny," as Reinhold Niebuhr put it. He is, as Percy points out, a Rip Van Winkle who has awakened from a long sleep and finds — again, himself. First he looks at his face, his body: is he intact, does he work? Then he looks at his habits: how and with whom does he spend his hours, to what effect and purpose? Then, maybe he is ready to do something with his discovery. He can pose questions. He can test out his muscles, physical and mental. He can start moving, try to reach a certain destination. He can begin the "search."

Lance's specific search, which sustains the story, is directed at his wife's adulterous behavior: with whom, where, and when. Lance's larger inquiry is stated in the question he asks his friend Percival: "Have you ever considered the possibility that one might undertake a search not for God but for evil?" And Lance challenges the psychiatric side of his priest-psychiatrist, by pointing out that these days such a search may be nearly futile. Is there anything we actually recognize to be "evil"? After Darwin, Marx, Freud, Pavlov, our behavior has been explained, put in "perspective," traced back or given a "context" or two. Margot Lamar sleeps with movie directors. We are not surprised. We don't get morally alarmed. We don't pray on her behalf. We may possibly become concerned enough to ask *why*. How is she "relating" with her husband? What "problems" does she have? How did her parents get on — especially when she was a young girl? Is she, by sleeping with X or Y, telling her husband and herself something she is not aware of? She is surely "acting out"; if she talked with a doctor, she might find out exactly what has prompted her to do so.

There is also the matter of her social class, the assumptions a well-to-do person of a certain background has learned to live with. When over half of America's families stay away from church, when "swapping partners" and "trying out relation-

ships" are considered by millions not only permissible, but
even desirable, then the word *adultery* becomes at the very least
old-fashioned — a moralistic hand-me-down from another age.
And so with other acts, forms of "behavior." Cannot everyone
be seen as a "victim," or as the "product" of various forces:
genetic (evolutionary); social, political, or more broadly, historical; and of course, psychological? If a man or woman becomes antagonistic, deceives someone, even violates the law,
we have learned not to pray, not to condemn so much as "understand," ask why. The person is "acting out" a psychological
conflict, or is desperate by virtue of his or her position in society, or perhaps "sick" in some way we only vaguely comprehend — though in time, with more research, things will become clearer: the biology, the neurophysiology of the brain,
and the effect of those "factors" on the way people act toward
others. With such a way of seeing things, where is the room for
evil — or, for that matter, good? Where is the room for the notion of will, either?

If a man or a woman does *not* commit adultery the reason
may be seen by many these days as psychological, sociological,
or the mixture that gets called "psychosocial." The man is "in-
hibited" or "repressed" or "guilty" or "passive"; the woman is
also one or more of those, or she is a victim of her
"background," her culture-bound practices, all of which have
to do with class, sex, political condition. Even the notion of
normality, a clinical rather than a moral or religious term, has
been explained away, so to speak — denied any authority, let
alone dignity, of its own. At a meeting of psychoanalysts in
1976, the issue of what is "normal" proved vexing indeed; a
number of doctors, quite reasonably extrapolating from
psychiatric theory, indicated that "normal" means "the relative absence of the abnormal." We are all neurotics, Freud
pointed out — those of us lucky enough not to be insane.

Where is the notion of good and evil under such circumstances? Whose good? Whose evil? "You people may have
been on the wrong track all these years with all that talk about
God and signs of his existence, the order and beauty of the
universe — that's all washed up and you know it," Lance tells

his priest friend. Then he observes: "The more we know about the beauty and order of the universe, the less God has to do with it. I mean who cares about such things as the Great Watchmaker? But what if you could show me a *sin*? A purely evil deed, an intolerable deed for which there is no explanation?" And a bit further on: "In times when nobody is interested in God, what would happen if you could prove the existence of sin, pure and simple. . . . If there is such a thing as sin, evil, a living malignant sore, there must be a God."

Shades of Catharism, the Albigensian heresy, Manichaeism, Jansenism — the long-standing temptation of many, under various guises, to insinuate Satan or Lucifer into God's Kingdom, indeed give the Devil power over not only man but God Himself? Probably not. Percy wants to know what others believe and why. He is not sure that many of us believe much of anything, but he rather suspects that the possibility of the apocalypse (absolute evil) weighs more heavily on our minds than the promise of salvation through "faith and faith alone." Some of us have even taken up with witchcraft, with "black magic," with demonology. And our scientists, who have found out so much about the physical and chemical "structure" of matter, down to the particles within the atom, have (of all people) come up with rather small products that can be dropped from planes, and kill in a flash hundreds of millions of people — even end virtually all life on the planet in a few hours. Perhaps everyone would agree that such an act is evil — committed by whatever pilots and bombardiers, in whatever cause. Or would some of us, dying, say yes, evil has been done, while others would with their last words express approval, in the name of "freedom," or "the proletariat," or whatever ideological abstraction held control of their minds?

Percy's *Lancelot* explores such vexing moral ambiguities and ironies of our contemporary existence. At times Lance is almost scientifically dispassionate as he probes his own wife's faithlessness. At other moments he is the philosophical questioner: was it, rather, a matter of sinfulness? There is no answer — not, at least, the kind we are used to asking for: the results of a "survey," the conclusions of a "research project," the insistence of the latest psychological theory. The pilgrim Dante found intelligent companionship at Vergil's side, and later received the sharp reminders of Beatrice — a prelude to what by earthly standards is ineffable, the grace of God. The pilgrim Lance has a friend Percival to help take stock of and figure things out. The novel tells us what there is to figure out — for Lance, and by no great leap of the imagination, the rest of us. In *Lancelot*, the cell and the figure Percival are all-important signs. We are at a symbolic remove from Louisiana, twentieth-century America. The novel begins and ends in the cell — two friends who have remained loyal to each other, for all the ups and downs of their respective lives. Even as Beatrice was at once a real person in Dante's life and a religious figure of transcendent significance, Percival is meant to be a fellow seeker — therefore, heir to the sins of the flesh — but also a representative of a particular Church and its faith. Although in every Percy novel the central character is strangely detached, indifferent if not hostile to the prevailing (and disintegrating) social order, in *Lancelot* there is a difference. The other Percy heroes (or rather, antiheroes) were "alienated"; Lance is a pilgrim — quite comfortable in his cell, and pleased to be talking with his friend, taking in a certain view, considering what was, is, might someday be.

Purgatory is not Paradise, but it is at least a distance from Hell. For many of this century's existentialists Hell is aloneness, so common a "condition." Our institutions fail to bind people together — even the family, never mind neighborhoods, churches, schools, and so on. *Lancelot* continues Percy's exploration of what Marcel kept calling "fidelity" — a commitment of one person to another, out of a shared commitment to a search for life's meaning. As Lance sits in his cell, thinks back to his home on Belle Isle, his grim and ultimately tragic experiences there, he tells Percival this: "I have to tell you what happened in my own way — so I can know what happened. I won't know for sure until I say it. And there is only one way I can endure the horrible banality of it: and that is that I sense there is a clue I've missed and that you might pick it up. It is as if I knew that one clue was buried somewhere in the rubble of

Belle Isle and that I have to spend days kicking through the ashes to find it. I couldn't do that alone. But we could do it."

The "we" is Marcel's "we." It is the "we" Percy has been writing about for years in his essays. It is the "we" that has to do with language as well as "fidelity." An Eskimo child from the village of Noorvik, Alaska, once told a visitor: "My grand-mother told me that when she looks at the snow, she thinks of me. When I look at the snow, I think of her. I hear her. If I looked at the snow and there was no one to think of, I would be blind and deaf. The snow would fall on me, but it wouldn't be snow for me." More elaborate and self-important theories of language, "communication," and "child development" have not said all that much more about the way we grow and learn to fathom the world and hold one another up, so to speak. And if we are on our hands and knees, dazed and groping, a return to "fundamentals" of the kind suggested by that Eskimo child may be our only hope — if it is our purpose to learn, once again, how to stand up, stand for something, other than our-selves.

Lance comes to life, undertakes an efficient, animated, if cold-blooded analysis of an adulterous situation — and as a result, comes face to face with his narcissism, his aloneness. In an earlier canto of the *Purgatorio* than the one Percy quotes, Dante views those whose fate it is to stay within the first circle or terrace of the Hill of Purgatory: "Proud Christians, wretched by your toils o'erspect." There he sees, significantly, artists and their like — the intelligent and the gifted, those tempted to take the world on their shoulders and feel (out of their keen awareness and the response to it of friends, readers, viewers, listeners) at the very center of things. Dante was, of course, himself an intellectual; yet, in the eighteenth canto he satirizes his own kind — the all too clever and knowing, who let the admiration and envy of others go to their heads, and who even-tually must suffer rather a lot: "Here of such pride is paid the forfeiture." One suspects Percy has in mind his own witty, wide-awake, discerning intelligence as he writes of the astute and fiercely determined Lance, who (given cause) can shake himself out of the doldrums and figure out everything. One can murder literally — or do so figuratively, with words the foils of one's preachy self-assertiveness. The *Purgatorio* was, after all, a brilliant writer's occasion for the most intense and unsparing self-scrutiny. If others are merely entertained or edified, or if they are frightened, hence moved to airy or scornful dismissal of the effort, then they had best beware. Dante knew that he was among kindred souls — writers and their interpreters or readers — when he ascended the hill of Purgatory. It is one thing to go witness and comprehend sad and doomed lives — in Auden's words, part of a tribute to Sigmund Freud: "Down among the Lost People like Dante, down/To the stinking fosse where the injured/Lead the ugly life of the rejected." It is another matter to look at oneself with the redemptive candor Dante eventually managed. Significantly, another person's unflinchingly honest and if need be critical but constant, faithful, and loving presence is required: Beatrice, whom Dante had first met at the age of nine, and Beatrice, whom he called upon much later, in his mind, to address him directly in the *Commedia* and spell out for him (in the thirtieth canto, from which Percy quotes) the details of a Hellish life. Percival is the Beatrice of *Lancelot* — yet another incarnation, for Percy, of the commitment between two persons Marcel had in mind when he used the word *fidelity*. One thinks of Christ the man, the unassuming itinerant, offering himself to particular, needy, friendless others — and thereby healing them.

Dante, and Bunyan after him, gave us the allegory of the pilgrim. Percy's novel is also an allegory: the talker and listener as contemporary Arthurian knights, as seekers after life's meaning. Percival, listening to Lance, the well-born and well-educated and watchful Southerner, is not hearing the details of a biography. He is hearing, through a vivid, sustained metaphor, what any number of reasonably sensitive and thoughtful persons, alive and well in today's bourgeois America, are likely to go through psychologically and spiritually. The moment for Lance, for Percival, for Percy, is Eliot's, in "East Coker": "So here I am, in the middle way. . . ." And the experience Lance has gone through that year, in the cell, after the murder and the hurricane and the several consequent additional deaths, is also Eliot's, in "East Coker": "The chill as-cends from feet to knees,/The fever sings in mental wires./If to be warmed, then I must freeze/And quake in frigid purgatorial fires/Of which the flame is roses, and the smoke is briars."

"I feel so cold, Percival," Lance tells him toward the very end of the novel. And a moment later: "So I have nothing to ask you after all, because there is no answer. There is no question. There is no unholy grail just as there was no holy grail." Lance realizes that he did not discover anything "at the heart of evil." In fact, he discovered that "there was no 'secret' after all, no discovery. . . ." Except, perhaps, that there is hope. Not the hope of yet another investigation by the biologist-psychologist Lance became as he tried to fathom the novel's parade of lusts, rivalries, jealousies — the murderous game of musical chairs we so often play with one another, without realizing what we are up to, what we are about. The hope, rather, Thomas Carlyle had in mind when he contemplated the *Commedia* of Dante and wrote, in connection with *Purgatorio:* "Hope has now dawned, never-dying hope, if in company still with heavy sorrow. The obscure sojourn of demons and reprobates is under foot, a soft breathing of penitence mounts higher and higher, to the throne of mercy itself."

So it is that Lance reminds himself to tell Percival of his "good news." So it is that the time of day and the weather change. The ruinous, killing hurricane, the stink of methane gas, the black night, give way to "morning sun bright and high and refracted through the clear crystal prism of northern air with that special moderation, the promise of warmth, of fine November days in New Orleans." As with Dante and Tennyson, the landscape, the climate, mirror the pilgrim's way. If New Orleans can be a place of corruption and deceit, a place where hurricane storms unleash their vengeance, it can also be some-thing else: "An odd thing about New Orleans: the cemeteries here are more cheerful than the hotels and the French Quarter. Tell me why that should be, why 2000 dead Creoles should be more alive than 2000 Buick dealers?"

Lancelot concludes with the word "Yes" — Percival's answer to Lance's question: "Is there anything you wish to tell me before I leave?" We are back to *The Last Gentleman,* with Barrett running after the Edsel, and the doctor at the wheel stopping and waiting for the troubled wanderer, who so much wants to ask, seek, find. The affirmation is there, if necessarily somewhat tentative. None of Percy's characters are all that sure of themselves, never mind "skilled" in something called "interpersonal relationships." Percival's "Yes," or Barrett's leap toward the Edsel, or the driver's decision to apply the brakes rather than the gas pedal, are the brief, awkward, but telling and unforgettable moments that companions on a long journey sometimes experience, amid the humdrum business of keeping on the move, working their often tedious and apparently meaningless way through space and time.

In Percy's *Lancelot* the two knights have yet to reach the end of the journey. There are days ahead. They will continue to live, to ask questions, to find answers hard to come upon, to be, to be "in between." With a twinkle in his eye, Percy sends Lance, upon his release, to Virginia, a border state — and one whose lovely, peaceable Shenandoah Valley is, unavoidably, near the "powers and principalities," with their temptations and corruptions. "For us there is only the trying. The rest is not our business," T. S. Eliot said in a moment of renunciation as well as affirmation. It is a mixture this particular Lancelot, upon "discharge," will be struggling for. His creator knows the considerable risks and occasional pleasures of walking through the forlorn, muddy, yet handsomely arranged and fiercely arresting, cemeteries of New Orleans, under that city's warm, kindly, promising suns — which, inevitably, give way to clouds, then wind and drenching rain.

Epilogue

As for the particular person that he is, Walker Percy appears to be diffident, quiet, unassuming. In his manner he reminds one, though with no moralizing intended, of what he has been writing about, struggling for — a personal vision that is modest, even self-effacing, because religious in nature. He is as unwilling to categorize himself as he is to pin down others with labels. In each of his novels the central character, once freed to make his pilgrimage and continue his search, becomes almost impossible to write about any further. From that moment on the character is "living a life," a phrase Percy uses in such a way as to set up severe barriers to "analysis": a person living a life is not to be confused with a patient analyzing his dreams, a writer putting down words on paper, a Democrat or Republican espousing an argument, a golfer extolling the art and joy of his hobby. "I suppose I could be called 'a failed doctor,' " he once said. More affirmatively and conventionally he has pointed out the obvious: "I'm a white Southerner." He announces himself this way, too: "I'm a Christian, and I don't think anything I write is unrelated to that fact." With regard to the last, he is not boasting, not apologizing or staking out cleverly "different" or "unusual" territory.

Percy, like other writers, works the particulars of his own life into the stories he writes — or, too, the various essays he is impelled to offer. He knows the bayous of Louisiana rather well. He can get a lot out of sitting with a friend in a small country bar, where Cajun fishermen hang out, taking their whiskey fast and without flinching, sometimes even without an afterthought of water, though the hand may, instead, reach for a hard-boiled egg, one of a dozen or so in a bowl, always there in some bars a few miles out of Covington, near Lake Pontchartrain. There is no class-consciousness when the doctor-writer is there; he is likely dressed in khakis, or casual trousers, and a sport shirt, and he talks plain, straight, in relatively short and simple sentences. Usually he is asking rather than telling: how goes the shrimping, or the fishing, or the planting?

He listens to words, to the ways they are strung into sentences. He listens to personal statements — the Southern habit, fueled by liquor, of saying frankly and at some length what is on one's mind, and, at intervals, what it all means, life; the Southern habit, too, of addressing issues of kin, of time and place and social position, through the telling of humorous, sometimes long-winded, memories. Faulkner unashamedly paid his neighbors heed. He went religiously to Oxford's courthouse square and came back a rich man: all he'd heard, which he could add to all he knew — the beginning, at least, of something to tell those anonymous readers who live elsewhere. Once, in a small-town bar, Percy observed this: "You sit here and listen, and it doesn't take long to realize that a lot of the 'existentialism' of the intellectual is close to the heart of the person next to you, having a beer after a day in a shrimp boat, or working on a farm, or on his way home from one of the businesses around here, but in need of a moment to get his head together."

He continues to keep a keen eye on those who are trying to make sense of what happens in the mind, and in the surrounding world — hence his continuing interest in psychiatry as well as sociology, and, not least, philosophy. But he turns to less academic sources as well. He will be shopping in a supermarket, or standing in the post office, and suddenly a remark, a manner of putting things, catches his attention. Like others of his trade, he has a notebook for thoughts, ideas, things heard or overheard as well as (more formally) constructed in the course of sitting down in order to "write."

As a matter of fact, he divides his working time between lying on the bed, with a setup that enables him to write, and sitting at his desk, often to type up pages of scribbled words. (His handwriting is extremely hard to read.) Magazines, books, notes may be strewn on the bed, even as they pile up on the desk. He learned in his youth, while fighting tuberculosis, to use enforced passivity as an active instrument of intellectual comprehension: all those Russian novels and Franco-German existentialist philosophers enlisted by a Southern physician stranded at Lake Saranac's sanitarium while the world went mad with the war of wars. To this day his qualities of mind and manner — wry detachment, quietness, evenness of mood, a tendency to ask briefly rather than come up with extended answers — signal a person who has not at all felt threatened at being, more often than not, an observer of the passing parade.

At times Percy does break out, travel to a college to speak, or up to New York to see his publisher. But he is not a writer who goes on the lecture circuit, and when he goes someplace, he does so because he wants in some way to help out — a writing project in need of moral support, a literary occasion he feels significant, or, for that matter, a medical or psychiatric observance he feels himself rightly obliged to attend and take part in. There are, also, the trips back to an old home — up to the Delta, to Greenville, to the old plantation of Uncle Will's. Some critics have wrongly connected the occasionally unfriendly asides directed toward stoicism in *The Moviegoer* as an indirect slap at William Alexander Percy, who was a self-professed stoic. He was, of course, many things — a romantic figure, a brave and solitary one, a sedate small-town lawyer whose world travels and worldly knowledge were exceptional for anyone of his time, never mind place. But he was, in a specifically human sense, a loving father to three boys who had experienced, during the late 1920s and early 1930s, quite enough loss, and who desperately needed the kindness of heart and decency and thoughtfulness Uncle Will rather gracefully had to offer, day in and day out. The love Walker Percy shows for his third and quite significant parent, so to speak, comes across in the introduction he wrote to a new edition (1973) of *Lanterns on the Levee;* perhaps more important, in the visits made to Greenville, visits enjoyed immensely — and not least, in the closeness of a family: three brothers who more than stay in touch, whose respective families are near each other, have stayed rather close literally and emotionally.

A number of reviewers have all too readily regarded Percy as yet another Southern writer; and in response, as indicated, he has taken pains to point out that his purposes are very much like those of the European existentialists who found in the novel or the drama a suitable, flexible, and suggestive mode of moral, psychological, and social inquiry. Actually, Percy not only lives in the South and comes of old Southern stock, but is indeed a Southerner. He is much conscious of the region's history, its considerable achievements and persisting flaws. He has lived both comfortably and anxiously with his heritage, but never allowed it to slip out of his hands — to become, thereby, yet another nameless, faceless member of a homogenized Levittown America (upper-middle-class version). In his novels the wandering Southerner or restless Southerner or besotten Southerner standing at the edge of a society's and his own extinction is, nevertheless, unmistakably someone who comes from below the Mason-Dixon Line: the words, the expressions, the preferences and habits, the rhythm, it seems, of the character's life.

Once, when talking about someone we both knew, Percy said that the individual badly needed "a case of the Alabama laziness." Such a phrase may be appreciated as delightful and humorous, a rather shrewd, "provincial" way of saying something exactly right about someone else's "mind" or "personality." But Percy was revealing something about himself — showing how a region can exert its imprint on a person, influence the way he regards qualities like ambition, talent, the energies that drive people to liquor, fun, and games, not to mention writing. And Percy knows his region, the South, exceptionally well. He lives in Louisiana, has lived in Mississippi and Alabama — and still goes to the latter (to the Gulf of Mexico, near Mobile) in the summer. He went to college in North Carolina. He spent summers in Tennessee, at his Uncle Will's place, near Sewanee. His mother's family comes from Georgia, and he is no stranger to that state; he lived there for a while as a child. The South is a region whose changing features he beholds with a steady, keen eye, and has written about extensively.

His sense of humor and his mixture of amusement and anxiety at the technological obsessions of America sometimes escape from him abruptly, unexpectedly — to his own surprise, it seems. He once approached his own car, looked at it more carefully than most of us are likely to do, smiled and wondered out loud what the "beast" had in store for him that morning. In these days when "advanced civilizations" seem to hang together only because the output of Cougars, say, stays at a certain level, such a comment manages to convey a certain attitude: studied distance from the temptation to self-satisfaction; and apprehension that the whole show (twentieth-century progress, much proclaimed) may soon enough collapse — the "ruins" his last two novels venture to anticipate as a distinct possibility.

He has been for over thirty-five years, still is, and will be to the last breath a doctor. Maybe once a doctor, always one; in his case, certainly. He not only uses medical words with a certain ease in his writing; he has the physician's familiarity with the workings of the body, and is not in awe of death. Once a pathologist, and once quite ill, he is doubly an existentialist — by philosophical inclination, and out of the physician's and patient's extended encounter with the ultimate shadow that awaits all life. And these days, when childhood is so often (and often so vainly) summoned in explanation of a person's gifts, let alone particular genius, one has to mention the doubly sad life of a boy who would lose both parents before graduating from high school. Still, Percy is a writer who deals with grim if not apocalyptic subjects drily, coolly, with humor — maybe with (by presumptuous Yankee designation) "the Louisiana aplomb." He is worried all right, but there is an absence of frantic self-centeredness in his concern — as if the believing Christian who writes articles and novels knows better than seeing man's trials, however severe, serious, or sad, as the beginning and end of all things.

He regards himself with a certain amused detachment. He

never planned that his life would come out one or another way. He has become a novelist, but years ago, he knows, had someone predicted that outcome, he would have been surprised indeed. He writes philosophical and theological essays; and, his protestations to the contrary, he may do so again — because, like Marcel, he seems to require an alternation of activity: from the abstract (his essays), with great relief, to the concrete (his novels, wherein specific individuals are fleshed out), then back again to the abstract, perhaps to prepare once more for the concrete. But he has little patience with endless adjectives or whole sentences and paragraphs meant to do the adjective's work: qualify. "I'm not sure what I'm trying to do," he once said when the subject matter of his fourth novel was under discussion. "I'd hate to have in my mind the notion that I'm writing a 'religious novel' — one more niche — though I guess I'm always on a search when I'm writing, and I think each novel of mine has in it considerable ethical conflict.

"I think I once wrote to you that I sit and wait, as Kafka told himself to do. I look out the window. I stare at the ceiling. Then I write. I'm not sure there's any more to say. It's always interesting to see what others have decided about what you've written. I'll read what they say, and sometimes I'll scratch my head: is *that* what I was trying to get at? But I'll tell you, a morning of work is enough. I'm happy to leave, be with my family. Faulkner once said he realized early on what a good job it is to be a writer: sit there and write! Sometimes I agree, but sometimes I wonder if there isn't a better way to make a living. The next morning, though, I'm ready for another go-around. I only hope that the result is worth a little to others. The writer explores ideas that come to him or he imagines stories, which he then develops. But the writer reaches out to others, and if the result can't be speech, a conversation between two people, one hopes there is another kind of exchange between him and someone else: the effort that has produced words on paper stirs a response in the reader — Pascal's 'motions of the heart.' "

Index